HOCHON'S ARROW

HOCHON'S ARROW

THE SOCIAL IMAGINATION OF
FOURTEENTH-CENTURY TEXTS

PAUL STROHM

With an appendix by A. J. Prescott

PRINCETON UNIVERSITY PRESS

PRINCETON, NEW JERSEY

Library of Congress Cataloging-in-Publication Data

Strohm, Paul, 1938–
Hochon's arrow : the social imagination of fourteenth-century
texts / Paul Strohm ; with an appendix by A. J. Prescott.
p.   cm.
Includes bibliographical references and index.
ISBN 0-691-06880-1 (CL) — ISBN 0-691-01501-5 (PB)
1. English literature—Middle English, 1100–1500—History
and criticism. 2. Chaucer, Geoffrey, d. 1400—Political
and social views. 3. England—Social conditions—Medieval
period, 1066–1485. 4. Literature and society—England—History.
5. Social problems in literature. I. Title.
PR275.S63S76   1992
820.9′001—dc20   92-9550

This book has been composed in Linotron Galliard

Princeton University Press books are printed
on acid-free paper, and meet the guidelines for
permanence and durability of the Committee on
Production Guidelines for Book Longevity
of the Council on Library Resources

Printed in the United States of America

10 9 8 7 6 5 4 3 2 1

10 9 8 7 6 5 4 3 2 1
(pbk)

To Caroline M. Barron

CONTENTS

ACKNOWLEDGMENTS

LAST SPRING Caroline Barron and I were talking about a text that has interested each of us, Thomas Usk's *Testament*. In one of those moments when engaged conversationalists both speak at once, I said, "There are still many things to say about it," and she said, "It still has many things to say to us." Our different statements epitomize differences in our disciplines. From my literary background, I emphasize protocols and strategies of analysis, viewing the questions we ask of texts as inextricably involved in the answers we receive. As a historian, she emphasizes a text's communicativeness, its potential to supply and revise knowledge. We have tested these and other assumptions in periodic conversations that have spanned the four years since I first seized on an invitation to attend her and Vanessa Harding's Medieval and Tudor London History Seminar at the Institute of Historical Research. These essays might be viewed as explorations of the ground between our respective assumptions. Her work appears repeatedly in my footnotes, but these notes offer incomplete testimony to her unfailing intellectual generosity.

I have encountered generosity in many forms while completing these essays. My colleague Sheila Lindenbaum has encouraged and informed my first efforts at archival research and shared the excitement of her own parallel investigations. Andrew Prescott of the British Museum, first transcriber of the accusations against Thomas Austin, not only loaned me his initial transcript but has generously edited the full text as an appendix to this volume. Dyan Elliott has assisted with several Latin translations. (Unless otherwise indicated, translations and paraphrases are mine. In the case of the *Westminster Chronicle* I have prepared my own translations, but always in consultation with the superb English rendering of L. C. Hector and Barbara Harvey.)

And I have continued to enjoy stimulating interchange with others who share my interest in textual environment, power and the written record, and cultural aspects of domination and subordination. Among those with whom I have discussed substantial portions of this volume are David Wallace, Susan Crane, Linda Charnes, James Simpson, Carolyn Dinshaw, and Alfred and Linda David. Although they have never been in one room at one time, they—together with the other people mentioned here—constitute the sustaining intellectual "circle" within which these essays were composed. I have also tried out several of these essays in seminars and lectures, including particularly helpful sessions on Hochon's encounter with Hugh Fastolf arranged by Derek Pearsall and Larry Benson at Harvard and Jill

Mann at Cambridge and on Usk's "Appeal" at the Institute of Historical Research.

Robert Brown of Princeton University Press has consistently supported this endeavor. Copyeditor Julie Marvin brought to her task a remarkable combination of sympathy, discretion, and independent knowledge. Most of the constituent essays appear here for the first time. A slightly earlier version of chapter 1 has appeared in the *Journal of Medieval and Renaissance Studies* 21 (1991), 225–49. Prior versions of the essays on Chaucer's "Lak of Stedfastnesse" and "To His Purse" are scheduled to appear, respectively, in a festschrift for Donald Howard (University of Delaware Press) and an essay collection on literature and history edited by Barbara Hanawalt (University of Minnesota Press).

Bloomington, Indiana
November 1991

ABBREVIATIONS

Annales	*Annales Ricardi Secundi, Regis Angliae.* Ed. H. T. Riley. Rolls Series, no. 28, pt. 3. London, 1866.
"Appeal"	Usk, Thomas. "Appeal of Thomas Usk against John Northampton." In *A Book of London English, 1384–1425,* ed. R. W. Chambers and Marjorie Daunt. Oxford: Clarendon Press, 1931.
CCR	*Calendar of Close Rolls, 1327–99.* London: Stationery Office, 1896–1927.
CFR	*Calendar of Fine Rolls, 1307–99.* London: Stationery Office, 1912–29.
Chronicles	*Chronicles of London.* Ed. C. L. Kingsford. Oxford: Clarendon Press, 1905.
CLBG, CLBH	*Calendar of Letter-Books of the City of London.* Ed. Reginald R. Sharpe. London: Corporation of the City of London, 1907.
CPR	*Calendar of Patent Rolls, 1327–99.* London: Stationery Office, 1891–1916.
EETS	*Early English Text Society*
EHR	*English Historical Review*
Hist. Parl.	*History of Parliament, 1386–1422.* Ed. Linda Clark and Carole Rawcliffe. London: History of Parliament Trust, 1992.
Historia Ricardi	*Historia Vitae et Regni Ricardi Secundi.* Ed. George B. Stow, Jr. Philadelphia: University of Pennsylvania Press, 1977.
Inventory	Royal Commission on Historical Monuments (England). *An Inventory of the Historical Monuments in London.* Vol. 1, *Westminster Abbey.* London: Stationery Office, 1924.
LBG, LBH	Letter-Books G and H. Manuscripts, Corporation of the City of London
KB	Sayles, G. O. *Select Cases in the Court of King's Bench Under Richard II, Henry IV, and Henry V.* Vols. 6, 7. Selden Society, vols. 82, 88. London: Quaritch, 1965, 1971.
KC	Leadham, I. S. and J. F. Baldwin. *Select Cases before the King's Council, 1243–1482.* Selden Society, vol. 35. Cambridge: Harvard University Press, 1918.

"Petition"   "Petition of the Folk of Mercerye." In *A Book of London English, 1384–1425*, ed. R. W. Chambers and Marjorie Daunt. Oxford: Clarendon Press, 1931.

Pleas   *Select Pleas and Memoranda of the City of London, 1381–1412.* Ed. A. H. Thomas. Cambridge: Cambridge University Press, 1932.

PRO   Public Record Office, Corporation of the City of London

RP   *Rolls of Parliament [Rotuli Parliamentorum]*. Vol. 2 (1326–77), vol. 3 (1377–1411). London, 1783.

Stat.   *Statutes of the Realm*. Vol. 1. London: Basket, 1763.

Traïson   *Chronicque de la Traïson et Mort*. Ed. Benjamin Williams. London: English Historical Society, 1846.

West   *The Westminster Chronicle, 1381–1394*. Ed. L. C. Hector and Barbara Harvey. Oxford: Clarendon Press, 1966.

VH   *Victoria History: Hampshire*. London: Constable, 1912.

HOCHON'S ARROW

Introduction

FALSE FABLES AND HISTORICAL TRUTH

> "Funny, sometimes, how things that aren't true are more true
> than the truth."
> —*After Dark, My Sweet* (1990)

THE PARADOX of the lie that might as well be true must interest anyone who seeks to understand texts in history or the historical influence of texts. For, strictly speaking, most texts—and not just a few celebrated forgeries or esoteric examples—must be regarded as untrue. Were we to shun texts that rely upon devices of narrative rearrangement, interested selection of detail, and spurious self-authorization, we would have to discard most of the written record. Yet, in other senses, the most blatantly made-up texts cannot help but reveal truth. Fabulists and romancers conceive episodes within imaginary structures or value systems their audiences embrace as true, and lies accepted as a basis for actions gain retrospective truthfulness through their influence on events. Whether announcing themselves as fictional or relying on an array of strategies to conceal their fictionalization, invented texts cannot fail to disclose the marks of their own historicity.

The texts to be considered in this study were mainly written in English, in and about London and Westminster, in the last two decades of the fourteenth century. Some treat actual characters, mainly in order to fictionalize them. Others treat actual characters who seem quite ready to collaborate in their own fictionalization. Some present invented characters within networks of representation extensively penetrated by real events. Some present documentable events (like the burning of Lambeth Palace in 1381) as if they were seasonal pageants or scripted performances, and others present scripted pageants (like Richard's reconciliation with the city of London) as if they manifested spontaneous feelings. In fact, we must finally remain impartial as to whether some events most carefully rendered and broadly accepted as fact (such as Queen Philippa's intercession for the burghers of Calais) happened at all. Yet all are finally composed within history—if not within a sense of what did happen, at least within a sense of what might have happened, of what could be imagined, of what commonly held interpretative structures permitted a late fourteenth-century audience to believe.

The texts themselves remain extremely divergent in their claims about truthfulness. Included are frankly invented fables of the poets, as well as chronicle narratives that assert considerable authority for their ordering and interpretation of actual events. Likewise included are other texts—such as statutes, parliamentary petitions, and legal pleas—that have been accorded unusual evidentiary value as a result of their pragmatic character or linkage with institutional practice. The distinctive claims of each text and the particular responses it solicits will, of course, be carefully noted. All will, however, be treated alike in one sense: less as records of events than as interpretations of events, inevitably reliant to one degree or another upon invention, upon fictional devices. A text's fictionality may derive from acts of commission (its imputation, for example, of motive) or omission (by what it evades or excludes); its fictionality may involve its utopianism, or, in the case of certain Lancastrian narratives, a willful and zestful plunge into sheer disinformation.

Insisting on fictionality as a common characteristic of the texts under consideration, I insist equally that fictionality should not be considered an embarrassment to a text's ultimate historicity. Composed within history, fictions offer irreplaceable historical evidence in their own right. Yet, for all their value as historical evidence, the fabrications of litigants and chroniclers and petitioners and poets will (in the fashion of certain crafty gatekeepers in folktales) refuse to yield their information unless tactfully approached. One element of tact is to be aware of the *kinds* of evidence they are, and are not, suited to divulge. Although these texts are valuable for the study of history, we must always remember to ask: the history of what? Only rarely can we expect them to tell us "what happened," or to contribute materially to our factual base. They offer crucial testimony on other, though no less historical, matters: on contemporary perception, ideology, belief, and—above all—on the imaginative structures within which fourteenth-century participants acted and assumed that their actions would be understood.

Consider the revealing moment when the chronicler Thomas Walsingham complains that the villeins ("villani") of St. Albans have been misled by a legend that King Offa granted them their land. He argues that in 1381 certain rebels instigated the St. Albans tenants to rise up and to seek liberties by means of long-standing lies, by false fables ("per falsas fabulas") persuading those younger than themselves to believe they once enjoyed liberties and privileges granted by King Offa and since unjustly removed by the abbots and monks of the abbey (*Gesta Abbatum*, 365). So vivid were these persuasions that they assumed in the villeins' minds the tangible status of a textual figment, a belief that their liberties were inscribed in an ancient charter with one capital of gold and another of azure ("quamdam chartam antiquam reposcerent de libertatibus villanorum, cujus litterae capitales fuerunt, de auro una, altera de azorio," 308)—a charter thought to be in the possession of the abbey, the return of which became one of the villeins' demands.

Walsingham is stirred to an energetic demonstration of the untruth of the villeins' claims. He seeks to show, historically, that the town of St. Albans was founded long after Offa's reign, and that by basing their claims on merciful intercessions ("suffragia") of Offa, who actually never laid eyes on the place ("qui villam Sancti Albani nunquam vidit," 366), the villeins have vainly fabricated lies. He is no doubt correct. But the legend of Offa's bequest bristles with historicity in a number of other respects. It reveals the villeins' respect for writing and written documents, and the contemporary function of writing as an instrument of power. It helps to explain why the rebels of 1381 sought emancipatory documents and also why they tried to burn restrictive ones. It reveals the essentially reasonable, and especially the conservative, nature of the rebel demands; for all the millennial talk, they essentially wanted title to work their land without excessive obligations or dues. It demonstrates the mutual reliance of laborers and monks on ideas of traditional land tenure, with the respective parties differing only on the particular tradition in question and the evidence required to sustain it. It suggests the enduring power of an ideology of benign kingship, latent but always available for use, as when briefly harnessed by the young Richard II when he instated himself as champion of the hapless rebels of 1381 at the climactic Smithfield meeting. It reveals the anticlericalism of the English populace, corroborated by the beheading of Archbishop Sudbury at the hands of the London rebels.

Like all texts, Walsingham's account of the Offa legend lies open to divergent readings. The villeins' credulousness provokes Walsingham to exasperation, even in the recital; it also contains elements of thwarted aspiration that must inspire sympathy. Either way, false or true, the legend of Offa's bequest possesses exceptional power. This power is historically rather than fancifully derived, because its assumptions about land tenure and literacy and benign kingship reveal the contemporary structures of practical knowledge and anticipation and belief within which the legend was formed and within which it spurred people to collective action. As I will say more than once in the course of this study, a text can be powerful without being true.

Fictive invention and suppression and distortion are normal properties of textual exposition, but we do everything we can to deny the fact. One reason past generations of academics maintained distinctions between "the literary," with its reliance on invention, and "the historical," with its adherence to fact, is the reassuring implication of such clearly bounded categories that fictional elements of a text can be segregated and controlled. Despite such earnest definitional efforts, fictive elements teem within historical narratives, trial depositions and indictments, coroner's rolls, and other officially sanctioned accounts. So, too, in the texts to be considered here. Admittedly, each text presents an issue of authorship, or element of narrative zest, or revelation of textual process that I have found attractive in its own right. But, in matters of fictionality and historical truth, I regard my texts as representative of the genres within which they occur—as exemplifying that inevitable and inextricable intertwinement of "fals and soth compouned" that Chaucer wryly describes in his *House of Fame* (ll. 2088–109).

At the center of my inquiry is the text itself, with the cryptic and paradoxical information it both offers and withholds. And the text is characteristically viewed within a larger field or "environment" of previous and contemporary texts, visual representations, pageants, social dramas, and political acts. This environment naturally includes texts commonly identified as "sources," though they are likely to be somewhat displaced from the central positions in which we have customarily instated them. Knowledge of a text's larger environment permits us to understand its social function in a way that source study never could. As I explain in more detail in my third and fourth chapters, this environment is the field of shared knowledge that allows an author to write in the confidence of being understood. It is, in other words, the guarantee of intelligibility that makes sense of a text as a communicative and social act.

An environment embraces not just words and textual conventions, but also schemes or structuring ideas functioning at an intermediate level of generalization. Factional loyalty and the role of a good servant in Hochon's case, the idea of queenly intercession in Anne's case, and a good many more: notions of *communitas* in the actions and accounts of the 1381 rising, the goal of civil order in the attack on livery and maintenance in 1388, the centrality of divine unction in the selection of a king in Henry's 1399 accession, the sanctioned rights of the *baron* as head of the medieval household. These structuring ideas may be labeled "ideological," and I occasionally do so, but only in a supple and deliberately migratory sense of the term. For I take "ideology" not as a set of inherently false and deliberately distortive beliefs, but more neutrally as the entire set of socially imagined ideas by which people explain their lives and places in a material order. Consequently, I regard ideological elements as unbound to any one political system—as unfixed, free-floating, and open to appropriation and use by contending centers of social power. Thus, we see both London merchants and Essex tenants struggling for designation as the "true commons," with the London merchant leaders coming out on top and achieving knighthood in the process while the rebels are stigmatized as uncouth beasts; we see both Nicholas Brembre and John Northampton struggling for possession of the idea of "common profit," with Brembre the temporary and Northampton the longer-term winner. Although I occasionally attribute an ideological thrust to an idea or structure, my real interest passes quickly to what I regard as the more important questions: who inscribed it in textual form and why, who appropriated it and to what effect, who laid claim to it by wielding it in a convincing way?

This emphasis on the contingency of texts, their reliance on a material reality beyond their own bounds, is my rejoinder to those notions of textuality that would view language and text as all there is, as our sole point of access to past events and their understanding. Texts do, indeed, regulate our access to the past, and especially to the crucially valuable terms of past self-understanding, of historical events as understood by their participants. This is why texts must be so respectfully interrogated—not just teased and mollified and cajoled, but above all attentively observed with respect for the way they create meaning and the status of the meaning they create. But the observer of texts cannot fail to note their ups and downs, their surprising changes of fortune, their varied and unpredictable uses. These vicissitudes register the presence of centers of authority beyond textual bounds, the ultimate reliance of the text upon those contending processes that determine reception and circulation, interpretation and application. This is why, after six chapters that may be read mainly as celebrations of textual versatility and power, I conclude this book with a cautionary chapter in which a brilliant act of textual self-creation is shown to be subject to revision and eventual effacement through the operations of political agency beyond textual control.

Believing that texts are subject to external manipulation and use, I have little allegiance to the idea of text and context as conventionally applied. My quarrel is not, to be sure, with "context" in its etymological sense, which I take to embrace everything that is "together with" the text, without particular specification of centrality or order of importance. The effect of much contextual criticism is, however, potentially misleading in its tendency to enthrone the text at the center of a surrounding field of contributory and client-like texts and events. This scheme, in other words, instates the text in a position of near-imperial privilege, its resonance enriched by cargos of meaning from its tributaries, which it in turn dignifies by elevating their inchoate impulses to a new level of significance. Chaucerians have every reason to understand this divide of text and context, for we have exploited it thoroughly in our author's interest. We have, after all, relentlessly hypostatized the masterworks of contemporaries like Langland and Gower, international masters like Jean de Meun, Guillaume de Machaut, and Boccaccio, and even events to which Chaucer dimly alludes like the rising of 1381, arraying them around his text in essentially static and subservient roles. Needless to say, devotees of Boccaccio and the rest have considered themselves fully entitled to ignore this particular prioritization and to reconfigure textual systems around their favored authors as well.

The question here is not who should be at the center, but process of centralization itself. I am proposing a belated Copernican, or even post-Copernican, revolution in our thinking about textuality, in which a Ptolemaic view of the favored text as the stable center of an ordered system gives way to an acknowledgement of a text as just one component of a less prioritized array, one that might itself stand nowhere near the center of any recognized textual universe.

My view of textuality has posed some organizational issues. An essay that begins with a text runs the risk of demoting all that follows to the role of explanatory context; an essay that ends with one runs the closely related risk of suggesting that the text is outcome, with everything preceding it existing merely to prepare the way. I have followed no single rule in these essays. Some, like "Treason in the Household," retrace my own investigatory path, while others, like "Queens as Intercessors," rearrange my conclusions for more convenient access. My general practice, though, is to seek an organization that returns my primary texts to the larger environment within which they were produced and their uses determined. This means that my essays usually begin and end in history, moving through a field of writings and events to the moment of the text's production, and then moving back out to the larger field that determined its disposition or use. This procedure certainly involves some deferrals and may place some burdens on my reader. It is, however, an element of the point I mean to make: that we need not consider historical events simply as "background" but may regard them as part of a large and unruly matrix within which new texts are constantly produced and received.

I have tried to go back to the written record in a fresh frame of mind, and "history" for me is more likely to refer to contemporaneous documents, and events and pressures registered in those documents, than to twentieth-century narrative histories and surveys. This practice has the advantage of avoiding the multiplication of received errors. An example might be the case of Henry IV's "proclamation" of his kingship, a document mentioned by most recent writers on his accession, for which I searched in vain for months before realizing that it did not exist, save in a host of nineteenth- and twentieth-century references derived from a fanciful nineteenth-century editorial invention. These comments are naturally not meant to understate my debt to the superb works of synthesis and analysis that have helped me to orient myself within this field—some of which appear in my notes and some not—by such landmark figures as T. F. Tout and J. G. Bellamy, and by such distinguished contemporaries as R. B. Dobson and Nigel Saul and Anthony Tuck. But I raise this matter in order to note a more particular obligation or—I should say—stimulus. The reexamination of texts in history has recently been advanced by a new generation of feminist historians, and my fifth and sixth chapters rely heavily on their work. I am particularly indebted in this regard to recent studies by Judith Bennett and Martha Howell.

Reconstruction of a textual environment exposes its practitioner to many new materials, and hence to surprises. None of these essays has ended up exactly where I thought it would. I began the essay on revelry as a discussion of the carnivalesque, but it ended as an inquiry into the production of oppositional action within a dominant system. I expected the discussion of Chaucer's *Purse* to reveal Chaucer's total reliance on a larger environment of dynastic theory, but ended by discovering evidences of his authorial intent. I intended for the essay on queens to show that female intercession served the interests of patriarchy, but became aware in the course of my research that any such structure can be captured and redirected from within.

My allegiance is, in short, less to a particular set of conclusions than to a continuing inquiry. This inquiry recognizes our reliance on the written record for what we can know of the past and seeks to approach texts with an appropriate mixture of skepticism and respect. It views texts not as finalized "sources" but as argumentative and interpretative documents in their own right, as historical contestants and as objects of contestation. Above all, it treats texts warily but without unnecessary ceremony, discarding outworn categorizations—like "literary" versus "nonliterary" or "fictional" versus "historical"—that might foreclose conversation among texts or between texts and events. It discovers in this conversation a rich cacophony of voices where monovocality had seemed to prevail, and it seeks to listen attentively, not only to the more strident but to some so slightly audible as to stand at the very edge of silence.

Chapter 1

HOCHON'S ARROW

THE MAYORAL ELECTIONS scheduled for 13 October 1384 at the London Guildhall must have seemed a sure thing to incumbent Nicholas Brembre and his party of merchant capitalists. Not only did Brembre enjoy secure majorities among the aldermen and members of the common council, but the opposition was in disarray, with previously defeated rival John Northampton and his closest followers under various forms of arrest and banishment. Nevertheless, Brembre and his party had left little to chance. Early in Brembre's 1383 term they had taken steps to discourage opposition, including a novel December 1383 proclamation, in English, against "congregacions." And, according to a subsequent accusation of the mercers, on election eve they smuggled arms into the Guildhall itself and laid ambushes about Cheapside to assure their effective control of civic space: "In the nyght . . . he did carye grete quantitee of Armure to the Guyldehalle . . . and certein busshments were laide" ("Petition," 34).

But those mercers, tailors, goldsmiths, and others who had supported John Northampton appear to have entertained some continuing political hopes of their own. They developed a credible alternative candidate in goldsmith Nicholas Twyford, an old Brembre adversary.[1] And they staged a demonstration on election day, a mixture of planned and spontaneous actions, involving a considerable number of armed men. Records of persons subsequently imprisoned, or for whose good conduct security was taken, suggest that the troublemakers were mainly guildsmen of "mediocris status," concentrated in the guilds that had supported Northampton all along (Plea Rolls, mem. 4b, *Pleas*, 62–63). The tailors and other guilds, for instance, planned a meeting at St. Paul's early on election day ("in quadam congregatione dicta diuersi homines plurimarum misterarum in ecclesia sancti pauli londonii die electionis maioris"), from which they proceeded to the Guildhall to make an uproar ("ad faciendum clamorem," Plea Rolls, mem. 4b, *Pleas*, 64). This demonstration seems to have elicited additional support. William Woodcock, tailor, showed up at the Guildhall and, after assessing the situation, returned to his shop to fetch a variety of

---

[1] Twyford's subsequent election as mayor in the more conciliatory climate of 1388 would, however, suggest that he was a less obdurate factionalist than Northampton himself (*West.*, 100–102; Bird, 68–69).

weaponry—sword, buckler, and poleaxe—in the hope that a riot would ensue.[2]

Showing his "stronge honde," Brembre carried the day with little or no actual bloodshed ("Petition," 34; *RP* 3:226). The would-be demonstrators seem to have been easily dispersed by the sorts of tactics later described by the mercers: "When free men of the Citee come to chese her Mair [Brembre's followers] breken vp armed cryinge with loude voice 'sle! sle!' folwyng hem; wherthourgh the peple for feere fledde to houses & other hidynges as in londe of werre" ("Petition," 34; see also *West.*, 100–102). Within days, a repression set in, with guild masters submissively complying with a request to furnish names of their own members who took part in the disturbances (Plea Rolls, mems. 4b-6b, *Pleas*, 62–69). As is generally the case with such repressions, the repression itself became an occasion for settling all sorts of scores, those connected with the disturbances and others as well; the masters of the cordwainers guild turned in one John Remes for a variety of charges including inflammatory words and other insubordinations, *and* for rebellion against their own leadership within the guild (Plea Rolls, mem. 4, *Pleas*, 61). So did this particular confrontation ebb away. Yet, for part of a day, the Guildhall and its environs had been a contested space, a staging ground for political actions expressed within— and expressive of—a charged factional situation.

The brief narrative of one such action—an action limited in scope but rich in symbolic implication—is the subject of this essay. This narrative is contained within a transcript of accusation or appeal ("accusatio sive appellum") launched by a disgruntled former apprentice, John Banham, against his master, mercer Thomas Austin, and other members of his household. This accusation occurs within a series of charges and countercharges exchanged between Banham and fellow servant John Hore on the one hand, and Thomas Austin and his brother Roger on the other, springing from a quarrel over Banham's and Hore's alleged misappropriation of funds. All the parties to the dispute were jailed at one point or another, as advantage shifted back and forth between them.[3] The accusation in ques-

---

[2] Plea Rolls, mem. 4b, *Pleas*, 67. Some participants in the demonstration were later to plead that they knew nothing about its inception, or that they mistakenly supposed it to be approved by the mayor and others; John Coraunt, for example, claimed that he had heard from two tailors (who later denied it) that the mayor, aldermen, and interested lords wanted guildsmen to show up in livery ("in liberationibus suis") for the election (Plea Rolls, mem. 5b; *Pleas*, 67).

[3] Following is a chronology of known dates in the case. 6 May 1387: Banham files a complaint in the mayor's court. As summarized by A. H. Thomas, "John Banham, late apprentice and servant of Thomas Austyn, mercer, . . . complained that his master had sued him . . . for £500, and though he did not owe that sum he agreed to judgment on the promise of his master that all previous accounts between them should be satisfactorily settled, but when he was committed to prison for the debt his master allowed him to remain there" (*Pleas*, 146).

tion represents Banham's attempt to gain an edge by launching a preemptive strike against Austin on new, political terrain. Dictated on 16 September 1387, at a time when the Brembre faction was still securely in the driver's seat, Banham's accusation seeks to incriminate Austin by associating him with the faction of John Northampton, and with that faction's misconduct on election day of 1384.

Charging Austin and his wife and brother with sundry seditious statements and suspicious contacts with Northampton loyalists, Banham moves to a close focus on the events swirling around the Guildhall before and after the 1384 election. On the night before, Austin is said to have hidden goods about the city in a suspicious manner, and to have communicated with Northampton's followers. On election day, he sent Banham into Cheapside to see whether dissident guilds like the goldsmiths and tailors and cordwainers were in fact approaching the Guildhall. Banham says that Austin advised the men of his own household to show up at the Guildhall armed, but that when he got there and saw Brembre's strength he abandoned his plans and told his men to go open the shop as if nothing had occurred: "Thanne Thomas Austyn saw here strengthe and a non he keste offe his harneys and seide 'al is lost that we hau ben a bowtyn' and bad his meyne privyly goeth to the schoppe and settythe opyn as no thyng were don."[4]

According to Banham, however, a residual encounter remained for that day, involving a Brembre supporter, Hugh Fastolf, and a group of Austin's

---

16 September 1387: Banham dictates his accusation, including the Hochon narrative. 21 September 1387: Fastolf is elected sheriff of London. 8 October 1387: A panel of four mercers has investigated Austin's allegation that he is owed sums for Banham's misappropriation of merchandise, garments, and goods, between Christmas 1382 and Christmas 1385. Basing their finding on their own investigations and on "les serement et main de John Hore un autre de ses servantz," they clear Banham, but with the understanding that he must remain responsible for any debts he might have incurred (LBH, fol. ccxxii; *CLBH* 317). 19 November 1387: Bond for Austin in relation to the accusation of 16 September is provided by a distinguished and politically mixed group of city politicians including future mayors Hadley, Venour, and Whitington, and a number of prominent mercers. Austin is said to have been detained as a consequence of impeachment; he is "sub custodia . . . pro quibusdam causis criminalibus vnde impetitus est" (*CCR* [1385–1389], 359; C54/226, mem. 26). 29 November 1387: A preliminary finding in favor of Austin: he is owed £110 by various persons for goods sold to them by John Banham (who evidently retained the funds) (*Pleas*, 146–47). 9 January 1388: Banham's 16 September accusation is forwarded to chancery, with an essentially corraborative statement from the mayor and sheriffs, including Fastolf. 29 January 1388: Final release of Thomas Austin, mercer, Alicia, his wife, and "Hugone Lytherpolle," as well as other unnamed persons (LBH, fol. ccxxiv; *CLBH*, 322). 18 July 1388: John Hore agrees, under pain of £100, to do or utter nothing harmful to the estate of Thomas Austin, and to assist Austin in recovering lost goods (*CCR* [1385–1389], 597).

[4] PRO C258/24, no. 9. Quotations from Banham's testimony are based on the edition of A. J. Prescott, printed as appendix 1. Spelling normalized, abbreviations expanded, and punctuation added.

servants, including Hochon of Liverpool, John Hore, and himself as participant and observer. It seems that, the Northampton people having scat-
tered "to houses & other hidynges" ("Petition," 34), Hochon, Hore, and
Banham remained behind, using a "chambre" as a "wayte" or ambush,
when Hugh Fastolf came onto the scene:

> Ther was that same day that Hochoun of Lyuerpoll his seruaunt stod in his
> chambre in a wayte and there cam Hewe Fastolfe and made water agens the
> cherche wal of seynt Laurenses and thanne seyde Hochoun of Lyuerpoll,
> "Yonder is on of the thefys," and thanne he seide, "wit thou sen how I schal
> naylen hym with an arwe to the wow [wall]," and forthe ther withe he teysed
> up his bowe for to hau keld hym and thanne seyde I . . .[5] "lad ben [let be],
> thou wilt on don us alle," and so it was ileft.

The fourteenth-century St. Lawrence's was located on the site of its successor, at the southwest corner of the Guildhall enclosure. Hochon and his
companions, described as within sight of it, presumably occupy one of the
rooms across Guildhall yard to the east. Since Fastolf is described as one of
the "thieves" who has stolen the election, the voting is now over, and Fastolf is probably to be imagined as exiting the Guildhall itself and crossing
Guildhall yard to St. Lawrence's, with Hochon and his associates viewing
him across the yard. Fastolf pausing to urinate, the disgruntled Hochon
issues his threat, but as a result of Banham's mollifying presence the threat
is defused.

Like most texts, this one is less innocent than it appears. If we are looking for unmediated data or other forms of "primary evidence," we are not
going to find it here, within a legal document dictated well after the fact
by an interested party for an audience of other interested parties. For,
whatever evidentiary qualities this narrative possesses, it finally exists to
promote an already interpreted scene, a scene that is at once knowledgeable
about the field of already existing interpretations within which it positions
itself and energetic in its attempt to refocus those interpretations in order
to discredit the Austins.

The interpretative situation is further complicated by Banham's own
precarious position. Needing to incriminate himself in order to explain his
presence at the scene, he recounts a situation in which he was indeed
aligned with the Austin household but acted as a moderating force. That
some instability of intent would slip into such a narrative seems inevitable,
and this inevitability is heightened by the intervention of other vocalities.
Confederate John Hore was probably present at the testimony and may

---

[5] The omitted phrase, "I John Hore," may have been a scribal slip, though it probably
indicates that Hore, another disgruntled former apprentice of Austin, was present along with
Banham at the oral interview. See appendix 1, 166–67.

have added his voice to Banham's own (see n. 5 and appendix 1, 166–67). And, despite the requirement that coroners take such testimony in something very close to verbatim form (Hunnisett, *Medieval Coroner*, 73; Kellaway, 80–85), the fact remains that this entire accusation was mediated through the ear and hand of coroner John Charney, whose terms of office had involved service on both sides of the factional fence.

Fissured and incomplete as we might expect this narrative to be in realizing its own apparent intent, it must also rely upon the cooperation of a receptive audience before it can fulfill its designs. Seeking to harness a highly contentious political situation for its own ends, it would be fortunate to enlist such cooperation. As it happens, this narrative is indeed subject to rival interpretations, not just as a consequence of ingenious twentieth-century reading, but as a result of alignments in London politics of the 1380s. The idea of a "pro-Brembre" reading and a "pro-Northampton" reading is, of course, a stylization, both because membership in the two factions ebbed and flowed and because any narrative may be read in as many different ways as there are people to read it. But, in this case, the existence of two communities of readers, each responding differently to Banham's account, may not only be inferred, but may be verified by actual shifts in the fortunes of his accusation.

BANHAM'S NARRATIVE AND ITS INTENDED AUDIENCE

The immediate audience of any accusation such as Banham's would have been the mayor, together with the two sheriffs and coroner of London. The mayoralty had been in Brembre hands since 1384. Brembre himself served from 1383–1386, and, after close associate Nicholas Exton assumed office in 1386, Brembre was appointed official spokesperson for London in its relations with the king (*CLBH*, 315). When Banham dictated his accusation, the sheriffs were two Brembre men—William More, vintner, and William Standon, grocer—and John Charney was coroner. New elections were held five days later, on 21 September 1387, and an even more conspicuously loyalist group was chosen, consisting of sheriffs William Venour and Hugh Fastolf, together with coroner William Cheyne.[6] In other words, not only could Banham expect his narrative to be read by Brembre loyalists, but by remarkable coincidence or shrewd anticipation on Banham's part it soon developed that one of his protagonists—Fastolf—was to be among the small group of persons responsible for the disposition of his testimony.

[6] Soon after Fastolf's and Venour's election, Richard wrote to Mayor Exton of his satisfaction in learning from Nicholas Brembre "that good and honorable men had been elected Sheriffs" (*CLBH*, 317).

Considering Banham's audience, and the date at which he dictated his testimony, any accusation of excessive Northampton partisanship would still have carried a great deal of negative force. And the force of this particular accusation is enhanced by the unobtrusive way in which it manages its effects. At first glance, Banham's narrative offers itself as a transparent and virtually authorless account of "what happened" that election day. Banham himself assumes the unobrusive role of objective observer, artlessly stringing together a series of clauses in the natural order of their occurrence ("and . . . and . . . and then . . . and then . . . and forthwith . . . and then . . . and so"). This effect is furthered by the way in which he finally does enter his text: erasing his own role in its creation, he *re*inserts himself in its action as a relatively minor character, intervening at the end on a prudent and cautionary note, bolstering his own position and credibility as a witness, and all but inveigling us into forgetting his importance as interpreter, if not fabricator, of the entire scene![7] And, on closer inspection, his natural order of events is essentially that of an "order of pleading," like those judicial narratives described in the *Rhetorica ad Herennium*, "in which the speaker sets out the facts and turns every detail to advantage in order to win a judgment" (I, 8).

The initial focus is on Hochon, skulking in a "wayte" or "ambush." Note that he is identified as Austin's servant. On a different social level than apprentices Banham and Hore, who possess at least remote hopes of someday entering the mercer's trade, Hochon is beholden to Austin in a more rudimentary way. His name, in fact, implies a servile—or at least humble—status. Banham and Hore possess actual surnames; Hochon is merely "from Liverpool." Moreover, to the extent that Banham and members of his audience were aware of it, the name "Hochon" itself introduces an added implication of loose living and near-vagabondage as a diminutive of the French *hoche*, meaning a "gambler" or "dice-player" (Dauzat, 329). Then, in contrast with the already partially discredited Hochon, we are given Hugh Fastolf, just happening along on no business at all, or on business of the most personal and least conspiratorial of sorts. He enters the scene as a known personage of undeniable eminence—an eminence sig-

---

[7] Readers of later fourteenth-century English literature will already be familiar with this narrative stratagem. One might compare it, on the grandest of scales, with Chaucer's self-insertion in the *Canterbury Tales*. Chaucer's self-effacing presentation of himself as an observer of other people's activities, and as the teller of one inept tale and another that laboriously follows its source, does not wholly eradicate his authorial role. But it certainly has the effect of effacing it temporarily in favor of the appearances in the near foreground of his vividly realized tellers. A still more proximate example is that of Thomas Usk in his "Appeal" of John Northampton. In that document, Usk inserts himself in a number of minor capacities—such as transcribing bills and carrying messages—that establish his own authority as a witness against Northampton's treasonous activities. (Usk's "Appeal" is discussed at length in chapter 7, below.)

naled by the fact that his resonant name alone (unaccompanied by the mention of his guild or profession or neighborhood customary in written records of London mercantile life) suffices to identify him.

Just as Hochon's humble station suits Banham's purposes, so does Fastolf bring a number of advantages to his role as Banham's aggrieved party. Technically a Great Yarmouth fishmonger, Fastolf actually accumulated his wealth as a monopolist and enterprise capitalist in collaboration with London merchants and financiers of the royalist party, such as Walter Sibile (*CPR* [1381–1385], 108, 109), Simon Burley (*CCR* [1381–1385], 232) and John Philipot (*CCR* [1381–1385], passim). His London ties began with membership in the powerful company of grocers in 1373 (*Hist. Parl.*) and multiplied in 1379, when he began to dispose of his holdings in Great Yarmouth and its environs (*CCR* [1377–1381], 30). Taking up residence in London on Thames Street by 1381 (*CPR* [1381–1385], 30–31), he represented London in Parliament in 1381 and possibly 1382 (*Hist. Parl.*). He served repeatedly as alderman for Tower ward in 1381–1382, 1384–1385, and 1385–1386, though relieved in the last case so he could attend to duties as deputy constable of Dover Castle under Simon Burley (*CPR* [1381–1385], 589), and for Bridge ward from 1386 to 1390. His association with prominent grocers of London would have marked him as a likely factionalist, and by 1384 he had already bolstered his partisan credentials by playing a role in the condemnation of Northampton at Reading (*CLBH*, 246). Banham's 16 September 1387 narrative catches Fastolf just at the brink of preferment: already deputy constable with Burley, he is now just five days from appointment as sheriff of London.[8]

So here we have Hochon, a mere servant, menacing a London citizen of considerable repute and substance. And, underscoring Hochon's dangerous intentions, Banham gives them to us via a mimed action (tensing the bow), a commentary on the action ("see how I shall nail him"), and his own expository conclusion about Hochon's intention ("to have killed him"). Hochon's violent enactment would presumably have been amply disturbing to members of the Brembre camp and of course to Fastolf himself. But what about those less committed—for example, the members of the jury that would consider the accusation? Even they might find occasion for distress in the violative aspects of Hochon's behavior.

Beyond its overt aggressiveness, Hochon's behavior possesses an element of social offense that may be specified within Erving Goffman's vocabulary of public interaction. In Goffman's terms, a violation occurs when someone is either intruded upon (illicitly disturbed or interrupted when

---

[8] Although Fastolf was never to become mayor, service as sheriff was an important stepping stone to that position. Since February 1384 the mayoralty had been reserved for former sheriffs (Bird, 145).

making a reasonable claim to public space) or is himself or herself obtrusive (in making an overextensive claim to personal space) (51). Seen in this way, the narrative suggests that Fastolf is intruded upon in the course of asserting an entirely reasonable claim to what Goffman would call "use space" (34). Elements of willful assertion are certainly to be found in the marking behavior by which Fastolf stakes his territorial claim. Still, in Goffman's terms, Fastolf is represented as trustingly depending on a kind of benign "civil inattention" on the part of his beholders, in which he may safely withdraw vigilance from his surroundings, in the confidence that even enemies with temporary advantage will "disavail themselves of the opportunities for various aggressions" (331). When Fastolf turns his back (as of course he must to urinate against the wall) he trustingly opens what Goffman calls a "lurk line," an area out of the individual's own line of vision, within which an unknown or unobserved adversary might connive against him (293). Ordinarily, a trusting person can allow "lurk lines" to exist without suffering harm. But not when inhabiting one of Goffman's "hot umwelts" (328), or aggressively supercharged environments. And, remaining for a moment with this terminology, I would say that the charge against Hochon and his master Austin is precisely that they have raised the temperature of their social environment.

In what I am calling the "Brembre" reading of this narrative, Hochon's aggressive behavior possesses the potential to give considerable offense. And evidently more than a few citizens were able to associate themselves with this reading. For, when documents relating to the Austin case were summoned into chancery in January 1388, Banham's accusations were supplied by the city officials, together with the information that More, Standon, and Charney had empaneled a jury to review the accusations, and that the jury had concluded upon its oath that all were true ("quod omnia in dicta billa contenta sunt vera") with the exception of one charge that Austin had stolen a thousand pounds from the king, presumably by bilking him out of customs duties. Given all the possibilities for manipulating a jury (Post, 65–77), not too much credit need be attached to this conclusion, but it does suggest that Banham's line of analysis, supported by the testimony of his fellow servant John Hore, was persuasive enough not to seem self-evidently outrageous to the already converted. Yet this reading, of Fastolf as an imposed-upon innocent, is hardly the only way in which this narrative could be read—or was read. Further reflection on the elements of Banham's narration, from a "dissenting" point of view, suggests its limitation as a reliable agent of its author's intention. Like other narratives, it will turn out to lead a subsequent life of its own, embracing evocative elements and drawing upon complicated associations that the author himself cannot finally control.

A Rereading: The Politics of Space

Implicit within the Banham narrative rests an alternative reading, in which Fastolf's perambulation shows such elaborate and inflammatory unconcern as to be obtrusive and provocative in its own right and in which Hochon's response may be seen as interactively provoked. This reading could be adduced simply as a matter of interpretation, as one of many possible construals of a multivalent text. More relevantly, though, it can issue from an analysis that links the interactional behavior portrayed in Banham's passage with institutions and finally with social and political power.

Banham's apparent intent in choosing Fastolf as a *named* participant was to suggest his standing as a person of independent repute and a Brembre supporter, against whom Hochon's impertinent threats would have seemed a particular offense. But, reading this passage from a point of view unbounded by pro-Brembre loyalties, we are reminded of the limits of authorial control. For a character intended to introduce one set of significations into a narrative cannot finally be counted on to introduce that one set alone. And a *living* person, especially a person enjoying an unusually complex social and political existence, can turn out to be an unruly signifier indeed. Hugh Fastolf, for example, possessed many attributes, well known to a general London audience of the 1380s, that would have ill suited him for the role of offended innocent.

Throughout Fastolf's career as monopolist, ship-owner, and London factionalist, he maintained a peculiarly charged identity, a high symbolic profile that seems repeatedly to have drawn his contemporaries into social contests and mock-contests with an aggressive content just short of actual mayhem. He is repeatedly mentioned as a participant in the largest social conflicts of his day, not just as a hapless bystander but as a protagonist who dominates a piece of the action in his own right. Whether we speak of the Good Parliament of 1376, the rising of 1381, or the assault on Richard's prerogative by the appellant lords in 1387–1388, Fastolf is there—if not in a leading role, at least in a role that attracts to itself, and expresses, issues of importance to significant numbers of participants.

Fastolf's first appearance on the national scene finds him treated—characteristically—as an exceptional and even infamous case. In the later 1370s Great Yarmouth was a site of intense factional struggle between a merchant patriciate (to which Fastolf naturally belonged) and a group of less prosperous merchants and guildsmen (Saul, 159–61). Matters came to a head in 1376, when the crown first supported the patriciate, and then reversed itself, requiring Fastolf and other *potentiores et maiores* to post bond for peaceable conduct toward the ordinary citizens who at least claimed to fear for their own life and limb (*CCR* [1374–1377], 415, 470; PSO C54/215, mem. 3d). Even though the Fastolf of 1376 may be considered more a local than a national figure, notice of his activities reached the Good Parliament of 1376, where, according to the records of the succeeding parliament of 1377, he was impeached, not in the usual way but "par clamor," because of the "malice & hayne" borne against him by some of his ill-wishing Great Yarmouth neighbors ("ses veisines, ses malveulliantz," *RP*, 2:375). Rescued in this case by the 1377 or "bad" parliament's determination to undo most of the reforming actions of 1376, Fastolf was soon to shift his base to London, but not to disappear from view.

As a visible capitalist with holdings in several counties, Fastolf might have been expected to suffer in 1381. He did in fact lose property to rebels (in July he received letters of authorization to repossess goods lost to insurgents in Norfolk and Suffolk, *CPR* [1381–1385], 24, 76), and he also came into conflict with other persons whose private motives temporarily coincided with rebel demands. An instance of the latter involves Fastolf's new residence on Thames Street, one evidently leased to Fastolf by Thomas Salisbury prior to his death, to which Fastolf appears to have laid de facto claim. On 14 June 1381, at the height of the "tempus furiosum," Salisbury's son Paul broke into the home together with a servant and other purportedly hired ruffians to seize the deed recording Fastolf's obligation to pay rent for the property as well as other documents. Fastolf was evidently not at home, but Paul terrorized his wife Joan, by threatening Fastolf with death by decapitation ("comminati fuissent quod idem Hugo esset decollatus, si ipsum ibidem invenissent"), by taking a sword and gauntlets, and by imbibing six casks of ale and a pipe of wine and destroying what could not be drunk ("sex cados cervisie et unam pipam vini . . . bibisse et vastasse").[9] Paul was evidently in the legal right, for these events are recorded in his letter of royal pardon.[10]

More troubles—including some concurrent with the Austin trial—were

---

[9] Réville, 207–9. Earlier on the same day, Paul had already shown a decided talent for improvised theater when he and his followers broke into the house of alderman William Baret and his wife, apparently with the same motives as in his visit to Fastolf. He forced them into the high street outside their door, where he made William's wife kneel to him and made both of them thank him for their long occupation of his home, as well as for sparing their lives: "Eos stare fecisse, et dictam uxorem ejusdem Willelmi coram eo per longum tempus genuflectere et dictos Willelmum et uxorem suam de longa habitacione in hospicio predicto et de vita eorum regraciari coartavisse" (Réville, pp. 207–9). This incident is discussed in Prescott, "London."

[10] Despite his exoneration, Paul was to remain legally liable to Hugh for any offenses. Paul would seem to have been simultaneously victimized by Fastolf's acquisitiveness and by bad guardianship. Stephen O'Connor has called my attention to a 29 May 1381 entry in LBH, in which Agnes Francis (widow of Adam Francis) renders account of her guardianship of Paul, son of Thomas Salisbury, knight (*CLBH*, 170). Paul evidently attained his majority shortly before he asserted his inheritance rights in the raid on the Barets and the Fastolfs.

to arise during Fastolf's term as sheriff in 1387–1388. Although Fastolf's real money came from capitalism and connivance, he was among those of Richard II's London supporters buoyed into visible and potentially lucrative posts in that rather hysterical period of royal favoritism that commenced in 1384–1385 and lasted until the rise of the anti–Ricardian Lords Appellant in 1387–1388. In addition to achieving posts like deputy constable of Dover Castle under Simon Burley (*CPR* [1381–1385], 589) and justice of the peace for Kent (*CPR* [1381–1385], 84), Fastolf advanced with fellow grocer and Ricardian William Venour to the position of sheriff on 21 September 1387 (*CLBH*, 313). Although this was an elective position, the *communitas* responsible for the election was still solidly pro-Ricardian, and this was the occasion when Richard wrote to Mayor Exton of his satisfaction in learning from Nicholas Brembre "that good and honorable men had been elected Sheriffs" (*CLBH*, 317). That this advancement was widely perceived as political is attested by a 1388 petition of the cutlers' guild, which singles out Fastolf's election for negative attention.[11] The cutlers argued that Exton had been handpicked by Brembre in order to continue "lez fauxete & extorcions qui furent comences par le dit monsieur Nichol & les autres de son affinite," and they asked that recorder William Cheyne and sheriff Hugh Fastolf "soient descharges de lour Offices pour tous iours" as "complices au dit monsieur Nichol" (Welch, 1:266).

The petition amounted to a request that the Merciless Parliament of winter/spring 1388 extend its scope to action against those Brembre loyalists like Exton, Fastolf, and Cheyne, who remained in city government, but either the fact that Fastolf's term would soon end or the flagging attention of the Appellants saved him from persecution. Nevertheless, his propensity for attracting speculation and comment had not deserted him. On 3 August 1388, the beadle of Cornhill ward was charged with having spread the false rumor that alderman John Churchman and sheriff Hugh Fastolf had been arrested by the king's council and had been tied up and taken on horseback to the Tower (with the reasons for their arrest written on a piece of parchment attached to Churchman's shoulder), and that, moreover, the Duke of Gloucester had dealt Churchman a blow on the head ("fregit capud praedicti Johannis" LBH, fol. ccxxix; *CLBH*, 329–30). Although the beadle was unable to produce the person from whom he had heard this rumor, and was disciplined for it, this quasi-event was nevertheless produced within an active grasp of the factional situation of the day: in August 1388 the royal council was still dominated by the Appellants,

---

[11] This petition is often dated 1386—for example, in *RP*, 3:225, Chambers and Daunt, 273, and Welch, 263. But the Westminster chronicler dates it early in the term of the Merciless Parliament (i.e., February 1388, see 334–36). The latter date is surely correct, since the petition of the cutlers must have been written after Fastolf's election as sheriff in September 1387.

with Gloucester as their most visible leader, and whether or not Gloucester cracked any heads the Appellants could not have been altogether pleased that their now waning efforts had left untouched so many of the king's supporters in the city of London.

We might assume that Fastolf's involvement in so many contemporary flareups was not just a matter of factional affiliation, but of a personality that was confrontational in its own right. Within two weeks after the Banham accusation, for example, four of Fastolf's friends would post a thousand-pound bond in chancery, guaranteeing that Fastolf would do or procure no injury or wrongdoing ("dampnum vel malum") to Ralph Ramsey or Henry Scogan (*CCR* [1385–1389], 443; PRO C54/228, mem. 32d). The circumstances of this extraordinarily large bond are unknown, and I can add nothing about Ralph Ramsey. But Fastolf's menace to the young Henry Scogan, recently arrived in London and later to be recognized as addressee of Chaucer's gently humorous poem and an earnest moralist in his own right, would seem to suggest a high level of continuing truculence.

How, knowing these things, could a contemporary audience not strongly disposed in Fastolf's favor have set them aside, or uncritically accepted him as the victimized innocent of Banham's narrative? Rearrayed in some of his contemporary significations, Fastolf acquires a certain contentiousness—even a certain swagger—that ill suits him for his assigned role.

Other difficulties arise with much that Banham says about the treasonous climate of the Austin household. On the face of it, the identification of Austin with Northampton was quite plausible. Austin was a prominent mercer—representing them, for example, in the Common Council during Northampton's first mayoral term (*Pleas*, 29)—and that guild had not only provided much of Northampton's original base but continued to support his positions throughout the 1380s. As late as 1388, for example, the Westminster chronicler describes the mercers, together with the goldsmiths and the drapers, as the *turbatores* who were continuing to agitate against the *vitallarii*, or victualers, within the city (334–36). These are the guilds, together with such allies as the cutlers, that petitioned the Merciless Parliament early in 1388 against the previous wrongdoings of the Brembre party—including its domination of the 1384 elections ("Petition").

But, whatever his private sympathies, Austin's career suggests that he was a more moderate proponent of the Northampton position than Banham makes him out to be. For one thing, although the names of literally hundreds of Northampton supporters of the period 1382–1384 are known, his name is nowhere mentioned among them. He is unmentioned among nearly one hundred Northampton supporters listed as principal conspirators or those who gave bond for the conspirators in or after January 1384 (*Pleas*, 57–60); nor is he listed in Usk's or the other indictments connected with Northampton's trial at Reading in August 1384 ("Appeal"; Powell and Trevelyan, 27–38; Bird, 134–40); nor does he appear in lists of the numerous other Londoners delivered under bail or left free on bond after the unrest on the election day of 13 October 1384 (*Pleas*, 60–69). Furthermore, Austin was present at a kangaroo meeting of 22 March 1385, among representatives from the ward of Cheap, when the mayor, aldermen, and additional "wise and discreet" representatives of the wards ("plusours bones gentz des plus sages et discretz des gardes de la citee") petitioned that Northampton be put to death in order to end division in the city (*Pleas*, A27, mem. 2; p. 56). In the superheated atmosphere of London factional politics, merely petitioning for someone's death does not necessarily register the petitioner as a strong opponent, but Austin's presence at least suggests moderation, since a pro-Northampton zealot would not have been invited to this patently stacked meeting in the first place!

Austin's civic posts likewise suggest a general posture of moderation, perhaps leavened by tacit Northampton leanings. He was first elected to the common council in March 1387, at a time when Brembre interests were still very much in control. His main posts were to come in 1388–1389, when the ruling oligarchy was in the process of opening its ranks to trustworthy members less securely identified with Brembre. His first term as alderman, for example, commenced in 13 June 1388, soon after Brembre's death and at the nadir of the city royalists' fortunes (*CLBH*, 325). And, on 21 September 1388, at a time of continuing royal eclipse, he was elected sheriff, to fill the position just vacated by Hugh Fastolf (*CLBH*, 332)!

That this reputable bourgeois spent the days before and during the 13 October 1384 election worrying about how to position himself is easy enough to believe. But that he cached armaments, armed his household, and even at one point took upon himself the responsibility of reminding Northampton's maintainers to be ready to act on election day, seems hardly credible.

A reading is, after all, based on a series of approximations, in which the reader applies an interpretative scheme, sees how it fits, and either accepts it or rejects it in favor of a better one. If one scheme, such as "a citizen of repute is wrongfully offended by a factional zealot" contradicts known facts, its audience is likely to try another, and presumably unintended one, such as "an arrogant factionalist provokes a loyal apprentice to a display of anger." Known facts about Fastolf and Austin promote such a rereading, and its likelihood is further enhanced when this narrative is fully rearrayed within its implied locale, of symbolically charged civic space.

Although none of the buildings of the fourteenth-century Guildhall precinct now stands, documentary and archaeological evidence assembled by Caroline Barron permits a reasonably assured mapping of the implied locale of Banham's narrative as well as a partial rescue of some of its contemporary symbolic resonances. Situated at the west end of the present, post-1411 Guildhall site was its precursor, a structure primarily of the thirteenth century, containing a "great hall" of about ninety by fifty feet, in which the commonalty would gather for the election of the mayor and comparable civic occasions. Some sixty yards southwest of the Guildhall stood St. Lawrence's, a structure dating from the twelfth century, then serving as parish church and ultimately (after the destruction of the Guildhall chapel) to become the site of important civic functions. The two structures were connected by the Guildhall yard, defined by the Guildhall to the north and St. Lawrence's to the southwest, and ringed by the Guildhall chapel, an endowed college, a common latrine, and other private and civic properties (Barron, *Guildhall*, 15–24). All were contained within a Guildhall precinct, defined at the south end by the south wall of St. Lawrence's and private tenements, linked by a gate opening on what was then Catte Street and is now Gresham Street.

The events of Banham's narrative could possibly occur at any point in the day and Fastolf's route could possibly be imagined to proceed from the south, through the ward of Cheap, with Hochon stationed across Catte Street. But the considerations that the Brembre people have supposedly already carried the day, that the election has just occurred and its outcome is now known, and that Hochon is tarrying at the scene rather than returning to open the shop encourage the impression that Fastolf leaves the meeting through the south door of the Guildhall, crosses the Guildhall yard, and pauses to urinate on the north or east exposure of St. Lawrence's. And the Guildhall yard, across which he passes to reach St. Lawrence's, must be regarded as a civic space of the greatest importance. Caroline Barron describes the yard as "an open space roughly 150 feet long and 45 feet wide . . . , the hub of civic life and yet . . . a place of quiet spaciousness cut off from the busy roads which encompassed it" (*Guildhall*, 24). Not only the hub of civic life, it was "common land," described as such in city documents (LBH, fol. 140v) and with rights of access of all citizens jealously guarded.

As common land, the Guildhall yard possessed a latent symbolic power, but a power that remained unrealized until it became an object of informed regard—until it was used or traversed in some way evocative of its meanings. Rearrayed in his contemporary factional identity, the Fastolf of Banham's narrative traverses the Guildhall yard in a manner that stakes a particular sort of claim—that lays, in a symbolic sense, factional claim to the whole city. Let me pause for a moment to emphasize the theatricality of Fastolf's reported gesture. Although the election is imagined to be over, Cheapside, and probably the Guildhall yard as well, had recently been swarming with armed belligerents of both parties. Not only might

Brembre have hidden arms within the Guildhall itself, but his men were said to have been armed, charging out at Northampton supporters as if actually at war. Armed Northampton supporters were abroad as well, including not only Austin and his men but probably many of the guildsmen who gathered at St. Paul's and certainly individuals like tailor William Woodcock. Many armed stragglers surely remained, with Hochon identified in this narrative as one of them. Fastolf's nonchalance in this situation virtually asks to be read as an assertion of control, less a politically neutral act than a public dramatization of the fact that, so securely does his faction now possess the city, none would dare do him harm.

And, while considering the symbolism of Fastolf's itinerary and actions, we cannot overlook the implications of his public urination. We tend to suppose that fourteenth-century Londoners were casual about public purgation, but contemporary evidence suggests otherwise. Some of the senses in which public urination might cause offense, and in turn serve as a focal point for larger civic conflicts, are embodied in an earlier fourteenth-century narrative brought to my attention by Caroline Barron. In Banham's narrative, the particular conflict involves representatives of two urban factions in a contested political situation. In this narrative of 1307, representatives of two other opposed groupings—the court on the one hand and the city on the other—clash over a matter of decorum within the city walls. As reconstructed from a badly damaged roll by A. H. Thomas [with my insertions from the manuscript], this narrative states that:

> Walter . . . and John, his servant [famulus], were summoned to answer Thomas Scott, groom of the Prince [garcioni principis], on a charge that when he wanted to relieve himself [. . . suum purgaret] in . . . Lane, they assaulted him and struck him with a knife, to his damage 100s. The defendants pleaded that they told the plaintiff that it would be more decent to go to the common privies of city [decentius foret adire communes cloacas civitatis] to relieve himself, whereupon the plaintiff wanted to kill Walter, and he in fear of his life defended himself. (Mayor's Court Rolls, roll 1, mem. 2, p. 255)

The fact that city latrines existed as early as 1307 and that use of them was regarded as the decent thing to do already has a bearing on the potentially insulting implications of Fastolf's act.[12] Although we often slip into casual assumptions about the Middle Ages as times of total laxity in such matters, this passage argues that Fastolf's decision to relieve himself against the wall of St. Lawrence's was more a flouting of public standards than Banham at first seems to suggest.[13] (The two situations may actually have been even

---

[12] Ernest Sabine documents the existence of at least thirteen common latrines, some large enough to accommodate many persons, in later medieval London (309).

[13] Attempts to restrain public urination seem also to have been made in late medieval and

more similar, given that just as citizen Walter was able to point to the existence of common latrines in the city, so was a common latrine located adjacent to the Guildhall yard, though with the issue of access unclear.[14]) Of course, as with Hochon's gesture, Walter and John's intervention involved more than "decency"; as indicated by jurisdiction of the case in the mayor's court, its real dynamism involved a clash between a city insider (a citizen with his servant) and an outsider (a retainer in the *familia* of Edward of Carnarvon) over a matter of conduct within the city walls. At stake, in other words, were matters of city prerogative, asserted against a member of a royal household known for its presumption and display, with the act of urination as occasion and pretext for aggressive rejoinder.[15]

One need not be an ethologist to grasp Fastolf's act as a particularly blatant and hence aggressive form of "marking behavior." Considering its election-day context, we would seem to have one of those cases described by Mary Douglas, in which an excretory activity at the body's margins (spitting, bleeding, crying, excreting) carries a special charge that cannot be fully understood "in isolation from all other margins" (121). The margins in question must be seen as political, in the operations by which factions lay or resign claim to control of civic space. Fastolf's traversal of public space, and urination at its verge, seems to announce: ours is not a partial claim; now that the election is over and the Northampton loyalists routed, this is *all* ours.

With respect to Fastolf's "notorious" identity,[16] to the symbolically charged nature of the space he traverses, and even to the contemporary implications of the act of urination, an alternative reading is emerging, within which Fastolf may be seen to provoke Hochon's response. These fragmentary observations may be drawn together within a sense of the

---

early modern Florence; Richard Trexler cites the fifteenth-century sermons of Bernardino of Siena as evidence that a red cross was employed on city walls to restrain urination (54).

[14] The city had taken pains to reserve its rights of access to this latrine (LBH, fol. cxl). Nevertheless, Caroline Barron, commenting on an early draft of this essay, pointed out that the access in question might not have encouraged its free use by citizens.

[15] The fray occurred two months before the death of Edward I and Edward of Carnarvon's accession as Edward II. On the "large and motley crew" constituting his *familia* of over two hundred noble wards, knights and esquires, yeomen, *garciones* or grooms, and the like, see Tout, 2:165–80. Tout regards the prince's household as a rival to the king's own and details its burdensome exactions. He observes that, though the prince was seldom resident in London, "the surplus of the income from the prince's domains was so constantly sent to his wardrobe in London that we are tempted to believe that there was with the prince, as with the king, some sort of standing wardrobe establishment, or treasury, in the capital" (2:178). On the first decade of the fourteenth century as a period of heightened political awareness on the part of London citizens and tradespersons, and resentment toward Edward I and Edward II, see G. Williams, esp. 264–68.

[16] I borrow this phrase from Linda Charnes, whose book on the formation of Shakespearean identities within preexisting expectations is forthcoming with Harvard Univerity Press.

larger factional struggle to which Banham's narrative alludes, with additional support from social theorist Michel de Certeau. De Certeau learned much from Erving Goffman but took another conceptual step by linking interactional behavior with facts of political power. He divides social practices into "strategies" and "tactics" (esp. 35–39). A strategy is launched by a person or persons who control space, who have appropriated a proper "place" as their own and from which opponents can be defined as the "other." Strategy is an art of the politically, economically, or militarily strong. A tactic, on the other hand, is a form of resistance launched by a person or persons who control no space, who must operate opportunistically within space controlled by another. Its medium is thus not space at all but time, as it poaches, surprises, and grasps opportunities to "seize on the wing the possibilities that offer themselves at any given moment" (37). Its opportunism reveals the tactic as an art of the weak.

Fastolf's progress across the Guildhall yard to St. Lawrence's, and his urination against St. Lawrence's wall, may be viewed not as random but as provocative behavior, as a strategy mounted by a successful factionalist, designed to celebrate and confirm his own faction's secure control of civic space. Hochon's symbolic display of aggression may be seen to issue from the weakness of his position. For what the dispirited Northampton followers have just learned is that they control no space, and that any actions they mount must represent shadowings, poachings, and the like, conducted within the territory of the now fully dominant Brembre party. Whether or not the actions of the Brembre party constituted "thievery," the election was theirs and with it the city. But Hochon seizes a momentary opportunity, a chance to grasp a possibility briefly presenting itself, to exemplify factionally based resistance to a state of affairs.

Secure in his party's control, the partisan of the strong flaunts his strength by meek behavior; controlling nothing, the minor functionary of the disappointed faction seizes a moment to behave as if he were strong. De Certeau's scheme, however, contains a consolation for those who must resort to tactics:

> Strategies pin their hopes on the resistance that the establishment of a place offers to the erosion of time; tactics on a clever utilization of time, of the opportunities it presents and also of the play that it introduces into the foundations of power. . . . The two ways of acting can be distinguished according to whether they bet on place or on time. (39)

The Brembre party, having scraped into office in 1383, set out to assure itself a long domination of the machinery of government and patronage. As late as October 1387, with handpicked confederate Exton as mayor and with loyalists Venour and Fastolf as sheriffs of London, this domination seemed secure. On 5 October 1387, for example, Exton floor managed an aldermanic oath of allegiance to Richard that included a denunciation of the "evil opinions of John Northampton," and he transmitted it to Richard with the suggestion that Brembre serve as the city's spokesperson with the king (*CLBH*, 315). On 28 October Richard was informed that members of the city were *unanimes* on his behalf, and on 10 November the mayor and citizens arranged an entry for Richard and his party at which all were clad in a single white and red livery as a token of their unanimity ("in una secta, alba scilicet et rubea,"—*West.*, 206). But the erosion of Brembre's position was hastened by the rise of the Appellants in the course of the autumn. The ascendance of the Appellants after their victory at Radcot Bridge on 20 December (*West.*, 222–24) and the arrest of Brembre by 21 December abruptly created a new state of affairs. By 27 December, Mayor Exton and the aldermen had peaceably received the lords (*West.*, 232), and when summoned by the Appellants that spring the mayor and aldermen effectively consented to Brembre's death by conceding (after some initial reluctance) that he might have been guilty of treasonable conduct (*West.*, 312–14). The events of 1388, during which Exton and the aldermen assumed a position of opportunistic neutrality and built a new oligarchy that included moderates like Austin while Brembre went to the block, show that welcome reversals often await those who "bet on time."[17]

A further, and undoubtedly related, reversal was to occur in the case of the Austin family. The entire case was reopened on 9 January 1388, at which time the transcript of Banham's testimony was forwarded to chancery by the mayor and sheriffs. But in January 1388, with Brembre on trial and Richard's city loyalists under cover or fully in retreat, Banham's accusation of treasonable association with an anti-Brembre faction would certainly have lost its sting. January 29, 1388, is the date of final release of Thomas Austin, mercer, and Alicia his wife, and his loyal servant "Hugone Lytherpolle" (LBH, fol. ccxxiv; *CLBH*, 322).

Fictional Truth

Banham's narrative shifts under our gaze, revealing new aspects of the faction-ridden situation it sets out to describe. Reinserted in the matrix of political claims and counterclaims that give it life, it seems less and less a repository of fact, or even to enjoy a unitary and consistent point of view. Are we therefore obliged to take the next step and to label it "untrue?" I

---

[17] Before their terms of office ended, both Exton and Venour would seek blanket pardons for themselves, apparently as a safeguard against subsequent charges associating them with the Brembre faction (*CPR* [1385–1389], 502, 505). For an excellent discussion of the city leaders' efforts to distance themselves from Brembre, see Bird, 90–98.

want to argue the contrary, that the narrative is to be valued for possessing its own kind of truth. But its truth is less documentary (in the sense of contributing hard fact to the record of contention in the 1380s) than fictional (in the sense of its realization within a broadly shared understanding of the topography and emotional tenor of factional contention). "True" or not, it embodies a fully historical grasp of the factional alignments, their members, their points of friction, the occasions at which they come into conflict, their lexicon of insult, and the possibility that violence might or might not ensue.

One venerable line of analysis concludes that, despite surface manifestations of struggle, later medieval London was actually a community and that community values normally prevailed over sectional interests. This is, for example, the contention of a recent study that finds Northampton to be an oligarch himself, turning to agitation only as an after-the-fact and "merely tactical" adjunct to his own schemes for aggrandizement.[18] And at times, when the city is threatened from without, such a corporate response is indeed in evidence—at least if we limit the responding group to males, and then further exclude unattached laborers, aliens, apprentices, and journeymen, and confine our attention only to the one-third or so of male citizens empowered to act on the city's behalf. This group, which did include followers both of Brembre and Northampton, showed an ability to orchestrate joint actions with remarkable celerity, as in their 1387–1388 switch of loyalty from Richard to the Appellants, the city's reconcilation with Richard in 1392, or the shift from Richard to Bolingbroke in 1399. And such instances of common purpose were, to be sure, dramatized in a host of official pageants and ceremonials, such as the 1387 reception of Richard by an entire patriciate clad in a single livery.

Nevertheless, evidence of other, less official social actions and dramas points in another direction, away from unity and common purpose and toward a highly fragmented political environment in which persons banded together along temporary lines of common interest to assert their immediate claims. These unofficial social dramas operate without the budgets, sets, and costumes of official pageantry and are likely to flare up in a moment and to use materials that come opportunely to hand. Official dramas, like de Certeau's strategies, involve institutional support, advance

---

[18] I am alluding in a general way to Pamela Nightingale's attempt at a new analysis of London politics in the 1380s, at once particularized in its microanalysis of individual motivation and general in its reliance on ideas of community. Nightingale's analysis would supplant that of Bird, with its emphasis on factional strife based on persistent differences between discernable class fractions. Bird's careful elucidation of actual points of economic and vocational difference within the upper strata of the London citizenry nevertheless seems to me to possess greater explanatory force than Nightingale's strained predication of a rather Thatcherite combination of extreme economic individualism and communitarian sentimentalism.

planning, and control of space. Unofficial dramas, like de Certeau's tactics, are more likely to enjoy only the sponsorship of those out of power, and to represent spur-of-the-moment improvisations within the space of the dominant adversary. These unofficial dramas, as I am describing them, do not necessarily require conscious or deliberate participation. They are defined less by intent than by a conjunction of other properties: an increased density of signification, which may include the appropriation of symbolically charged devices or the conferral of special significance to an everyday object; a momentary enlargement of referential scope, in which local events are saturated with larger political or institutional meanings; and provision of a hypothetical frame within which dangerous social or political conflicts can be addressed in an atmosphere of lessened risk.

Such improvised dramas appear and reappear in accounts of events treated elsewhere in this volume: when the London rebels of 1381 raise John of Gaunt's *jakke* on a lance and use it for target practice; or when Richard under pressure from the Appellants seeks to rally followers by wholesale distribution of badges in the countryside; or when John Northampton, invited to come with friends to Whitefriars, brings four hundred representatives of London crafts; or when Paul Salisbury guzzles and smashes Fastolf's casks of ale. Often a drama openly enjoys the status of an invention, as when ill-wishers generate the rumor of Fastolf trussed up and taken to the Tower on horseback with accusations written on parchment attached to his confederate's shoulder, or when Henry of Derby, seeking to legitimize his usurpation, assembles a solemn committee of *doctores* to compose the narrative of his accession. But, even when not provable or "true," these improvised dramas embody a kind of truth, by summarizing and epitomizing the realities of social struggle beneath the more placid productions of communitarian ideology.[19]

Hochon's intervention is an example of improvised social drama, in which a chance provocation (Fastolf's perambulation and urination), a ready-made audience (Banham and his associate John Hore), and a vivid symbol of anger and frustration (Hochon's weapon) are knit together to exemplify a situation of factional rivalry. Perhaps Hochon really drew his bow, and Banham observed and reported his action, and Banham's narrative order reiterates an original order of events. Perhaps Banham's account is, like the rumor of Fastolf trussed up and taken away, a case of sheer invention. Either way, his account is realized within a set of commonly held ideas about factional strife: that such strife is real and likely to boil up in everyday interaction, that it engages momentary passions and fosters

---

[19] Divisive elements operating behind some of the ostensibly unifying structures of Richard's reign in general and the city of London in particular are discussed in detail in David Wallace's forthcoming *Chaucerian Polity*, to be published by Stanford University Press.

long-term grudges, that possession of mayoral and shrieval and aldermanic posts secures effective power and is worth caring about, that alignments involve not only individuals but also larger units like craft guilds and *meynes*, or households. These are the kinds of interpretative structures within which London citizens of the 1380s made sense of their world and organized themselves as participants in its social struggles. Without common assent to these and other ideas, Banham's narrative could probably not have been composed and would certainly not have been intelligible to the public to which it was addressed.

Hochon's arrow never flew, never struck a real target. But Banham's narrative offers privileged access to an environment of factional struggle now largely closed to us, with all its accompanying solidarities and antagonisms and personal risks and material enticements. It enjoys, in other words, a densely complex and richly communicative historicity, as John Banham's fiction of truth.

Chapter 2

"A REVELLE!": CHRONICLE EVIDENCE
AND THE REBEL VOICE

PRESENT-DAY theoretical practices offer powerful tools for disclosing the historicity of fabulous narratives and the fabulousness of historical narratives. As a result, we are left in a contradictory and rather embarrassing relation to the historical claims of the later medieval narrative chronicles. We are less likely to end up looking foolish when we seek historical information from outright inventions like romances and novels than from these deceptive compendiums of narratized fact and wild speculation. The unreliability of the chronicles is due in part to the properties of narrative itself, with its propensities for selective treatment, imputation of motive, and implicit moralization. But the chroniclers accentuate these aspects of narrative, adapting their texts to serve clerical partisanship, bolster royal authority, and uphold hierarchy and vested privilege. Further distortions result from compositional reliance on what Derek Pearsall has described as preexisting "interpretative models" (69), unabashed and often unacknowledged borrowing, rumormongering, and overt fabrication.

Rather than denying the chronicles any historical value at all, however, I propose to adopt the harder task of trying to understand the *kind* of historical information they may legitimately be supposed to provide. Certainly, the chronicles offer an abundance of information about the historically defined vantage point of the chroniclers themselves, about their own favored interpretative models or schemes, and about the ways in which they wield them in support of a highly partial view of social experience. At the same time, these highly interested observers devote little attention to the rationales for resistance to their own most cherished beliefs. Least of all would we expect to learn much about my chosen subject, rebel ideology and intent in 1381, from narratives designed to deny the rebels either coherent ideology or rational intent. Yet, as Jean-Claude Schmitt has observed, even the most unremittingly elite texts contain precious information about the motivations of the unlettered, silenced, and decidedly nonelite; in his words, "It is not so much the documents that are lacking as the conceptual instruments necessary to understand them" (171).

My own inquiry into the largely effaced basis of rebel actions will proceed in two conceptual stages. The first depends upon an observable feature of argumentation, or of narration employed for argumentative purposes, that an action must be at least partially evoked before it is condemned. Thus, resting within the chroniclers' unrelentingly hostile renditions is often an implied or shadowed representation of a rebel rationale. One might well ask how an observer as fully invested in the status quo as a monastic chronicler could even begin to conjure a believable basis for rebel action, and I reply to this question in the second of my conceptual stages. In my treatment, interpretative schemes are likely to be the property not just of a single social segment but of a society as a whole. As a result of this Janus-faced quality, a single scheme might make a dual appearance, wielded by a chronicler to condemn a rebel action and (rotated on its axis) wielded by the rebels to produce that action in the first place. Some of the most interested formulations of the chroniclers will turn out to have been not theirs alone, but only available to them, on loan as it were, for temporary use, even as these same formulations were available to the chroniclers' adversaries for very different application.

(Mis)representing the Rebels

> Wherever men oppress their fellows, wherever they enslave
> them, they will endeavor to find the needed apology for such
> enslavement and oppression in the character of the people
> oppressed and enslaved.
> —*Frederick Douglass*

The chronicles employ a broad range of strategies designed to discredit the social standing, judgment, and objectives of the rebels at every level of representation. These strategies—representing the rebels as yokel interlopers, as shifty manipulators of traditional oaths and understandings, as a purposely undisciplined rabble, as playacting juveniles or besotted revelers—repeatedly recur, sometimes in succession and sometimes tumbled together.

I want to begin by arguing the paradoxical position that rebel motives and desires are most clearly illuminated within these stigmatizing strategies rather than beyond their bounds. This position acknowledges a practical reality, that since little narrative material about the rebels is to be found outside the chroniclers' presentational strategies, we will find our evidence there or nowhere. Beyond that, however, lies another aspect of stigmatizing narrative: a narrator who wishes to discredit an actor or group of actors must first, in however grudging or distorted a fashion, *represent* their actions or words. Once oppositional actions or words have been represented, they lie open to subsequent interpretation. So opened, in however closely regulated a context, the chronicle-produced blunderings and murkily motivated atrocities of the clownish "peasants" of 1381 often turn out to possess a representational underside, a dim and inadvertent area of implication in which a coherent and admirable motivation may be discerned.[1]

The whole gamut of stigmatizing strategies is to be found within the Westminster chronicler's description of the first phases of the 1381 rising and the burning of Lambeth Palace:

> Ignobilis turba rusticorum surrexit. Eodem anno pridie Idus Junii coadunata fuit maxima multitudo ruralium Estsexie pariter et Cancie; et hii quidem qui de Cancia per plures partes Cancie uti rabidissimi canes discurrentes plurimo-rum domos et maneria solotenus diruerunt, nonnullos decapitaverunt, et quos-que sibi occurrentes qui de eorum contubernio non fuerant ut eis adhererent et cum eis in defensionem regis Ricardi interposito juramento constringebant, pretendentes se defensuros regem et regni commoditatem contra suos tradi-tores. Quare concrescente eorum turba longe lateque debachabantur, magis-trum Simonem de Sudbur' tunc archiepiscopum pariter et Anglie cancella-rium proditorem esse asserentes et morte dignissimum; unde ad manerium suum de Lambhuth' descendentes libros, vestes, mappas, et plura alia inibi

---

[1] The proposition that (in the words of Gurevich) "the Latin writings of scholars and the teachers contain substantial elements of the non-literate folklore tradition almost against their authors' will" (xvii) has been widely entertained but not always satisfactorily explained. Gur-evich himself explains the presence of popular alternatives in literate works in terms of a communicative function, the need to reach an illiterate laity, which would not apply to chron-icles destined for limited circulation. The same phenomenon has been explained in terms of inevitable linguistic interchange or cross-contamination, as with Michael D. Bristol's conten-tion that texts are produced within "a 'heteroglot' world of socially diverse speech types. These speech types overlap, interpenetrate, exchange terms and expressions, and in general shadow each other so intimately that no monopoly of knowledge is ever achieved without contamination by what it purports to exclude. Instead of an inference that popular culture cannot be observed anywhere, it seems more useful to assert that popular culture existed everywhere, though never in a 'pure' and uncontaminated form" (45–46). The relative advan-tage of my approach is that it specifies a mechanism—intended narrative stigmatization—by which the suppressed motives enter the text in the first place and are thus rendered available for analysis. Relevant to this approach is Annabel Patterson's recent and highly illuminating discussion of textual "ventriloquism," in *Shakespeare and the Popular Voice*, especially in her essay "The Peasant's Toe: Popular Culture and Popular Pressure," in which she seeks to re-trieve a popular voice from the words of biased commentaries and fallible spokespersons (32–51). Another very congenial convergence with my analysis occurs in John Ganim's *Chauce-rian Theatricality*, especially the chapter on "The Noise of the People," in which he discusses the pressure of the popular voice on artists otherwise inclined to deflect or contain its claims (108–20). On the larger problem of reconstructing rebel ideology see Rosamond Faith, "The 'Great Rumour' of 1377."

relicta igne combusserunt; dolia vino referta confregerunt et hauserunt, et quod vini fuerat relictum in terram effuderunt; singula coquine vasa adinvicem collidentes fregerunt; et ista perpetrantes velud de re laudabili plaudentes "A revelle! A revelle!" exclamarunt. (2)

A base mob of peasants rose up. On June 12 a large multitude of countryfolk from Essex and Kent gathered together. And indeed, those from Kent, running through their country like rabid dogs, completely destroyed many homes and manors, beheading not a few, and forced those not belonging to their sworn association to adhere to them and to swear an oath of alliance with them, in the defense of King Richard, imagining themselves as defenders of the king and the welfare of the realm against their traitors. Now, their throng thickening, they rampaged far and wide, claiming that Master Simon Sudbury, then both archbishop and chancellor of England, was a traitor and deserved to die; whence descending on his manor of Lambeth, they burnt books, vestments, linen, and many other things left there; they broke open and drained casks of wine, pouring out what was left on the floor; they broke all the kitchen utensils by beating them together; and while doing these things, as if applauding a praiseworthy accomplishment, exclaimed, "A revelle! A revelle!"

The chronicler's scandalized response is actually fabricated from several different tropes and representational strategies, which may be disentangled for consideration:

Rebels as peasants/outsiders. Immediately to be noted is the chronicler's description of the rebels as *rustici* or peasants, entering the city from Essex or Kent. Walsingham separately amplifies this usage when he explains that *rustici* is the normal term for those also called *nativi* or *bondi*, "serfs" or "bondsmen" (*Historia*, 1:454). *Rustici* is thus reserved for the lowest order of agricultural workers: those peasants who, even in the last decades of the fourteenth century, remained bound to the land in customary or sworn relations.[2]

This characterization of the rebels' social composition has been enormously influential; we continue to register its effect by styling the risings of 1381 as "The Peasants' Revolt." But judicial and other historical evidence indicates that other strata were consequentially involved, that peasants—bound or otherwise—played a relatively minor role in the London uprisings. Arguing from escheators' inquests taken after the insurrection, Rodney Hilton finds well-to-do yeomen among the ranks of the rebels, and argues that nearly a third of the rural rebels appear to have engaged in crafts and trade rather than agriculture as such (176–85). Using court rolls and other public records, Christopher Dyer has drawn our attention to the

---

[2] For further discussion of contemporary terminology, see Hilton, 176–77.

leading role played in the rural revolts by members of the "village elite"—
reeves, constables, bailiffs, and holders of multiple parcels of land—with
bound peasants in a decided minority (9–42). Andrew Prescott has used
records of the king's bench to show that, when the rural rebels reached
London, they were far outnumbered by adherents from local suburbs and
the city itself, many of whom were among the leading tradesmen and officials of their communities ("London," 125–43). Hilton appears to be correct when, taking all evidence together, he argues that, far from being confined to serfs or bondsmen, "the rising was one of the whole people below
the ranks of those who exercised lordship in the countryside and established authority in the towns" (184)—everyone, that is, below the ranks of
the gentry and the principal merchants of the largest cities.

As often with the chroniclers, telltale traces of a largely effaced alternative linger to affirm the imaginary nature of their interpretative schemes.
In his case, the social breadth of the rebellion is the obscured element that
intermittently shows things. Although the Westminster chronicler normally uses terms such as *rustici*, he immediately qualifies his initial characterization by calling the rebels *rurales*—or "rural folk"—implying or at
least admitting in theory a more socially diverse grouping. And Walsingham, having likewise introduced the term *rustici*, and advanced *nativi*
and *bondi* as synonyms, offers a similar qualification: "Rustici namque,
quos 'nativos' vel 'bondos' vocamus, simul cum ruralibus accolis in Est-
sexea" (the peasants, whom we call "serfs" or "bondsmen," together with
neighboring rural folk in Essex) (*Historia*, 1:454). And the chroniclers
concede, infrequently, that some of these "other" inhabitants of the countryside might be influential. The Westminster chronicler notes in passing,
for example, that "nobiliores de villa" or upper-class townspeople were said
by the abbot and prior of St. Albans to have supported the local commo-
tions (15). And several chroniclers admit the involvement of Londoners in
the disturbances there (Froissart, 9:395, 402; *Anonimalle*, 141; *Eulogium*,
352; Walsingham, *Historia*, 1:456). These fragmentary admissions culmi-
nate in a momentary but piercing analysis by the Westminster chronicler,
who explains the paralysis of the city during the massacre of the Flemings
in terms of the disposition of disaffected classes within the city itself to
rebel:

> Formidabat quidem ne si invalescentibus servis resisterent, communes tan-
> quam suorum fautores cum servis contra reliquos civium insurgerent, sicque
> tota civitas in seipsa divisa deperiret. (8)

> It was feared that, if the ever-stronger serfs should be resisted, the commons
> [of the city] might rise as their accomplices against the rest of the citizens, and
> thus the whole city should be lost as a result of its internal divisions.

Given the marginal awareness that the rebels were something other than a band of ignorant rustics from Essex and Kent, why then the insistence of the chroniclers that this was the case? Why does Walsingham insist on describing them as the lowest of peasants or *vilissimi rustici* or as "unshod ribalds" or *discaligati ribaldi*, and not only as serfs but as the most lowly of that station, *vilissimae conditionis servi* (*Historia*, 454, 456, 459)? Several interrelated explanations immediately present themselves. One, at the level of imaginative process, is proposed and used with effect by Peter Stallybrass and Allon White: that (in the formulation of Barbara Babcock) "what is socially peripheral is often symbolically central" (20). For the chroniclers, the dynamics of this particular social upheaval are most vividly exposed as reversal and substitution of "low" for "high," and the more marked the contrast the more tellingly its mechanisms are revealed. Thus, in the passage in which Walsingham denounces the peasants in the Tower as the vilest of serfs, he completes this imaginary formation by elevating the knights present in the Tower to the highest levels of status:

> Nam quis unquam credidisset, non solum rusticos, sed rusticorum abjectissimos . . . audere . . . quorundam nobilissimorum militum barbas suis incultissimis et sordidissimis manibus contrectare, demulcere. (*Historia*, 1:459)

> For who would believe, not only peasants, but the lowliest of peasants, would dare to stroke and to touch with their most unrefined and filthy hands the beards of the most noble of knights.

This abundance of superlatives exaggerates a difference, establishing a polarity that exists mainly at the imaginative level. The soldiers garrisoning the Tower (the king and his party then being absent at Mile End) are elevated to the status of most noble knights; the rebels themselves (who probably represented the kind of social cross section described by Hilton, with a high proportion of Londoners) are described not only as dirty-handed peasants, but as the most abject of that rank. Additionally, whatever imaginative satisfaction these exaggerations might possess as an epitomization of transgressive inversion, they also possess the practical political advantage of isolating and stigmatizing the rebels as beneath consideration or respect. Characterized by the chroniclers as serfs, bondsmen, and plowmen, the rebels are the more easily excluded from a rightful share in governance of the realm.

I have already suggested that—despite the intelligent correctives of Hilton, Dyer, Prescott, and others—we continue to show our acquiescence to the chroniclers' strategy when we style the risings of 1381 as "The Peasants' Revolt." Yet, as we have seen, the chroniclers' own accounts contain contradictory information that permits revision from within. Their highly interested characterization of the rebels' social standing may be treated as interpretative hypothesis rather than as fact, and need not be allowed to stand in the face of contrary evidence.

Abuse of sworn association. The English upper classes of the fourteenth and first decades of the fifteenth centuries engaged in a continuing debate about new and illicit forms of association, in which stable and hierarchically ordered ties of vassalage were challenged by short-term and lateral arrangements for personal advantage.[3] The ties of vassalage were sworn and sanctified and irreversible; those of congregation or covinage or affinity were sustained by improvised oaths of a sort entered into lightly, or by contract, or by the simple acceptance of a badge or other emblem of livery. The unease occasioned by aristocratic retinues formed through such processes was palpable, especially among those property-owning lesser gentry and already prosperous urban merchants unlikely to benefit from a loosening of restrictions on association. And, we learn in accounts of the revolt, this unease was focused and brought to bear in a series of accusations and suggestive innuendos against the uses of new forms of association for purposes of rebellion. Recall, in this regard, a nearly incidental observation by the Westminster chronicler in his description of the rebels on their way to Lambeth: "Quosque sibi occurrentes qui de eorum contubernio non fuerant ut eis adhererent et cum eis . . . juramento constringebant" (they forced those not belonging to their sworn association to adhere to them and to swear an oath of alliance with them) (2). The chronicler's use of the prevalent language of adherence in a sworn association or *contubernium* (in Middle English, *conturbation*) points to a constantly recurring scandal in the chronicle accounts: the rebels' novel and illicit appropriation of forms normally employed by their betters. Thus, Walsingham describes the rebels stopping pilgrims on the way to Canterbury, whatever their condition of life, and compelling them to swear—*jurare*—to support Richard and the true commons (*Historia*, 1:454–55). Froissart claims that some sixty of them including Tyler wore *jupons* (of a presumably matching livery), (9:411), and jurors at Scarborough claimed that the local rebels employed a livery of hoods in order to further their conspiracy against kings and nobles (Dobson, 291).

Of course, everybody in the fourteenth century habitually accused everybody else of employing novel techniques of association, including the swearing of oaths and the distribution of liveries to unite persons with shared interests in temporary association to pursue selfish ends. The claims by Froissart and the jurors at Scarborough that the rebels formed a fellowship and distributed liveries to their members would appear to be striking instances of such "projection" of motive on the rebels, serving at once to indict them of conspiracy and to ridicule them for aping the associational

---

[3] See Strohm, *Social Chaucer*, chapter 1, and chapter 3 of the present study, esp. 57–58.

strategies of their betters. Yet the frequency with which the chronicles return to the rebels' use of oaths and other devices of sworn association invites further consideration. In the same passage in which Walsingham speaks of the rebels' attraction to ideas of community, for example, he also argues that they swelled their ranks by Wat Tyler's technique of demanding fealty from their followers, "fidem eis facere"; that the crowd before the abbey gates joined their right hands and swore fealty to each other, "jungentes dexteras, fidem acceperunt ab invicem et dederunt"; and that inmates were released from the abbey prison on condition of their inseparable adherence, "eis inseparabiliter adhaererent" (*Historia*, 1:471).

However scornful the tone in which such associational gestures are reported, their cumulative effect is contrary to what Walsingham and the others obviously intend. For, grudgingly but persistently, the rebels are shown as able to attract adherents, to command loyalty, to manipulate existing forms creatively in order to constitute themselves as a new kind of community. An attempt is made to argue that the associations effected by these means are coerced; Walsingham says that those refusing fealty are beheaded and their homes destroyed. But his text is strewn with indications of a more voluntary sort of association; a crowd of two thousand gathered at St. Albans, he tells us, "non inviti"—not reluctantly (*Historia*, 1:471).

Ironic references to community and true commons. Moving from oaths and sworn associations to the kinds of social formation they create, the Westminster chronicler derides "agrestis illa societas," "that boorish society" (4), and judicial processes mention rebel membership in a conspiratorial body called *magna societas* (Dobson, 256).

Of course, ideas of community or society could cut either way. Consider, for example, the idea of *communitas*, or community, as identified by Walsingham in a scathing passage on the preference of the St. Albans rebels for the appellation of *communes* or the commons:

> Ita enim tunc temporis gloriabantur eo nomine, ut nullum censerent nomen honorabilius nomine "communitatis," nec quemquam de caetero reputaturi fuerunt dominum, juxta aestimationem suam stolidam, nisi Regem solummodo et communes. (*Historia*, 1:472)

> For at that time they gloried in the name, and considered that no name was more honorable than that of "community," nor, according to their stupid estimation, were there to be any lords in the future, but only King and commons.

If I am not mistaken, Walsingham's attribution of the idea of community to the rebels sits two-sidedly in his narration. It may be read, as he obviously intends it to be read, as self-evident absurdity, a notion held only during a brief period of tumult by a group of befuddled people. Or it may be read more sympathetically, as a rationale for revolutionary conduct with its own very deep and ultimately respectable implications in the social thought of the day. Closely connected to the idea of community read sympathetically is the idea of a rejuvenated and enlarged commons, a commons containing within its ranks members of many diverse social groups, all enjoying a condition of equality.

When not deprecating the rebels by calling them rustics or comparing them with animals, most contemporary commentators simply style them the *communes* in Latin or *cummuns* in French. This is what Walsingham calls them in the passage just quoted, and in his account the *communes*, acting in concert with the king, becomes the vehicle of the rebels' ideas of *communitas*. The notion of governance by king and commons alone, or, as it was often described, king and bishop and commons alone, may be seen as a very plausible rebel adaptation of the traditional notion of the three estates in a form favorable to the claims of commonality. In radically emptying the category of lordship, this formulation expresses a dissatisfaction with intervening hierarchies, with persons who interpose themselves at every level between king and commons, or bishop and commons: imagined is a life without middlemen, without *domini*. Thus, the Anonimalle chronicler attributes to Tyler the view that England should have only one king and one bishop, together with a commons whose members should be "de une condicione" (147).

Anonimalle says that the rebels have adopted a watchword: "Et les ditz comunes avoient entre eux une wache worde en Engleys, 'With whom haldes yow?' et le respouns fuist, 'Wyth kynge Richarde and wyth the trew communes' " (139). Of course, the idea of a "trew communes" might simply have been produced by a chronicler seeking to put reasonable words in the rebels' mouths. But recourse to English in any of the fourteenth-century chronicles is rare enough to station the idea of the true commons on a distinct ground, a ground with potentially extratextual affiliations.[4] Certainly, the phrase "trew communes" possesses a polemical force that argues for its independent value to the rebel cause. For one thing, "trew" reverses such condescending or derogatory phrases as "menues communes" (*RP*, 3:100), standing them on their heads. For another, it affirms a tenet that is rarely contradicted, which the rebels appear to have found indispensable: that of loyalty to Richard, a king led astray by bad counsel. For yet another, it sets an enlarged and regenerated commons against that group of usurping and self-aggrandizing middlemen who had ironically claimed the very

---

[4] The claim of the rebels to represent a reasonable cross-section of the ordinary folk of the realm is certainly borne out by historical research. See, for example, Rodney Hilton's argument that the rising embraced "the mass of the population," as opposed to "the lords, the lawyers and government officials" (184).

title of commons, those rural landowners and urban entrepreneurs who were constituted as the commons of Parliament.[5]

The peasant turba or "mob." The Westminster chronicler describes the rebels at Lambeth as an *ignobilis turba*, a base rabble or mob. This characterization is repeated many times over, in a variety of forms: they become *turba maledicta* (Walsingham, *Historia*, 1:462), *furens turba* (*West.*, 4), and *multitudo terribilis* (*Eulogium*, 353), and a host of related terms and epithets. The point, at any rate, concerns lack of control, direction, or clear objectives. Thus, Froissart tells us that the peasants entering London had no idea what they wanted, no ability to plan actions; a third of them, he says, did not know what they wanted or sought but just followed one another like beasts, like the peasants of the failed crusade: "les III pars de ces gens ne savoient que il demandoient, ne qu'il quéroient; mais sievoient l'un l'autre, enssi que bestes et enssi que li Pastouriel fissent jadis" (9:390). Such disparagement is, of course, prevalent in the chronicles. Walsingham, seeking an explanation for the uprising, finds it in the unruly conduct of the *vulgi*, including their preference for spending sleepless nights drinking liquor, wallowing in drunkenness, and committing crimes: "noctes insomnes in potationibus, ebrietatibus, et perjuriis transigentes" (*Historia*, 2:12). Froissart, getting to the heart of the imagery of misrule, accuses Wat Tyler as having no program beyond the encouragement of riot or "le rihotte" (9:412). Walsingham takes pleasure in characterizing the rebels as a sort of Falstaffian army, ill-organized and ill-equipped:

> Quidam tantum baculos, quidam rubigine obductos gladios, quidam bipennes solummodo, nonnulli arcus prae vetustate factos a fumo rubicundiores ebore antiquo, cum singulis sagittis, quorum plures contentae erant una pluma. (*Historia*, 1:454)

> Some had only sticks, some rusty swords, some only axes, a few bows more reddened on account of smoke from their own hearths and old age than from old ivory, with arrows, of which many had only a single plume.

A corollary is that this undisciplined rout—more often compared, as with the Westminster chronicler's *rabidissimi canes*, to animals than to men—is able to pursue no coherent objectives but simply runs wild in city and countryside.[6] Thus, in the Westminster account of the descent on Lam-

---

[5] The contemporary Rolls of Parliament attempt a rudimentary distinction, using the plural to describe the parliamentary commons ("les Communes") and the singular to describe the ordinary people of the realm ("la Commune," or often "la povre Commune"); the rhetoric of the "trew communes" erases this distinction, asserting the primacy of the one and only truly inclusive estate of the realm.

[6] The ultimate repository of such beast-imagery is, of course, the first book of Gower's *Vox Clamantis*, in which rebels are represented as asses, oxen, swine, dogs, cats, foxes, birds, flies, and frogs, led by a jay.

beth, the rebels are portrayed in an orgy of pointless destruction, guzzling and pouring out wine, breaking up kitchenware, and the like.

Despite the refusal of the chroniclers to concede the rebels any purpose or plan, their narratives contain ample evidence of their deliberation. With respect to the assault on Lambeth, consider that Sudbury, in his capacity as Chancellor of the Realm, is repeatedly listed in the chronicles themselves as sharing the highest position with John of Gaunt at the top of the rebels' "enemies list" (see, for example, *Anonimalle*, 145); in this respect alone, the rebels' early destruction of Sudbury's palace at Lambeth and Gaunt's Savoy Palace seems entirely purposeful and selective.[7] Further, as outlined by a number of chroniclers, a central objective of the rebels was the destruction of those customary records by which their liberties were curtailed. Walsingham, for example, notes their determination that court rolls and muniments should be burnt so that, the memory of old customs having been rubbed out, their lords would be unable to vindicate their rights over them: "Statuerunt omnes curiarum rotulos et munimenta vetera dare flammis, ut, obsoleta antiquarum rerum memoria, nullum jus omnino ipsorum domini in eos in posterum vendicare valerent" (*Historia*, 1:455). And this is in fact the very program followed at Lambeth, according to the Anonimalle chronicler; in his alternative account the rebels suddenly become purposeful, burning the registers and chancery rolls found there: "mistrent en feu toutz les livers des registres et rolles de remembrauncez de la chauncellerie illeoqes trovez."[8]

The disparagement of rebel discipline coupled with contradictory evidence that indicates unusual discipline in the rebel ranks runs throughout

[7] A detailed argument for the highly organized nature of rebel actions, based largely on the "astonishing speed of their concerted movements" (268) has recently been mounted by Nicholas Brooks (268). He notes among other evidence of forethought that the rebels deliberately refrained from burning archiepiscopal manors in Kent, knowing that, as Sudbury's main residence and main archive, Lambeth Palace was their proper objective (264–65).

[8] 140. On the rebels' purpose in destroying muniments and other written records of seigneurial restrictions and tenant obligations, see especially Susan Crane's brilliant "Writing Lesson of 1381." As nearly as we can judge from the chronicles, such actions were motivated in part by a desire to return to a customary past of wider license or lighter obligation. Walsingham reports that one element of the Kentish rebel program was to limit taxation to past practices, to levels that their forefathers and ancestors had known and accepted, "quam patres et antecessores eorum solummodo noverunt et acceptaverunt" (*Historia*, 1:455). And he argues simultaneously that the rebels act for a better future ("pro meliori futura"), that, the memory of old customs having been wiped out ("obsoleta antiquarum rerum memoria"), their future could be shaped by common decree (*Historia*, 1:455). The rebels' attitude toward written records thus contains some evidence supportive of the contention that their ideology looked back nostalgically to a traditional past (Faith) and that it depended upon hopes for a transformative, millennial future (Cohn); the rebels' attitude was, as Walsingham reports it and as it can be inferred from other sources, compounded in an intelligent and practical way from the mixture of backward- and forward-looking materials available to them.

the chronicle accounts. Consider, for example, the Westminster chronicler's account of the rebels' next act of destruction, their move on John of Gaunt's palace at Savoy:

> Agrestis illa societas totum stimulata in rabiem . . . hospicium ducis vocatum le Savoye invaserunt, omnes clausuras disrumentes, nichil quod preciosum erat parcentes quin illud aut igne combusserunt aut in Thamense flumen demergendum projecerunt. Cerneres ibidem rem nostris seculis insolitam, nam dum preciosissima cernerent, tractarent, et colligerent, non audebat rustica manus preciosa furtivis manibus surripere, quia si quis in aliquo furto fuerat deprehensus, sine processu sive judicio ad mortem rapiebatur decapitandus. (4)

> That uncouth society, wrought up into an animalistic rage, attacked the duke's palace called the Savoy, bursting every barrier, sparing nothing of value from destruction either by fire or by throwing it into the Thames. You might have seen an event rare in our time, for perceiving highly precious objects while handling and collecting them, the peasant band did not dare to steal any of the precious objects, since anyone apprehended in theft was hastened away, without judicial process or judgment, to death by beheading.

The chronicler emphasizes the rebels' abstinence from looting for fear of punishment but neglects to mention that the sources of their discipline were internal, a matter of self-policing rather than simple abjection. Other accounts clarify the matter. Walsingham repeats the Westminster chronicler's assertions about tumultuous disorder but includes revealing evidence of internal self-regulation. On the one hand, he characterizes the rebels as madmen, "amentes"; on the other, he reports that they actively policed themselves, proclaiming to the community at large that no one should retain any object found there for his own use, under penalty of execution, "ut patesceret totius regni communitati eos non respectu avaritiae quicquam facere, proclamari fecerunt, sub poena decollationis, ne quis praesumeret aliquid vel aliqua ibidem reperta ad proprios usus servanda contingere" (*Historia*, 1:457). He follows this observation with an account of the destruction of the duke's belongings, including grinding up his rings and jewels in mortars so they could never be used again (*Historia*, 1:457). And Knighton adds an illustrative anecdote, to the effect that one would-be thief, apprehended with a hidden piece of silver, was thrown into the fire by his fellows, who said that they were lovers of truth and justice, not thieves or robbers, "zelatores veritatis et justitiae, non fures aut latrones" (135).

As with the eighteenth-century food "riots," revealed through E. P. Thompson's analysis as highly disciplined actions (76–136), descriptions of these supposed mob scenes cannot seem to resist the intrusion of details that reveal purposeful order. Although realizing their narrative accounts within the most stigmatizing frames, the chroniclers repeatedly lapse into contradictory details—rebels as madmen, rebels as spellbound by symbols of absent authority, rebels as a threateningly disciplined military force—that serve inadvertently to reveal the very discipline they mean to conceal.

Revelry. Thus far we have encountered a cluster of interpretative schemes, all the common property of several chroniclers who wield them to dismiss rebel conduct as the haphazard actions of persons too lowly and irrational to mount a sustained plan. Some of these schemes (the rebels as serfs, as cunning conspirators, as members of a mindless rout) contradict each other; all in one way or another embrace contradictory evidence from outside their own boundaries. But, even as these schemes can shown to be imaginative rather than soberly descriptive, their imaginative status in no way lessens their persuasive power. So with the interpretative scheme that interests me most here: the representation of rebel action as a variety of revelry, festive inversion, and grotesque play.

Revelry and festivity have, of course, been under sustained scholarly discussion at least since the work of E. K. Chambers and F. M. Cornford early in this century, but I refer particularly to the influential discussion of the carnivalesque in Bakhtin's *Rabelais and His World*, available in English translation since 1968 and particularly influential during the last ten years. Bakhtin identifies the carnivalesque as a distinctive patterning of behavior, marked by such characteristics as inversion of hierarchies and distinctions based on status, and the elevation of "low" to "high" estate; accompanying derision of the static, solemn, or "high"; erasure of the line between participants and spectators; and preference for the temporal temporary over the timeless and static, with acceptance of the temporary nature of the carnivalesque itself. I have, in fact, only one serious qualification to introduce to Bakhtin's magnificent formulation, involving its ahistorical tendency. Like other schemes for the production of human actions (and episodes in the narration of human actions) the carnivalesque is subject to varied appropriation and use. Its essence, rather than remaining always the same, is liable to change, depending on the circumstances in which and the motives for which it is employed. The paragraphs that follow will both depend on Bakhtin's formulation and modify it, insofar as they attempt to reveal the differing uses of revelry in the hands of the chroniclers, and the rebels.[9]

[9] Bakhtin and his commentators have shown a tendency to "essentialize" ideas of carnival, to suggest that they always operate in the same way—on the side of time, change, and the people. Sometimes the carnivalesque is indeed a vehicle for social change. But frequently, as "sponsored" merriment, it can also serve more limited and conservative ends as a release of pressure, ultimately dependent upon the status quo it pretends to subvert. Actually, carnival can be used in either way, depending on circumstances. Paumier, leader of the artisanal-peasant faction in Le Roy Ladurie's magisterial *Carnival in Romans*, transgresses boundaries when attired as the Candlemass bear, but so does his adversary Guérin, leader of the notables, seize

Revelry surfaces as an interpretative category in the Westminster chronicler's account of the burning of Archbishop Sudbury's Lambeth palace,
during which the rebels are said to have repeatedly exclaimed, "A revelle!
A revelle!" The effect of the chronicler's invocation of revelry at this point
in his narration is clear enough: he describes the frenzy of rebel destruction
in terms of revelry in order to suggest essential heedlessness and blindness
to social desert and preference for temporary indulgence over long-term
responsibility. The chronicler's invocation of revelry may, in fact, be ade-
quately explained without recourse to any notion of historical accuracy or
referentiality whatever. Lest he be misunderstood, the chronicler inscribes
his own interpretation of the Lambeth rebels' exclamation. He says that
while "perpetrating" these acts, the rebels uttered these words just as if
applauding something worthy of praise, "ista perpetrantes velud de re laudabili plaudentes exclamarunt" (2). And, through his use of *perpetrare*,
neutral in classical Latin, but already possessed of a potential negative val-
uation in the fourteenth century, he suggests that no congratulations are
warranted and that nothing worthy of praise has occurred. Beneath his
annoyance at the rebels' unconcealed self-congratulation, however, rests a
further critique, implicit in the very invocation of revelry. On the textual
surface, he suggests that this revelry is unearned, that people who destroy
property have no right to feel so good about themselves. At a somewhat
less explicit and more imagistic level, the rebels are incriminated by all the
additional associations that revelry bears for its scandalized observers: its
overprivileging of the "low" and insufficient respect for the "high," its invitation to bystanders to imagine themselves as participants, and its encouragement of temporary license. So are we constantly shown the rebels
engaging in varieties of revel, play, and festive inversion—carnivalesque
forms treated as inappropriate in their very joviality to the grim crimes they
accompany, but also as disturbing in their own right on account of the
images of insubordination and misrule they inevitably bear.

Walsingham tells us, for example, that subsequent to the execution of
Archbishop Sudbury the rebels continued in a "solemnis ludus," a solemn
play or game, executing those who refused fealty or incurred hatred (*Historia*, 462). The ludic or theatrical analogy is continued: those to be executed are rushed "in plateis," "the street" in classical Latin, but any of a
variety of open spaces in medieval Latin, including that "open space" or
"stage" in which a play is performed. Walsingham means, of course, for his
oxymoronic "solemn play" to express a sense of inappropriateness, of hor-

---

on the occasion of the carnival parade to reproduce a conservative and hierarchized version
of society (310, 321–22). Stallybrass and White correctly assert the "banal but often ignored
truth" that there is no inherent revolutionary vector to carnival and transgression nor no
conservative vector either, that "the politics of carnival cannot be resolved outside of a close
historical examination of particular conjunctures" (16).

ror and dislocation. But the effect of his description is also to impute to the rebels an essential unseriousness and arbitrariness, in a disturbing importation of the hypothetical and the improvised into the realm of civic process.

The chroniclers find other ways to depict festive conduct and displays as both inappropriate and disturbing. Walsingham says that the rebels, unable to capture John of Gaunt at the Savoy Palace, set up one of his garments for target practice, in a familiar game of the carnival season:

Arreptum quoddam vestimentum pretiosissimum ipsius, quale *jakke* vocamus, et impositum lanceae, pro signo ad sagittas suas statuerunt. (*Historia*, 1:457)

They seized one of his most precious vestments, which we call a "jakke," placed it on a lance, and stood it up as a target for their arrows.

Walsingham's concern does not seem to involve impiety; the *jakke* is according to the *Middle English Dictionary* a quilted tunic rather than an ecclesiastical vestment. As in the Westminster chronicler's description of destruction at Lambeth, the narrator seems more concerned about the value of the item than about the violent impulses the rebels are enacting. But the homicidal wishes that inform their game are amply evident in his account. Walsingham continues with an additionally disturbing suggestion that festive forms are potentially inadequate to contain the passions they localize and produce. As with many festive popinjays, especially in times of declining talent at archery, the rebels are said to have tired of shooting at the surrogate garment and to have taken it down and hacked it to pieces with axes and swords: "Depositum securibus et gladiis confregerunt" (*Historia*, 1:457). This pattern, stressing an apparently festive gesture's potential to go demonstrably bad, is repeated elsewhere. The Anonimalle chronicler tells us, for example, that after the decapitation of Sudbury the executioners bore his and other heads "en processione" through the city, to the shrine of Westminster Abbey (145). His description evolves a religious or civic *ridyng* with inevitable festive associations. This visitation, contrasted with Richard's own more reverent conduct at the abbey the next day, seems to the chronicler so inappropriate as to call down the vengeance of God soon after. And, at the episodic level, his account shifts directly from the procession to the massacre of the Flemings, an outbreak of violence of a sort attributed to popular celebrations of the Middle Ages (145).

The chroniclers most typically impute a carnivalesque outlook to the rebels through their depictions of festive inversion, in which the rebels refuse to accept customs of polite deference to those above them on the social scale. Instead, their behavior exhibits that "grotesque realism" that, according to Bakhtin, has the effect of localizing and materializing static ceremonial and rendering ridiculous its deferential habits and forms (24).

The rebel "body"—both collective and individual—is in this sense a grotesque body, Bakhtin's body of carnivalesque license, behaving with rudeness, effrontery, and an unwillingness to accommodate itself to established forms and precedents, and hence threatening the divinely ordained social hierarchy of tradition.

We have already encountered Walsingham's account of the "vilest of peasants" wandering the Tower with their sticks and stroking the beards of most noble knights. Not content with these outrages, the rebels of Walsingham's imagination then loll on the very bed of the king, proferring indecent invitations to no less revered a person than the king's mother, Joan of Kent, "et sedendo, jacendo, jocando, super lectum Regis insolescerent; et insuper, matrem Regis ad oscula invitarent quidam" (*Historia*, 1:459). The point here partially involves transgression of boundaries: all this violation of the king's most private space, and deliberate lying about and insult to the queen, is presented within the domain of *insolentia* or deliberate affront. But the effrontery itself goes past simple transgression or insubordination to a more ambitious inversion, in which the rebels, temporarily brought high, are imagined to issue invitations to the queen mother as if she were a common wench. The extremity of this inversion parallels the conduct of one provincial "Rex Communium," who, taking advantage of the reversal occasioned by a local rebellion, forced *milites honorabiles* to taste his food, kneel to him at meals, and carve his food as he ate (Walsingham, *Historia*, 2:6).

Wat Tyler is represented as conducting himself toward King Richard at Smithfield with a mixture of rude or insubordinate play and seriously vainglorious presumption, proceeding, if not from a position of lordship over Richard, at least from a conviction that the upward momentum of his fortunes has raised him to a position of temporary equality. In the *Anonimalle* account, he not only addresses Richard as "Frer" and proposes that the two of them become "bones compaignons," but he is accused of shaking the King's hand "durement et fortement," and of calling for ale and rinsing out his mouth rudely and villainously before the king, "rynsa soun bouche ledement et vilaynesment avaunt le roy" (147–48). The point is not just that Tyler lacks good manners, but that he refuses to limit his own patterns of behavior to those that connote lower station, humility, and restriction of his own claims. His refusal to accept hierarchical assignments of "low" and "high" is epitomized in his refusal to dismount in the presence of the royal party; according to Walsingham, the quarrel that licensed the royal party's fatal attack on Tyler was provoked by a disagreement over whether the mounted rebel leader was to be approached on horseback or on foot (*Historia*, 1:464). In these scenes Tyler is not only described as fraternal but as downright boisterous—in something like the carnivalesque state described by Bakhtin, including "special forms of marketplace speech and gesture, frank and free, permitting no distance between those who came in contact with each other and liberating from norms of etiquette and decency imposed at other times" (10).

In keeping with this licensed atmosphere, Tyler is depicted as engaging in varied forms of menacing play. Although he would have been unlikely to mount an attack against his sovereign, he is described as coveting a dagger and then wielding it disconcertingly. Froissart has him requesting the dagger from one of the king's followers and playing with it: "il en commencha à juer et à tourner en sa main" (9:412). Knighton has him throwing his own dagger from hand to hand like a boy playing a game: "de manu in manum jecit quasi pueriliter ludens" (137). Though his precise intentions remain unspecified, he is revealed as frivolous, unpredictable, out of control.

Tyler and his followers are regarded, not as an alternative center of authority and power, but as a carnival rout—heedless of established status distinctions, disrespectful of the rightful dominance of the "high," thrusting themselves into unwelcome participation in the world of civic event and ceremony, able to muster only a tumultuous and transient appearance on the stage of real history. Little wonder that this inherently evanescent band is portrayed as sinking to the ground, paralyzed, melting away at the approach of a disciplined force representative of civic structure of the city of London, as when, in the description of the Anonimalle chronicler, the aldermen arrived in array, leading with them the guardians of the wards in diverse bands with a fine company of persons well armed in great numbers: "les aldermen viendrent sarrement, amenaunt ovesque eux les gardeyns de les wardes en diverses routes ove bele compaignye des gentz bien armes a graunde noumbre" (149).

Even so, the attempt of the chroniclers to represent the rebels as members of a feckless, temporary, classless multitude, a carnival throng, ultimately works to mixed effect. Scandalous as the rebels' vernacular cry of "A revelle!" while destroying the archbishop's fine palace might have seemed to the Monk of Westminster, it arrests the nonmonastic reader in ways he might not have intended. Part of its effect may simply be that, as one of the very few scraps of vernacular in a Latin chronicle, it permits the surmise (although by no means the certainty) that it represents a scrap of actual utterance, a key to the rebels' understanding of their own actions.

Entertained as a hypothesis, the idea that conceptions of revelry may have offered a staging ground for rebellious actions makes a good deal of sense. For, where the chroniclers see only insolence and pointless riot, the reader can often with equal plausibility glimpse a harnessing of festive inversion in ways that permit the production of genuinely transgressive acts.[10] The account of revelry at Lambeth Palace is followed in the chron-

---

[10] The inherent duality of later medieval renderings of the carnivalesque is emphasized in Michael Mullett's *Popular Culture and Popular Protest*. On the one hand, he notes that "the

icles by the more extensive action against the Savoy. The disrespectful inversion attributed to the rebels in the Tower—plucking beards, lolling on the king's bed, offering to kiss the queen—precedes, in Walsingham's account, the shocking invasion of the chapel and seizure of Archbishop Sudbury. So, too, in a reminder of the potentially repugnant consequences of populist fervor, is a carnivalesque procession to Westminster followed in the *Anonimalle* account by the massacre of the resident Flemings. Tyler's insubordinations before the king may also be viewed as explorations of new forms of egalitarianism, though with a different and probably unanticipated result.

Imputations of revelry clearly enough serve the stigmatizing purposes of the chroniclers. But the imagery of carnivalesque inversion simultaneously serves the purposes of the rebels in their attempt to invent themselves as a new kind of community with "carnivalesque" characteristics, a community disrespectful of hierarchy, bent on the reversal of "low" and "high," eager to involve its members in the production of transgressive actions. Knighton, describing the origins of the revolt in Kent, tells us of the formation of a joyous throng, bent on common action:

> Qui maximo tripudio suo more gaudentes catervatim ruere coeperunt, laeti admodum effecti quod diem viderent quo sibi invicem succurrere possent in tanta ac tali necessitate. (131)

> Who, rejoicing, began to gather together in companies with great celebration as they were wont to do, quite filled with joy that the day had come when they were able to succor each other in such and so great need.

Knighton writes with an obvious sneer. Yet consider this conjunction of images and associations: the rebels gather in companies or bands, intent on working collectively for the common good; their time of submissive deference at an end, they seek to become actors or participants in shaping their own circumstances; their temper is joyous; and, as is their habit, they display *tripudium* or joy. To linger for a moment over this unusual word choice: evidently originating in Roman augury as a description of corn rattling on the ground prior to its consumption by sacred chickens, it came to be associated with a ritual dance. I do not, by the way, mean to suggest that either the chroniclers or the rebels knew about the chickens. But the word in medieval Latin retains its implications of frivolity, suggesting fes-

---

carnivalesque features in revolts were the ones that made it easier for their enemies to discredit them and their pretensions to peace, conservatism, sobriety, chastity, religion, moderation, and respect for traditional symbols" (96). On the other hand, he notes the indispensability of carnival, with its traditions of "formalized impertinence," for the production of oppositional actions (99). Also germane to this subject are the studies of Yves-Marie Bercé, emphasizing the contribution of festivity to a "langage gestuel," that lies open to appropriation and use by varied parties and interests (Bercé, 1976, pp. 55–92).

tivity, jubilation, and the dance; according to Latham the palace at Eltham possessed a *camera tripudiantium*, a ballroom or chamber devoted to the dance (495). Knighton, preparing to describe enormities, chooses a word marked by deliberate incongruity, a word that in this context borders on the grotesque. But his description of an outpouring of festive, associational joy cannot fail to evoke a subversive countercurrent, constituted by affirmative ideas about community, inclusive definitions of citizenship and the commons, a dramatically broadened base of participation in associational ceremonies, and a suspension of social difference within the festive throng.

REVELRY AND THE RECOVERY OF REBEL IDEOLOGY

> Ask the slave what is his condition—what his state of mind—
> what he thinks of enslavement? and you had as well address
> your inquiries to the *silent dead*. There comes no *voice* from the
> enslaved. We are left to gather his feelings by imagining what
> ours would be, were our souls in his soul's stead.
> —*Frederick Douglass*

With the possible exception of a few quoted scraps, such as the watchword about Richard and the "trew communes" and the cry of "revelle" at Lambeth, we have not heard the rebel voice and we are not going to hear it. But we naturally wish to know something more about rebel belief and motivation than may be inferred from a "ventriloquistic" translation of the chroniclers' fulminations. For, even when we have turned the chroniclers' condemnatory words back on themselves, we are still operating within their terms. Does any sense exist in which the revolt can be understood in its *own* terms?

The accusations of the chroniclers notwithstanding, no event occurs unless the actors possess some structured understanding of what they are doing, some way of proceeding in the confidence that their actions are intelligible to themselves and their fellows. Anthony Giddens has observed that structure is essential to the production of actions in the first place; in his view, "structure is not to be conceptualized as a barrier to action, but as essentially involved in its production" (70). He moves beyond the production of actions within structure to insist that actions depend upon structure for their intelligibility, that commonly held ideas of structure enable social actors and beholders to make sense of an event. He treats these commonly held ideas as "interpretative schemes," which he describes as "standardised elements of stocks of knowledge, applied by actors in the production of interaction." He argues that such interpretative schemes "form the core of the mutual knowledge whereby an accountable universe of meaning is sustained through and in processes of interaction" (83). The issue, if Giddens is right (and I believe him to be), is not to find our way to the rebellious events of 1381 as naked or arbitrary actions, occurring outside of theory, but rather to seek a fresh understanding of the terms or "structures" within which the rebels themselves produced their oppositional actions.

Giddens may help in another respect here. In his formulation, interpretative schemes are by no means the exclusive property of the actors who employ them. Rather, their tendency is to be very broadly held within a society, and their common possession as knowledge mutually held by actors and by observers is what renders actions intelligible. My proposal is this: that some of the very schemes wielded by the chroniclers to stigmatize rebel actions were elements of "mutual knowledge," available to—and in fact employed by—the rebels for the production of oppositional acts. The number of really powerful and galvanizing schemes available within a society is, of course, limited, and the evocative and explanatory force of ideas like community and revelry cannot be presumed to be the property of a single class of actors or commentators, or to function the same way in every situation. These schemes are inherently flexible, varying in their application according to whoever appropriates them for use and how effectively they are employed. That a given scheme might be wielded in more than one way, both in the production of a rebellious posture in the first place and in the condemnatory reframing of that posture in a subsequent narrative account, is not only possible but highly probable.

Some interpretative schemes possess more migratory potential than others. Few of the London rebels were in fact peasants or outsiders, and we would hardly expect them to rally around self-characterizations of themselves as rustics or yokels. Nor, despite frequent chronicle reference to the rebels as animalistic (as mad dogs, sheep, peacocks, and the like), do the rebels appear to have appropriated animal imagery for their own use.[11] The particular schemes most eligible for rebel appropriation—and in fact generally attributed to the rebels by the chroniclers—are those involving collectivity and collective association. With only the slightest of adjustments, the scorned *turba* or mob of the chronicles could become a commonality or true commons; suspect or coerced practices of sworn association might be asserted as new and legitimate ties; and we have already seen that, with hardly any adjustment at all, revelry might offer an alternative vantage

---

[11] That such appropriations were at least a possibility is suggested by the continental example of LeRoy Ladurie, who describes the self-identifications of the Romans artisans with the bear, sheep, hare, capon, and donkey, while the patricians captured the more auspicious symbolism of the rooster, eagle, and partridge (214–15).

point on an entrenched hierarchy and a staging ground of oppositional actions.

My argument is that the chroniclers' appropriation and use of these schemes is not novel, and that these schemes do not originate with them; their habit is to reproduce the rebels' actions in terms closely related to the rebels' own, but now rotated on their conceptual axes and wielded derisively for purposes of condemnation. I have suggested that ideas of the carnivalesque were employed by rebels to produce actions, as well as by the chroniclers to condemn them. This suggestion receives additional support from the timing of the rebellion, the fact that the burning of Lambeth Palace is usually placed on 12 June, in 1381 the day of the eve of Corpus Christi, "acta sunt hec pridie Idus Junii . . . que dies tunc erat vigilia Corporis Christi," with the destruction of the Savoy on Corpus Christi itself (*West.*, 4). This feast day was a traditional occasion not only of religious procession and observance, but of more generalized revelry. Miri Rubin reminds us that an element of turbulence was inevitable on Corpus Christi in any event, that "the element of disorder, the excitement of a populous event, percolated and erupted in a variety of ways," with pilgrims and travelers, and spectators and prostitutes swelling the crowds, and with a galaxy of informal celebrations augmenting the already festive atmosphere (263–64). The elements of revelry were, in other words, at hand; the rebels would not even have needed to evoke them, but only to claim them as a vehicle for actions already ripe to be produced.[12]

Certainly, the London rising possessed many elements of a giant carnival: flaring up suddenly, involving spectators as participants, obliterating distinctions of rank among those taking part, encouraging inversion of established hierarchies, and yielding with sudden docility to the reassumption of established roles once the appointed period is at an end. The idea that all participants on both sides shared certain ideas about rebellion as carnival would help to explain a matter of repeated mention, the initial ineffectiveness and near-passivity of the forces of authority. On this point, Walsingham describes the lords of Kent and Essex remaining quiescent, as if asleep, in their homes while the rebels gathered a great force, "velut stertentes, domi quiescentes immobiles permanebant" (*Historia*, 1:455); the Anonimalle chronicler finds the king's counsellors inexplicably abashed, "si abaiez qe mervaille fuist" (144); Walsingham muses over the strange impotence of the garrison of the Tower (*Historia*, 1:459). And, at the far end of the revolt, the suggestion that the rebels depended upon the tonalities and rhythms of the carnivalesque to produce oppositional actions would

[12] The connection between popular disturbances and religious holidays (including Corpus Christi) is fruitfully explored by Natalie Zemon Davis (esp. 170–73), although her instances, drawn from the sixteenth century, deal more with religious rivalries than with manifestly political or economic unrest.

help to explain the repeated insistence that the rebels switched abruptly from determined opposition to complete abjection upon the death of their leader. The Anonimalle chronicler is typical in causing them to fall to the ground like corn, pleading for mercy, when they see the death of their leader, "et purceo qils virent qe lour chieftayne Wat Tyghler fuist mort en tiel maner, chaierount al terre en my les blees come gentz descomfitez, criaunt al roy de mercie" (149). To be sure, the rebels were subject to a number of divisive strategies, including bogus (or at least promptly retracted) letters of pardon, at which Richard is said by Froissart to have set thirty clerks at work (9:406). Even so, the death of Tyler bears an eerie resemblance to the deposition of a Mardi Gras king, whose followers melt away when the Lenten procession comes.

Somewhere close at hand would appear to be the generalization that carnival, inherently temporary and ultimately deferential to the established order, is bound in the end to be "contained" and subservient to the status quo; that, in the carnivalesque, the rebels committed themselves less to an oppositional structure than to an inherently evanescent antistructure.[13] I am, however, reluctant to remove the idea of carnival so far from the stream of history, to adopt so essentialist an idea of what it is and must be. Ideas of "carnival" per se remain relatively unprescriptive of social consequences, except as they are articulated or fail to be articulated with other ideas in a more comprehensive oppositional ideology, except as they are either embraced or rejected by actual centers of social power. The failure of the carnivalesque to eventuate in social change must finally be sought in these areas, rather than in the temporary or inherently conservative nature of "carnival" itself.

Despite promising beginnings, the rebels appear never to have developed a comprehensive associative or communitarian ideology. We have

[13] The carnivalesque may, in this sense, be seen in Giddens's terms as indispensable to structuration of action, both produced within the events of the revolt and rendering their production possible. Alternatively, it may be seen in Victor Turner's terms as "anti-structure," as an intersubjective awareness uniting the peasants in communal relations that are "egalitarian, direct, nonrational" (as opposed to formal and hierarchical), linked with "spontaneity and freedom" (as opposed to obligation, morality, law) (45–49). Giddens's view of structuration presupposes a contentious social situation in which different centers of social power vie to assert their claims via structured actions (esp. 80–88); Turner imagines a more hierarchized and static social situation in which *communitas* and accompanying role reversal are periodically produced, not out of contention between alternative centers of power but as sponsored and temporary antistructure designed to confirm existing social roles (esp. 52–53). Because I see the English society of 1381 as contentious in the extreme, I prefer Giddens's model, in which parties with widely divergent interests seek by variously structured actions to grasp social power. Seen in this sense, production of rebellious action within the forms of carnivalesque is not just temporary "anti-structure," but rather hoped-for *alternative structure*—alternative structure that in 1381 fell short of institutionalization but was not foreordained to containment.

already discussed the latent presence of a rudimentary communitarian ideology in an anathematized form in the chronicles, and ideas of revelry and *tripudium* appear to have been part of such an ideological formation. Yet, however galvanizing the idea of a "trew communes," uniting diverse strata in sworn association and animated by the ordered disorganization of the carnivalesque, it seems never to have issued in a usable theory of rule. For, as mentioned previously, the idea of the "trew communes" originated in a radical stripping and reworking of the traditional theory of the three estates, retaining a king and a prelate together with a commons while eliminating unnecessary intermediaries. The persistent idea of loyalty to a king, woven into the very oaths the rebels were said to have sworn, was to prove a fatal limitation. This was the ideological element that Richard was to invoke when, Tyler slain and the rebels stirring among themselves, the young king evidently offered himself as their sole leader—not only in the less reliable account of Froissart but in the more authoritative accounts of Walsingham and the Westminster chronicler. The latter, for example, has Richard leading the commons from Smithfield to a nearby field, with the words "I am your king, your leader, your captain, and those of you loyal to me are to go at once into the open field," "Ego sum vester rex, vester dux, vester primicerius; et si qui ex vobis michi adherent, exeant statim in campum" (12). So deflected, the rebels followed their acknowledged leader to Clerkenwell, where by all accounts they were surrounded and undone.

If the unformed state of their ideology left the rebels in fatal dependence on the beneficence of their king, it also foreclosed the possibility of alliance with other, nonmonarchic sources of social authority. For both the definition of the "trew communes" and the practical composition of the rebel throng appear to have excluded the effective centers of potential armed opposition to monarchic power. The townspeople allied with the rebels included a sprinkling of citizens and burgesses, although most were journeymen, apprentices, and casual laborers (Hilton, 186–207); the rural rebels included significant numbers of reeves, jurors, constables, and landowners, although the largest single group held land by customary tenure (Dyer, 14–19). In other words, the ranks of the rebels were socially inclusive, but with the significant exclusion of what Hilton calls "any group which had a part to play in the accepted political game" (221). Absent were the wealthy urban merchants and other citizens and burgesses of parliamentary strata, the landholding knights and gentry of the countryside, as well as such other functionaries as civil servants, lawyers, and sergeants-at-arms. Also absent, of course, were the aristocracy, some of whose members actually would oppose Richard later in the decade, and members of the ecclesiastical hierarchy.

Walsingham suggests that the rebels made some effort to win the allegiance of the garrison of the Tower (*Historia*, 1:459), but few or no alliances appear to have been consummated. For this reason alone, the conclusion at Clerkenwell, or something like it, may be regarded as foregone. Credit for dispersing the rebels is variously assigned in the chronicles and other narrative sources. True to his chivalric assumptions, Froissart assigns a major role to the mercenary Robert Knolles and the foreign knight Perducas d'Albret (9:414–17). Walsingham mentions the notables of London or "optimates de Londoniis" (*Historia*, 1:466), and the heavily doctored account in Letter-Book H imagines the brunt to have been borne by a band of "citizen warriors" (*CLBH*, 166). Whichever account we accept, however, we are reminded that none of the real sources of existing civil authority was allowed a place in rebel ideology or canvassed for possible alliance.

For these and other reasons, rebel actions produced within the codes and trappings of the carnivalesque did indeed fall short of institutionalization. Their temporary carnival of misrule at an end, the king whom they had wrongly trusted would, according to Walsingham, pronounce a harsh epitaph: "Rustics you were and rustics you will remain; you will remain in bondage, not as until now, but in a state even more vile," "Rustici quidem fuistis et estis; in bondagio permanebitis, non ut hactenus, sed incomparabilitier viliori" (*Historia*, 2:18). And this same king would charge his commissioners to punish rebels "according to the law of our kingdom of England or by other ways and means, by beheadings and the mutilation of limbs, as seems to your discretion the best and most rapid way of proceeding," "secundum legem regni nostri Anglie, vel aliis viis et modis, per decollaciones et membrorum mutilaciones, prout melius et celerius juxta discreciones vestras vobis videbitur faciendum" (Réville, 234).

More striking than the rebels' failure, however, is the distance that their improvised ideology enabled them to traverse. Although pervasive, social conflict in later medieval England was more often mimed than enacted. In this case, however, the imagery and associations of revelry—its disrespect for hierarchy and status, its encouragement of reversal, its erasure of the line between spectatorship and participation—offered a vehicle by which a heterogeneous group of rebels, inflamed by individual and collective social grievances, were able at least briefly to set aside customary deference and to stage genuinely transgressive acts.

Chapter 3

THE TEXTUAL ENVIRONMENT OF

CHAUCER'S "LAK OF STEDFASTNESSE"

NEW SOCIAL TENDENCIES achieve representation under the most varied conditions. Their first appearance is often within hostile texts that seek to proscribe them or to regulate their effect. Negative treatment, intended to contain or control new developments or even to proscribe them out of hand, may be regarded as the normal tariff placed upon the entry of innovative social practices into representation. But the paradox known to all hucksters and most politicians—that the most negative publicity is better than no publicity at all—would seem to operate here. For, however stigmatizing in intent, written treatment puts new tendencies into play, opens a discursive field within which they can be figured and refigured, promulgated both as textual and social practice.

A case in point is a new syntax of personal relations that became available for use and possible abuse between the late thirteenth and mid-fifteenth centuries. Newly permissible forms of association were offering unscrupulous lords and enterprising upstarts the opportunity to thrive by colluding for economic advantage in ways that diluted or abused traditional social practices. These new social tendencies were first textualized in late thirteenth-century complaints about "trailbaston" or roadside thuggery. Bands of brigands were thought to strengthen their ties and expand their influence through such devices as ingenuous oath-swearing, fealty, common livery, and mutual pleading. The brigands were, of course, only imitating their betters, and in any event these devices were too potent to remain exclusively in their possession for long. Thus, discussion was soon broadened, no longer to focus on brigands alone but on the practices themselves and all those local lords and others who were responsible for them. These practices were brought into textual consideration under a variety of headings, such as covinage, or conspiracy to oppress neighbors by force; maintenance, or connivance in joint legal pleading; champerty, or the instigation of legal pleas; improper swearing and oath-taking to bind the fortunes of a single group; and nontraditional retaining, especially through the use of livery or emblematic apparel to secure and advertise short-term alliances for mutual profit.

These new associative practices were discussed across the widest possible range of textual genres. We might expect them to appear in such official and quasi-official forms as parliamentary petitions and statutes and judicial records—and they do. But their emergence within self-consciously "literary" genres, including those seemingly most aloof from contempory developments, was nearly as rapid. Of course, each genre remained predominantly faithful to its own expressive circumstances and conventions and objects of attention. A statute might emphasize the permissible forms of retaining, a petition the destructive consequences of improper retention, a poem the retainers' own prideful display. Nevertheless, wholly absent was any sense that the subject of retention belonged exclusively to one genre or expressive register, whether legal or parliamentary, "literary" or not.

The whole body of contemporaneous texts on this subject, together with related ceremonials and performances, constituted an "environment" or field conducive to the production and interpretation of yet more texts and more related actions. By the closing decades of the fourteenth century, every stratum with access to writing, or with the least ability to mount a ceremony or social performance, was contributing written analysis and social drama to the debate. Lords concocted new ceremonies and celebrations of personal loyalty and relatedness. The king's council sought to cool the situation by drafting restrictive ordinances. The parliamentary commons produced denunciatory petitions. Conservative satirists (as well as socially innovative brigands) wrote poems on the subject. The king himself alternately inveighed against unsanctioned alliances and practiced them, condemned liveries and distributed them wholesale in his own behalf.

Within this outpouring of texts and performances, I am interested in one three-year period of particularly heightened representational activity, in which texts themselves readily attained the status of political events. This is the period between 1388 and 1390 in which Richard lost, and then regained, his royal prerogative. In this brief period originated the texts to be examined here: a petition generated by the parliamentary commons; a royal self-representation as described by a sympathetic chronicler; and a deceptively slight poem, *Lak of Stedfastnesse*, by temporarily on-the-shelf civil servant and Ricardian loyalist Geoffrey Chaucer.

A Petition of Commons—Cambridge, September 1388

The Westminster Parliament of 1388 had dragged on from early February through early June with just one significant recess, earning its designation as the "Merciless Parliament" by condemning Brembre and Burley and other supporters of the king and by severely circumscribing Richard's own power. By its end, all participants appear to have been in a state of stressful exhaustion and glad for a respite. Petitions advanced by commons were more perfunctory than usual, dealing mainly with matters related to the impeachments and their immediate aftermath (*RP*, 3:246–52). But the commons, already looking ahead to matters ignored during the struggle between king and Appellants, called for another parliament at Michelmas "pur Amendement du Roilaume, en confort de sa Commune" (*RP*, 3:246).

At this parliament, which convened in Cambridge on 10 September 1388, the commons presented a composite or "comprehensive" petition dealing with an accumulation of concerns and grievances, of which the opening sections and most or all of the rest have been preserved in the *Westminster Chronicle*.[1] Noting that this text consists of "separate petitions concerning the public interest . . . 'edited' to form a series," its most astute analyst treats it as something of a miscellany of statements on discrete matters (Tuck, "Cambridge Parliament," 230). But I find in its provisions a common productive impulse, grounded in an idea of public order based on respect for central and hierarchical authority.

The petition's concern with public order is expressed in its first provision, calling for the lords of the realm to desist in granting liveries called signs or badges, "lez liverees appellez signes" (*West.*, 356). This is hardly a novel request. The parliamentary commons pleaded again and again, throughout the reigns of Edward III, Richard II, and Henry IV, for restraint upon the easy exercise of temporary forms of association—affinities, congregations, confederacies, covins, and other gatherings for purposes of extortion or local domination. A statute of 1 Richard II, for example, complains of the ease with which the petty aristocracy form retinues of esquires and others to maintain their quarrels. Specifically at issue is the ease of enlistment: retainers can be enrolled for one hood or other livery a year, from which—the framers of the statute note in dismay—the grantors often collect full value from the recipient, or even turn a profit, "repreignantz vers eux la value de cel livere ou par cas la double value" (*Stat.*, 335)! A concerted, though unsuccessful, initiative of commons occurred again in the Salisbury parliament of 1384, framed as a complaint that locally powerful persons, supported by the signs or ornaments of lords, "per dominos

---

[1] 354–68. The "comprehensive commons petition" was first described by Howard L. Gray, who commented that "the commons petition of early parliaments was a petition of several articles. Although each article was in itself a petition and demanded its own response, there was a certain appropriateness in enumerating in a series the commons' requests" (203). A. R. Myers doubts Gray's conclusion that the comprehensive petition persisted into the fifteenth century (593–610), but Gray's observations about the parliamentary processes of the fourteenth century in general, and the Cambridge Parliament in particular (227), retain their force. Granting Gray's point, and that of Tuck ("Cambridge Parliament"), any consistency within the provisions of the petition of the Cambridge commons must be seen to result less from any tradition or imperative of unity than from persistent elements in the larger situation within which the petition was composed.

regni signis quasi ornamentis diversis," sought to oppress poor persons in the countryside (*West.*, 80–82).

Exemplified in these initiatives is no mere concern with apparel or ornament, but an urgent unease about the forms of appropriate relation between persons. That distress about temporary and unsanctioned associations should intensify in the new labor situation of the second half-century should occasion no surprise. In the 1388 petition itself, this distress, and an accompanying impulse to limit new forms of association through regulation, is manifested in a number of ways.

Unease over unsanctioned associations for illicit ends resurfaces, for example, in the petition's discussion of "touz manerez de meintenance, extorcions, et oppressions faitz ou affaire al poeple." The extent of its framers' concern with maintenance is revealed in their care to include an extensive definition of the practice, a definition too long to include here, but from which the following extract is taken:

> Et purceo qe diverses opinions sont en quel cas meintenance doit estre ajugge . . . , declarissement ensuyt: cest assavoir quant ascun seignur espirituelle ou temporelle ou dame ou femme de religioun ou qeconqe autre de quele estat ou condicion qil soit emprent ou susteigne ascun querele dautre homme a qi il nest pas partie cosyn nalye . . . et quant ascuns soy assemblent en grantz routes et multitude de poeple outre lour degre et estat . . . en destourbaunce de la ley ou en affray de poeple, ou feignent diverses querels par autres de lour assent devers plusours lieges du roiaume. (*West.*, 358)

Some of the points of particular concern here—all inimical to the stability of sworn relations—are that such associations involve alliance of persons not otherwise related, that they represent a temporary and voluntary association for concerted action, and that they seem to involve transgression of the normal constraints of personal degree. Subject to particular condemnation, in other words, is the idea of collusion outside the boundaries of the sanctioned order for purposes of self-advancement or gain.

This same concern about illicit association and transgression for purposes of advancement underlies a number of seemingly unrelated provisions of the larger petition. One of its most puzzling sections, for example, involves the abolition of "touz lez gildes et fraternites" and the expropriation of their funds. Tuck explains this proposal in terms of a desire to fleece these establishments, together with a prevailing fear of sedition; pecuniary motives (including the capture revenue for land held in mortmain by these organizations) almost certainly underlay an ensuing inquiry into the rules and resources of guilds, fraternities, and mysteries ("Cambridge Parliament," 237–38). Inspection of the details of the original petition suggests, however, a further source of unease on the part of the parliamentary commons, involving neither sedition nor finances. The original petition provides for the *exemption* of those guilds and fraternities "ordenez al honour de seint esglise et encres de divine servise, sanz livere, confederacie, meintenaunce ou riotes" (*West.*, 356). Spared, in other words, are those religious fraternities and confraternities that do not aspire to political influence, and that reject the new forms and practices of short-term association for civic or economic advantage. Remaining under suspicion are two categories of organizations. The first consists of urban craft guilds. Later fourteenth-century usage, as signaled by the language of the dual writs issued to gain information about guild structures as a consequence of the Cambridge petition, was to distinguish between "gildae et fraternitates," or *religious* guilds, and "misterae et artificia," or *craft* guilds (PRO, C54/229, mem. 32d). The implication of the petition, and the writs subsequently issued as a result of the petition, is that the parliamentary commons regarded *all* craft-guilds (though not, presumably, the more prosperous mercantile guilds) as potential sources of economic and civil disturbance. Similarly under suspicion are *some* religious fraternities that refuse to confine their activities to keeping their candles lit, and that venture into organizational techniques involving livery, confederacy, maintenance, or worse.[2]

Revealed in this suspicious approach to socially innovative guilds and fraternities are several critical social divisions within the middle strata: first, between those prosperous mercantile citizens and burgesses in Parliament and the artisanal tradespersons of more middling stature who served as masters of the craft guilds; and second, between any and all guild masters and the disenfranchised journeymen or *servientes stipendiarii* who served them. Or, to put it more simply, between the prosperous merchant-capitalists who tended to dominate the parliamentary commons and other, less favorably situated, artisan-workers of all categories.[3] Apparently expressed in this provision against socially unruly guildsmen is a mistrust by the parliamentary commons of those persons—whether above or below them on

---

[2] Organization for economic and civil influence behind a screen of pious fraternalism evidently did occur in the 1380s and 1390s. Caroline Barron is currently editing a previously undiscovered English guild return—that of the "yeomanrie of the curriers"—in which the journeyman curriers touch a few religious bases and then launch into a series of tough-minded economic provisions: "No man of that Craft ne shall sette non vncouth man a worke," etc. That such activities did occur under guild cover is evident from a 1387 complaint of master cordwainers that journeymen were seeking to organize contrary to the 1383 ordinance against covins, under cover of a religious association (LBH, fol. ccxix); additional attempts of relatively dispossessed workers to work within religious guilds for wage-gains and other objectives are signaled in the 1396 complaints of the master saddlemen against their own journeymen or yeomen (LBH, fol. cccix b).

[3] With respect to the domination of commons by a mercantile patriciate, May McKisack observes in her study of parliamentary representation that "during the fourteenth century the election of parliamentary burgesses was in nearly all towns the exclusive privilege of a few of the wealthier citizens" (38); nearly half were gentle in the first quarter of the fifteenth century (Roskell, 161), and the proportion of royal officers was growing apace (Brown, 120).

the social scale—who might benefit from unsettling practices of livery and maintenance that had proliferated so rapidly in the middle years of the fourteenth century.

A similar vision, fusing both a desire for social order and a prudent self-regard, informs the petition's treatment of those workers who wander the countryside without official permission, seeking to better their circumstances. The proposed treatment of those arrested without letters patent is revealing: they shall not only be placed in jail but returned to a condition of servitude, bound, if claimed by no other, to the person by whom they are apprehended "soit tenuz de servir a luy qi luy ensi prist" (*West.*, 360). An underlying element of self-regard is apparent; as Tuck points out, the commons contained many small landowners and petty capitalists who stood to gain from a clear subordination of the work force and control of its wages ("Cambridge Parliament," 236). Yet the self-interested substructure of this argument would not necessarily have been evident to the commons who promulgated it, precisely because of the degree of their investment in the whole idea of social order grounded in patterns of domination and subordination. The very idea of masterless men would have seemed so evidently repugnant to the commons that its members would hardly have had to probe their motives in advancing an argument for the reinstitution of social hierarchy at every level of society.

The petition embraces other concerns that I will not examine here, including establishment of appropriate wages for laborers and servants according to their degree, "solonc lour degre," orderly administration of justice and conduct of trade, and payment of parliamentary and judicial expenses according to schemes more favorable to the commons than to the aristocracy (with free tenants of lords to contribute to the expenses of shire knights and other charges "en supportacion del comune poeple," and with only "villeins de sanke" or hereditary villeins exempted).

However diverse, the different provisions of the petition originate within a body of propositions and assumptions favorable to civil order and to the interests of commons. The dominant proposition asserts the necessity of stable hierarchy at every level of social experience—with the centrality of "degre" everywhere asserted, and with prevailing condemnation of those seeking to operate "outre lour degre." We may notice, on the other hand, that this principle of hierarchical order is selectively imposed. Lords are to keep retinue, but the ranks of their followers are drastically limited, to tenants "de sanke" and (by inference) to lifetime retainers or retainers fully indentured to their lords. Laborers, and especially rural laborers, are bound to serve, but we are told little about the obligations of the middle strata. Aligning themselves with social stability and order, the successful merchant-capitalists used their parliamentary influence to assail the very configurations designed to advance the interests of others through collective action—K. B. McFarlane's "bastard" retinues on the one hand and those guilds and fraternities that employed the new tactics of livery and maintenance to increase their effectiveness on the other.

RICHARD ON LIVERY AND MAINTENANCE, 1388–1390

The commons generated petitions on livery and maintenance with regularity. A crucial difference is, however, that the 1388 petition achieved unprecedented notice, especially in the form of Richard's own support. In order to understand Richard's sudden solicitude for the commons' position on public order, we must step back from the petition itself to consider the general situation in which it was composed and within which Richard framed his response.

The Merciless Parliament had dealt severe blows to Richard's kingship. Although Gloucester and his fellow Appellants abandoned their briefly held plan to depose Richard (*RP*, 3:379), and although commons would renew homage to Richard and he his coronation oath to them (*West.*, 294), the parliament nevertheless ended with severe circumscription of his prerogative and with a continual council still in place "pro gubernacione regis continua" (*RP*, 3:248; *West.*, 232). Thus began that summer of Richard's eclipse when, the Westminster chronicler tells us, the king spent June through autumn engaged in the chase, "venacioni indulsit" (*West.*, 342). And when Parliament next convened in Cambridge on 10 September the king remained in a weak position, effectively barred from rule by the residual prestige of the Appellants and the continuing activities of the council. Yet the Appellants had left the door open for a reassertion of royal authority by their failure to institutionalize their own gains, to advance domestic reform, or to inspire military success (Tuck, "Cambridge Parliament," 225–27). And Richard was set to capitalize fully, even brilliantly, on these omissions.

The Westminster chronicler's account of the Cambridge Parliament highlights the concern of commons with those very forms of retaining addressed in their petition; at this parliament, the chronicler observes, the commons complained about the badges or *signa* issued by lords, since those who wore them, buoyed up by insolent arrogance, were practicing various extortions in the countryside:

> Item illi de communitate in isto parliamento de signis dominorum graviter sunt conquesti eo quod ea gestantes propter suorum potenciam dominorum in tam cervicosam superbiam sunt elati quod varias extorsiones in patria circumcirca ausu temerario committere non verentur. (*West.*, 354)

The lords (as they had in 1384) responded defensively, assuring the commons that any offenders handed over to them would be appropriately dealt with. "Ista promissio illis non placuit," comments the chronicler, making clear the commons' resolution not to be so easily satisfied. And this is the point at which Richard came forward with a surprising offer of his own, offering for the sake of tranquility to set an example by abandoning his own use of badges: "Ad hec rex, affectans ut tranquillitas foret in regno pro bono pacis et ut aliis daret exemplum, optulit se deponere sua signa" (*West.*, 356).

Note the elements of conscious self-representation involved in Richard's performance. Whether through forethought or momentary inspiration, he chooses exactly the right moment to put himself forward as a mediator of disharmony: a moment of total standoff between the lords and commons. At this moment, he does not simply express an opinion but makes himself into an exemplum, an example of correct behavior. And, as if in recognition that they have witnessed a performance, the commons constitute themselves as an approving audience: "quod summe placuit communitati predicte." Certainly the chronicler was converted. He emphasizes throughout that Richard's motives are of the highest order: "Ut tranquillitas foret in regno . . . volens comune dissidium evitare . . . ut omnis materia dissencionis radicitus exstirpetur." The extent of Richard's victory is figured in his final response to the lords, to allow them to go on using their signs until the next parliament—"concessit dominis sepedictis uti eorum signis usque in proximum parliamentum"; hitherto so enfeebled as to be excluded from affairs of state, he has now repositioned himself to make "concessions" to the lords, out of an evident reserve of civil power.

As several commentators have pointed out, this intervention marks a decisive stage in Richard's reassertion of sovereignty (Tuck, "Cambridge Parliament," 235; Tuck, *Richard II*, 133–37; Goodman, 50–51; Storey, 135–40). Richard's success at the Cambridge Parliament paved the way for his resumption of sole governance at Westminster in May 1389. And his own recognition of his successful self-representation as an exponent of public order and enemy of new forms of association is embodied in his proclamation upon resumption of power; to his subjects he promised a full program of public order, including the suppression of illicit congregations and associations, for purposes of maintenance or oppression: "congregaciones, oppressiones, manutenencias, seu coventicula illicita . . . in perturbacionem pacis" (*RP*, 3:404). Nor did Richard immediately abandon this profitable stance toward public order. He instituted new peace commissions in the fall of 1389, with members drawn not from the aristocracy but from the strata of parliamentary commons (Storey, 140–42). He engineered a compromise at the Westminster parliament of January 1390, in which the lords agreed to retain only persons "de privata familia," receiving a fixed annual annuity (Walsingham, *Historia*, 2:195–96). He oversaw a comprehensive, if ineffective, council ordinance on retaining in May

1390.[4] This ordinance was his last significant effort to woo the parliamentary commons with issues of public order. By November 1390, he had abandoned his efforts to reform the peace commissions (Storey, 149–52). Yet, for a period of nearly two years, he had exploited this strategy with marked success.

That Richard's opposition to abuses of retaining owed more to political expediency than personal conviction is evident from his own behavior before September 1388 and after May 1390. The very heart of his anti-Appellant strategy in the summer of 1387 had been the widescale retention of personal followers, in part through the activities of deputies who would distribute badges to influential citizens who were to swear to hold with the king, "jurare quod postpositis ceteris dominis quibuscumque cum ipso utpote eorum vero rege tenerent, datisque eisdem signis, scilicet coronis argenteis ac deauratis" (*West.*, 186). Likewise, Richard instituted his own Order of the White Hart at the tournament at Smithfield in October 1390, "ubi datum erat primo signum uel stigma illud egregium in ceruo albo" (*Historia Ricardi*, 130), a "liveray that he yaf to lordes & ladies, knyghtis and skquiers, for to know his housholde from other peple" (*Brut*, 343). For his own manipulation of *signa* in the course of his career, Richard would in fact become known as a primary abuser. (See appendix 2, 182–84.) Nevertheless, at a crucial period, Richard showed himself able to suppress his own inclination to exercise bastard feudalism on the grandest of scales, in pursuit of a longer-term, ultimately absolutist, goal.

Chaucer's Poem

Chaucer's "Lak of Stedfastnesse" has been treated as a tissue of commonplaces, so thoroughly dependent on its predecessors that it cannot possibly address a particular situation.[5] Alternatively, it has been treated with equal

---

[4] For a rare instance of attempted enforcement within the spirit of the ordinance, see *Esturmy v. Coutenay*, 1392, in *KC*, 77–81; for a 1393 complaint of Commons about nonenforcement see *RP*, 3:307.

[5] The argument for conventionality has been thoroughly made by J. E. Cross, who seeks to demonstrate by extensive reference to classical Latin, Old French, and Old Swedish that the poem's "seemingly unique statements" are actually so "commonplace" as to frustrate any attempt to connect it with contemporary circumstances, that it must remain "undated and unaddressed" (283, 302). On inspection, however, the language and conceptions of the poem turn out to be freighted with a good deal more historical specificity than Cross's line of argument would suppose. Cross argues, for example, that there is no essential difference between "Lak's" "Trouthe is putte doun" and such precedental texts as Isaiah's "Et conversum est retrorsum iudicium" and Juvenal's "Probitas laudatur et alget." But in fact the deepest historical and cultural differences separate the Hebrew and Latin emphasis on the judicial system in *iudicium* and the Latin emphasis on personal responsibility in *probitas* from the

conviction as a highly topical utterance that can be connected unproblematically with any of several burning issues of the day, including the activities of the Merciless Parliament, Richard's extension of his prerogative in 1397, as well as the Rising of 1381.[6] For all the earnestness with which commentators have sought to historicize this poem, they would still seem to have run afoul of what J. Hillis Miller has called "the apparent canyon between history and language" (291)—or, in this case, between a highly conventional text and specific moments in history. Temporarily pursuing this metaphor of the canyon, one might observe that the conjectures with which the poem's commentators have sought to bridge it have a decidedly improvised quality, a look of not being ready to bear much weight.

My objective is to overcome the incommensurability of texts and actions, and hence to narrow the gap between them, by delineating an environment within which both texts and actions are produced and received. If the petition of commons, Richard's intervention, and Chaucer's poem are seen to originate within a common environment of ideas about collusion and maintenance, extortion and representation, and princely redress, then less conjecture needs to be focused on their special relation, one to another; at the same time, discussion of their legitmate interrelation within a larger situation will rest on a less particular and more defensible argumentative ground.[7]

Although it does embrace many traditional elements, Chaucer's poem nevertheless does inhabit a specific place of its own in a larger discussion of public order, new forms of retention, and the social responsibility of the nobles and the king. Generally and appropriately typified as a poem about

---

fourteenth-century concept of *trouthe*. *Trouthe* is deeply involved in medieval convictions about the permanence of sworn understandings and the possiblity of securing sworn relations from temporal decay by associating them with the divine.

[6] For these views see Pollard, 123, Brusendorff, 274, and Brewer, 41. The most persuasive observation on this poem is that of V. J. Scattergood, who acknowledges the difficulty of moving between unique historical particulars and self-enclosed texts, reminding us that Chaucer's habitual strategy is to talk "about the particular by way of traditional genres" (474). In effect, Scattergood recognizes the need for what must be considered a scholarly "leap" across the gulf between texts and circumstances. His own conjecture—that the poem's exhortation to its addressee to maintain his "estat" alludes to Richard's defense of his prerogative in 1386–1387—is more interesting and persuasive than most. That it must remain a conjecture is implicit, however, in his formulation of the problem.

[7] My conception of a productive "environment" may be associated with J.G.A. Pocock's description of the textual "matrix," and he is persuasive in his description of the sense in which interpretation may emancipate itself from the overly particularized (and overly ingenious) insights of which literary critics are sometimes accused. Arguing that "languages are the matrices within which texts as events occur," he observes that "if we have succeeded in demonstrating that continuities of discourse were historically actual, that they were resources of language available for use . . . over periods of historical time, then we have escaped the reproach that we are merely reading them into the record" (28).

"the world upside-down," it is nevertheless implicated in contemporary history at a number of points, including the particular terms of its explanation for contemporary malaise. Here is the poem:

Somtyme the world was so stedfast and stable
That mannes word was obligacioun,
And now it is so fals and deceivable
That word and deed, as in conclusioun,
Ben nothing lyk, for turned up-so-doun
Is al this world for mede and wilfulnesse,
That al is lost for lak of stedfastnesse.

What maketh this world to be so variable
But lust that folk have in dissensioun?
For among us now a man is holde unable,
But if he can by som collusioun
Don his neighbour wrong or oppressioun.
What causeth this but wilful wrecchednesse,
That al is lost for lak of stedfastnesse?

Trouthe is put doun, resoun is holden fable,
Vertu hath now no dominacioun;
Pitee exyled, no man is merciable.
Through covetyse is blent discrecioun.
The world hath mad a permutacioun
Fro right to wrong, fro trouthe to fikelnesse,
That al is lost for lak of stedfastnesse.

Lenvoy to King Richard

O prince, desyre to be honourable,
Cherish thy folk and hate extorcioun.
Suffre nothing that may be reprevable
To thyn estat don in thy regioun.
Shew forth thy swerd of castigacioun,
Dred God, do law, love trouthe and worthinesse,
And wed thy folk agein to stedfastnesse.

The basis of the current inversion of values in the world is, we learn at the outset, the subversion of an earlier system of "obligation," in which people were bound (*ob-ligo*, "to fasten" or "to bind") in a stable relation based on the certainty of *trouthe* or "mannes word." This system of stable obligations, presented as an object of nostalgia in the poem, may be understood to allude to the sworn hierarchy of feudal tradition, a system whose devotion to the common good is suggested by its distance from rampant individualism (or "wilfulnesse") and proclivity for social fracture (or "dissensioun"). So much an object of nostalgia is this system that its economic basis in the rents derived from proprietorship is wholly concealed; only its successor-system is described as having an economic basis, in individual greed or "covetyse" exemplified in the desire for "mede."

What might seem to be taking shape here is a sweeping claim on my part about the "transition from feudalism to capitalism." I would not deny the broad pertinence of such a formulation, though at a level of grand abstraction still fairly remote from the actual dynamics of Chaucer's poem. The greater specificity of Chaucer's poem is that it lodges its indictment of covetousness in a contemporary social practice, a practice that might possess a few precapitalist elements but that is essentially a function of a fourteenth-century state of affairs: that of short-term "collusioun" with others for the purpose of doing "wrong or oppressioun" to neighbors. The means of this oppression—whether through force, intimidation, or maintenance in legal proceedings—remain unspecified. But the result is "extorcioun," the act defined by the *Middle English Dictionary* as "wresting money . . . by force, intimidation, or the undue exercise of power or authority."

This emphasis on collusion for purposes of extortion in turn draws Chaucer's poem into close association with maintenance as defined in the 1388 petition: that situation when a lord or other takes up a quarrel to which he is not party by reason of blood or marriage ("a qi il nest pas partie cosyn nalye") in order to gain reward, or colludes with others to feign quarrels ("feignent diverses querels par autres de lour assent") to assault lieges of the realm or to occupy their lands, or to maintain or retain ("mayngtenent ou retiegnent") brigands or other shady characters (*West.*, 358). The authors of the petition seek an inquiry into all forms of "meintenance, extorcions et oppressions" practiced upon the people; the result of *collusioun* in the poem is "oppressioun" and "extorcioun" of neighbors. The emphasis on oppression and extortion within both petition and poem is explicable not because one document is a "source" for the other, but because both petition (with its condemnation of connivance in suits and quarrels) and poem (with its condemnation of collusion against neighbors) draw upon current language and concepts to address a current situation of abuse of power.

Even in the weakened condition in which he first received the parliamentary petition, Richard is its addressee; in fact, his response to the provisions on livery ("le roy voet") is interpolated within the text of the petition preserved in the *Westminster Chronicle* (356). So, too, would Richard appear to be the "prince," and hence addressee, of Chaucer's poem.[8] Not only does

---

[8] That Richard might be Chaucer's addressee is, of course, suggested by Shirley's manuscript heading, "Lenvoye to kyng Richard" (*Minor Poems*, 83–84). Yet Shirley's attributions are notoriously fanciful and self-serving and can at best be taken only as evidence of one reasonably acute fifteenth-century reader's response, rather than evidence in the usual sense.

the poem's emphasis on public order coincide with Richard's own program, but the role imagined for the prince in Chaucer's poem coincides
with a public stance Richard had already devised and enacted for himself.
This role is, of course, that of princely mediator. In Parliament, Richard
had bound himself to an act of voluntary self-submission, in this case to
the demands of commons for curtailment of lawless retinues, in order to
mediate between rival factions. At once principal practitioner of lordship
as head of the royal household and meek subject in voluntary submission
to the wishes of commons, he possesses the prerequisites for mediation: an
ability to place himself, at least imaginatively, in each camp, and a willingness to refrain from pressing his own claims. In the envoy to the poem, he
is urged to do very much the same: to submit to a series of voluntary self-
curtailments ("Dred God, do law, love trouthe and worthinesse") and to
efface his claims, in order to serve as mediator, go-between, and priest in
the wedding between his subjects and their own lost virtue ("And wed thy
folk agein to stedfastnesse").[9]

That Chaucer should address Richard at such a time and in such a way
is consistent with what we know of his career. In May 1388, during the
last frenzies of the Merciless Parliament, Chaucer had severed his last royal
and London or Westminster ties by relinquishing his exchequer annuities
(Crow and Olson, 336–39) and completing the process of prudent with-
drawal to Kent that he appears to have adopted in order to ride out the
emergency. But no sooner was this process complete (on May 1) than the
Merciless Parliament adjourned (on May 4), and the condemnation, exile,
and banishment of Richard's followers came to an abrupt end. Some residual prudence might have been in order, and Chaucer's continuation of his
Kent sojourn during the summer of 1388 may be likened to Richard's decision to spend the summer apolitically, indulging in the chase. The difference, however, is that Richard had a job; Chaucer, effectively unemployed

---

More persuasive are the coincidence of the poem's admonitions to defend the people against
extortion with Richard's own campaign for public order, and the fact that Richard's campaign
occurred at a point in Chaucer's own career when a flattering poem addressed to his monarch
would have made most sense. Most modern critics have assumed that Richard is the addressee
of Chaucer's poem; for an attribution and dating consonant with mine see Donald Howard,
388–89.

[9] In fourteenth-century England the role of mediator is traditionally played by women;
Richard's mother Joan of Kent and his first wife Anne of Bohemia were, of course, renowned
for their intercessions. (See below, chapter 6.) The prince as voluntary intercessor, withhold-
ing his own spousal claims in order to promote a marriage of his subjects and their own lost
virtue, would have borne a strangely gendered charge for many readers of Chaucer's poem.
In this sense, the highly assertive "swerd of castigacioun" that has posed interpretive temp-
tations and difficulties for some readers of the poem might simply be thought compensatory:
a visible emblem of incontestable phallicity to offset any less-than-princely elements in
Richard's chosen role.

since 1386, appears to have been in serious financial straits (Crow and Olson, 384–91). With tensions subsiding in the course of the summer of 1388, and then with Richard's remarkable reemergence at the Cambridge Parliament, Chaucer's hopes of renewed preferment surely quickened. Events now unfolded quickly. In September 1388 Richard launched his campaign for public order. In May 1389 he resumed sole governance. In July 1389 Chaucer was among the first of the Ricardian adherents reappointed to office, with his assumption of the clerkship of works. In May 1390 Richard's campaign for public order came to an effective end. Between September 1388 and May 1390 Richard was an appropriate addressee of a poem about the responsibility of the prince to preserve order in the countryside, and Chaucer, first as petitioner and then as grateful client, had good reason to write such a poem.

This is as specific as I wish to be about the possible timing of Chaucer's poem, since my objective is less to "date" it than to position it within a broad array of roughly contemporary statements and gestures. In this sense, I am less concerned to argue that the petition is a "source" for the poem, or that the poem depends upon a specific knowledge of Richard's parliamentary self-presentation, than that all three were created and understood within a much larger and more diffuse environment of language and ideas and expectations. Once these disparate performances are seen in this way, less emphasis needs to be placed upon their special relationship, one to another. Acting in a common environment of texts, gestures, and assumptions about public order and new forms of retaining, the commons frame a petition, Richard launches a campaign, Chaucer writes a poem. We need not wonder that certain words and concepts surface and resurface in each.

CHAUCER, RICHARD, AND IDEOLOGY

Chaucer's relation to Richard is, in some senses, that of poet to patron as traditionally conceived. But, in another sense, his address to Richard is not a direct communication from petitioner to patron at all, but is rather produced, and undoubtedly received, within the larger environment that encloses them both. Many components of this environment may be seen as implicitly *ideological* in nature, and conceptual ground may be gained by the use of this term, if its risky power is fully respected and employed in a focused way.

I use the term *ideology* not as distortion or false consciousness, but more neutrally as an essential element of social organization, as a system of imaginary representations and enactments through which persons approach understanding of their historical situation (Geertz, 218; R. Williams, 153–

57). Ideology so conceived functions as a crucial middle term in literary production, mediating between what Bakhtin and Medvedev call the "literary environment" upon which the text depends for its form and style and the "socioeconomic environment" that, although not necessarily represented directly in the work, exerts an absent influence upon it (26–27). I would argue, as well, that it exerts a crucial influence on reception, establishing the terms and expectations within which a text is assimilated to the experience of its reader or hearer.

The propositions on social order produced and sustained within this ideology are broad and supple: the prince is responsible for maintenance of public order; society depends on orderly degrees of domination and subordination; augmentation of local authority is suspect; collusive attempts to deprive others of their rights or property are to be condemned. Such propositions are hardly the property of Richard, or Chaucer, or the commons, or, for that matter, any individual or single class of persons. They are available throughout the later fourteenth century for varied appropriation and use in a variety of tactical situations.

For example, the 1388 petition invokes these and related propositions in its condemnation of unruly aristocratic retinues and disorder in the countryside. But, earlier in 1388, the aristocratic Appellants had made their own use of similar reasoning to indict Richard's followers, condemning the king's involvement in newfangled practices of "covyn," "affinite," "meyntenaunce," and retinue-building: "les ditz traitours . . . firent le roy de faire grant retenue de novell' des diverses gentz et a doner a eux diverses signes autrement que il ne soloit estre dancien temps" (*West.*, 256; see also 242, 244, 248). Then, the wheel having come around again, Richard and his followers at the law-and-order parliament of 1397 indicted Gloucester and the "senior" Appellants "for the great number of "Extorsionibus, Oppressionibus, Gravaminibus, & aliis Malefactis" visited against king and people (Rymer, vol. 3, pt. 4, 131). Then, the wheel having come around *yet* again, followers of Henry IV stripped certain lords who had profited by the death of Gloucester of their right to give "Liverees of Sygnes," the more so because of clamor among the people that "some of her men have done grete extorsions, wronges, and oppressions to the poeple" (*RP*, 3:452). Chaucer's poem, written in 1388 or 1389, casts Richard as the agent of social stability, well able to castigate disorder. But Gaunt and the great lords invoked the same principle of princely responsibility, though at the aristocratic rather than monarchic level, when they replied to the complaint of commons that their retinues were oppressing the countryside. Gaunt and the lords founded their reply on the assertion that every lord was able to punish his own dependents for any outrages (*West.*, 82).

Such examples testify to the broad currency of an ideology of civil order, sanctifying old ties and deploring new and opportunistic social arrangements. It might even be styled a "dominant" ideology, although not in the Althusserian sense that it wholly set the terms of contemporary self-understanding, or that it functioned in the same way for all social groups. The varied uses to which the discourses of social order might be bent suggest that, rather than setting the limits of self-understanding, ideology actually produced concepts of varied applicability, available for appropriation and manipulation by different groups in their own behalf. Far from disavowing central conceptions of social order, each of the dominant centers of later fourteenth-century authority and power—including the royal party, the aristocratic opposition, and those upper gentry and merchant-oligarchs represented in commons—sought to advance its interests through acts of imaginative appropriation.[10]

In "Lak of Stedfastnesse," Chaucer performs an act of appropriation on Richard's behalf. He assembles a body of powerfully suggestive statements linking steadfastness, sworn relations, reason, virtue, and pity, and the honorable rule of law, and he opposes to it a nightmare of collusive greed, wrong, oppression, fickleness, and extortion, associating the former with Richard and the latter with his opponents. Part of the tact and presumed effectiveness of Chaucer's poem is its alignment with Richard's campaign to present himself as an agent of social tranquillity, both in the Cambridge Parliament and in the following year. That is, for all its severe and hortative tone as a poem of advice, "Lak of Stedfastnesse," actually flatters and supports Richard by its very consistency with his own program of self-representation. In this sense, it is the most welcome kind of advice, advice that the recipient does not really need. John Gower, in the first version of his *Confessio*, offers to Richard what he describes as "wisdom to the wise" (bk. 8, l. 3059*). So does Chaucer offer to Richard a course of action and a rationale that he does not really need, a pretended instruction for one whose plentitude of power and wisdom eliminate any need for instruction.

One view of ideology would have it as a reservoir of possible social solutions, of "answers to questions posed by the situation in which it arose" (Kenneth Burke, in Geertz, 230). Yet the dynamics of Chaucer's address to Richard in "Lak of Stedfastnesse" suggest an expanded view of how ideology works, a view that treats ideology as still more diversely involved

---

[10] Alternative discourses were simultaneously available, and sporadic and fragmentary appeals to principles of fraternity, brotherhood, and even fair profit may be found in guild ordinances and among the occasionally insurgent peasantry. Members of the more secure social groups tended, however, to define themselves by self-interested application of traditional social principles rather than by introduction of discourse encouraging to new social arrangements. New social arrangements do surface within discourses of social order sponsored by these dominant groups, but in highly stigmatized forms, as when new patterns of association are branded "collusive" in Chaucer's poem or guild activities are suspected of "riotousness" in the 1388 petition.

in the production of meaning. Chaucer's poem poses a series of questions about how to respond to the threat of retinues and collusive practices and then bases its answer on the availability of the prince as go-between, reeffecting the union between his people and their own traditional virtue. I would suggest that the "problem" of civil disorder to which Chaucer's poem is a response and the "solution" of the prince who can rejoin his people to their own virtue are both shaped within an ideology of civil order and kingship.

All this being said, I want to stop a good deal short of saying that ideology determines the content of texts or of human actions, for those symbolic elements we call "ideological" are a good deal more diverse and less unified than such a view would imply. Operative elements in Chaucer's text and in Richard's performance include ideas of civil order, sworn association, the common good, voluntary restraint, princely redress, and selfless mediation—ideas potentially at strife with each other, and ideas that only the most adroit of social actors could align even briefly within a single and apparently coherent formation. Moreover, these elements were far from resting secure in the possession of any social group, but were available within a broadly accessible oral and textual domain to be claimed by any of the contestants for political power. Such contestants were hardly lacking in the crucial years of the late 1380s, and they included such groups as the landed aristocracy, with its attempt to extend its power through retinue formation; the monarchy, with its attempt to regain the prerogatives of sole rule; the parliamentary commons, with its mistrust of new forms of guild organization; journeymen seeking their own organizational base; and civil servants, some of whom were displaced or in jeopardy as a result of continuing turmoil involving the highest offices of the land. For each of these groups, secure possession of the principal elements of ideology would have conferred unquestioned practical advantage.

There is a paradox here: ideological commonplaces are the *means* of symbolic assertion (in the sense that they constitute those ideological forms by which, according to Marx, people become aware of struggle and fight it out), but they are also the final *objective* (in the sense that their possession, by any of the major groups, would contribute enormously to its success). The resolution of the paradox is that a group asserts its claim to possession of an ideological structure by using it effectively. By producing arguments, representations, and enactments through the apt deployment of ideological materials, the group not only gains their assistance in its own process of self-constitution but also demonstrates its right to them by disclosing their rightful place in the narrative of that group's ascendancy.

In these terms, Chaucer's poem may be seen to render Richard an extremely valuable service. It captures a number of crucial elements of the ideology of public order, employing them both to state a problem and to define its solution. And it effects this capture on Richard's behalf, offering him within ideology as the final "answer" to charged "questions" that ideology had already posed. Yet Richard is finally not ideology's creation. He is rather, if not its master, at least its beneficiary. For, within the space of Chaucer's poem, it is bound over and delivered to the magnification of his regality and the service of his rule.[11]

[11] A starting point for my thinking in this section was the classic essay of the *Cahiers* editors on the cinema of John Ford, developing the concept of ideology as a source not only of answers but of questions—of "questions posed after the fact ["post-posées"], the existence of which is made possible because their answer has already been given" (Texte collectif, 33). The longer I have thought about ideology, though, the less inclined I am to view it as a dominating force within which meanings are determined and the more I tend to view it as an object of desire in its own right, whose possession bolsters the authority of the social group that demonstrates title to its use. I have been influenced in this ultimately anti-Althusserian view of ideology by several readings, including Giddens, 184–97, and Oscar Kenshur's strictures against ideological essentialism, shortly to appear as a volume in the University of California Press's "New Historicism" series.

Chapter 4

SAVING THE APPEARANCES: CHAUCER'S
"PURSE" AND THE FABRICATION OF
THE LANCASTRIAN CLAIM

THE AURA of inevitability still surrounding Henry IV's seizure of the throne in 1399 results in part from our own lingering captivation by the Lancastrian genius for manipulating public opinion. Recent studies, especially Caroline Barron's "Deposition of Richard II," have suggested that Henry IV's triumph was neither as inevitable nor as secure as has commonly been supposed. Yet in the years and months before Henry's accession the Lancastrians generated a blizzard of bogus genealogy, false prophecy, anti-Ricardian fabrication, and novel ceremonial, punctuated by deft employment of the emergent English vernacular in parliamentary and other unprecedented contexts. So thorough was this campaign that it virtually crowded out non-Lancastrian discourse in the crucial autumn months leading to Henry's accession, and it continued to function with undiminished energy to efface non-Lancastrian accounts once Henry was on the throne. The success of this prototypical propaganda machine was so great that its products gained a self-perpetuating momentum, pervading the symbolic and discursive environment within which subsequent works—including Chaucer's "To His Purse"—were composed.

THE ARGUMENTATIVE ENVIRONMENT

The particular logic and sequence of Henry of Derby's actions upon his return to England in July 1399 remain concealed behind the discrepant and unreliable chronicle accounts through which we attempt to know them. Nevertheless a general pattern does emerge, a pattern mixed, whether through Henry's uncertainty or deviousness, but moving by its own logic ever closer to a claim on the throne. Swearing to the northern lords at Doncaster that he aimed only to secure his heritage and to put Richard "in gouernaunce" (Hardyng, 350), and through his emissaries to Richard at Conway that he wished only to be hereditary steward or "Anglie senescallo iure hereditario" (*Dieulacres Chronicle*, quoted in Clarke and Galbraith, 51), he is described by Creton as assuring Richard at their first meeting at Flint Castle that his goal was to aid in governing the people, "sil plaist a nre seigneur ie le vous aideray a gouverner mieulx quil na este gouverne le temps passe."[1] But from that moment in mid-August when he took the king under control, no doubt remained that Henry would be king. Only to be determined were the procedure and the argumentative rationale by which Richard's deposition and his own advancement would occur.

Numerous indications suggest that Henry and his allies spent much of the period from mid-August to the very eve of his climactic 30 September meeting with the estates in Westminster Hall generating and canvassing different routes and rationalizations leading to his elevation. On 19 August, writs were issued, in Richard's name but presumably under Henry's direction, summoning the relevant estates of the realm to Parliament, in order to conduct "ardua regni negotia" (*Annales*, 251–52). The fact that Henry summoned the estates does not necessarily mean that he possessed a final plan. Whatever steps were to be taken—whether to secure Richard's abdication, seek his deposition, argue for Henry's legitimate descent, or seek some combination of election or acclaim—the parliamentary summons would assure the presence of an appropriate body to witness and to weigh their impact. That Henry meant to furnish the assembled estates with a yet-to-be-determined argumentative avenue to the crown is signaled by a nearly simultaneous letter to abbots and major ecclesiastics, asking them to examine "cunctas Chronicas regni Angliae statum tangentes, et gubernationem," and inviting persons competent to expound the chronicles, together with the relevant texts, to come to the site of Parliament.[2] The aims of this inquiry become clearer in the light of Henry's creation, early in September, of a committee of *doctores*, *episcopi*, and others to consider the matter of deposing Richard and choosing Henry in his place, of how it was to be done and for what reasons, "et qualiter et ex quibus causis" (Adam of Usk, 29).

This committee provided a focal point for the political and argumentative pressures that were generating a rich variety of rationales or *causae* for Henry's advancement. Because none of the existing accounts of the events surrounding Henry's usurpation predates the climactic 30 September

---

[1] Creton, 374. The tactical nature of Henry's oaths at Doncaster and Conway and the "unsystematic" but keenly opportunistic route by which Henry moved toward a claim on the throne are admirably canvassed by Sherborne. He observes that 10 September was the first date by which Henry may be said with certainty to have resolved upon kingship (as opposed to stewardship or other capacities), but that his strategy had been tending in this direction for several weeks ("Perjury," 240).

[2] *Annales*, 252. *Annales* places both writs and monastic letters in early September, subsequent to Richard's arrival in London and incarceration in the Tower; Lapsley, relying on evidence dating the writs to 19 September, also thinks the letters were sent at an earlier date.

gathering at which he claimed the vacant throne, the reconstruction of these *causae* involves a good deal of guesswork. Nevertheless, an environment of partially realized preaccession dynastic theory can be derived, from among those arguments finally instated as official Lancastrian explanation, from rejected alternatives and other evidences of contradiction embedded within Lancastrian chronicles, and from those few surviving sources—belated and mostly French, together with some cobbled-together fifteenth-century Yorkist texts—located outside the scope of the Lancastrian propaganda machine.

Descent. The fifteenth-century chronicler Hardyng claims that attempts to assure a Lancastrian succession predated the actual usurpation. He relates that John of Gaunt, taking note of Richard's childlessness, sought to have himself rather than the earl of March declared legitimate heir to the throne:

> I herde the . . . erle of Northumberlonde saie divers tymes, that he herde duke
> Iohn of Lancastre, amonge the lordes in counsels and in parlementes, and in
> the common house, amonge the knyghtes chosyn for the comons, aske þe bille
> forto beene admytte heire apparaunte to kyng Richarde, considerynge howe
> the kynge wase like to haue no issue of his bodie. (Hardyng, 353–54)

Checked in this regard by the adherence of the lords and commons to the earl of March, Gaunt turned to another, and longer-term, stratagem, by which his son Henry's claims might be bolstered. This stratagem hinged on a bogus claim that Edmund, second son of Henry III, was in fact his first son and legitimate heir but was set aside in favor of the future Edward I on account of his spinal disfigurement: "When the duke of Lancastre wase so putt bie, he and his counsell feyned and forgied the seide Cronycle that Edmonde [Crouchback, son of Henry III] shuld be the elder brother [rather than Edward I] to make his sone Henry a title to the croune. . . . Whiche Cronycle, so forged, the duke dide put in divers abbaies and in freres . . . forto be kepte for the enheritaunce of his sonne to the croune" (Hardyng, 354). The advantage of this account is that Edmund, as Duke of Lancaster, was great-grandfather of Duchess Blanche, Gaunt's wife and Henry's mother, and Edmund's reinstatement would thus enhance the matrilinial side of Henry's claim.

Gaunt's stratagem seems so farfetched that we might suspect Hardyng—himself an inveterate forger (Kingsford, "First Version," 468) writing with clear purpose of undermining the Lancastrian claim—to have invented it. But other sources less partial to Richard portray Gaunt carrying his tale of Edmund Crouchback to parliament.[3] And, unlikely as the idea that Gaunt

---

[3] According to the continuation of the *Eulogium Historiarum*, "Dux dicebat quod Rex Henricus Tertius habuit duos filios, Edmundum seniorem et primogenitum, et Edwardum. Qui

planted forged chronicles in diverse abbeys and friaries might seem, Henry's own invitation to "certas personas instructas in Chronicis" to show up with relevant texts suggests that he had some hope for their contents (*Annales*, 252). Finally, several sources suggest that Henry's most ardent or impatient supporters did resurrect the argument for his legitimate descent within the committee of *doctores*, in the last days before his elevation. Hardyng says that "kyng Henry, vpon saynt Mathee daye afore he wase made kinge [that is, on 21 September], put forth that ilke cronycle claymynge his title to the crown be the seide Edmonde" (353). This suggestion is seconded by the more authoritative Adam of Usk, present among the *doctores*. Adam, struggling with the rest of them to find some justification for Henry's accession, nevertheless has his limits. He notes that the Crouchback story was raised by certain members ("per quosdam") of Henry's select committee (30). But even this pliant group finally admitted that the evidence of authoritative chronicles argued against it, and Adam goes on to provide a lengthy list of contrary citations (30–31). The argument basing Henry's title on birth had, in short, been repeatedly refuted throughout the decade, and no reputable person appears to have accepted it. Yet, the skepticism of Adam and the other pro-Lancastrian *doctores* notwithstanding, it was to resurface on September 30 and repeatedly throughout the period of Lancastrian rule.

Conquest. The Frenchman Creton, reaching England in July with Salisbury and Richard's vanguard, learned that Henry had already substantially succeeded, "avoit Ja conqui / Dangleterre la plus grant pt" (315). Richard's subsequent loss of two armies in two weeks through a combination of incompetence and treachery and Henry's good fortune in tempting Richard out of Conway and into his power on August 14 and 15 enabled Henry to enjoy nearly complete success without the necessity of a single real battle. Although this conquest would eventually be shown to be more precarious than anyone in September and October 1399 could have imagined, and though it would have to be periodically reconfirmed, it nevertheless represented a stunning momentary success. Still to be determined from mid-August onward, however, was the role of this conquest in securing Henry's title. Everyone knew by mid-August that Henry would be king; the question was whether the blunt *fact* of conquest could be brought to bear argumentatively in order to rationalize Henry's accession.

Henry was a realist, and we cannot doubt that the fact of conquest was central to his perception of his claim. Yet his contemporaries, including those of his own party, remained committed to the development of a rationale that did not rely on the embarrassing fact of his seizure of power. The

---

tamen Edmundus dorsum habuit fractum, et propter hoc judicavit seipsum indignum esse ad coronam; quare pater eorum eos sic componere facit, quod Edwardus regnaret" (369–70).

officially sponsored account of the Lancastrian accession is contained in a document known as the "Record and Proces del Renunciation"—a document with the advantage of after-the-fact verbatim adoption in the Rolls of Parliament (3:415–24), also existing in an excellent Middle English translation in Julius B II (19–47), as well as exerting an influence on the accounts of Walsingham (*Historia*, 2:234–38) and other pro-Lancastrian chroniclers. All these sources agree in citing Henry's assurance that conquest was a minor element of his argument for the throne and that no one need think that "be waye of Conquest I wold disherit any man of his heritage" (*RP*, 3:423). That a story exists behind the story is, however, hinted by an additional passage contained within the equally pro-Lancastrian *Annales Ricardi*. According to the *Annales*, Henry first proposed to claim the kingdom through conquest, but this claim was discouraged by Justice Thirning and the community of opinion he represented because of the legimate fears it would engender among the populace.[4] Whether Thirning, the *doctores*, or other persons are to be thanked, Henry's argument for the consequences of conquest was moderated—though, as we will see, it was not to be withdrawn.

Resignation versus deposition. Henry could "chalange" or claim the realm only after its throne had been vacated; all parties agreed on that. But some uncertainty seems to have existed throughout the fall of 1399 as to whether the Lancastrian party should seek Richard's abdication or his deposition. As embodied in the various after-the-fact textualizations upon which we must depend, a clearcut decision between these two alternatives was never made; whether through thoroughness on the one hand or disorganization on the other, the Lancastrians simply pursued both at once.

With regard to abdication, not one but two stories were placed in circulation, neither with any apparent basis in fact. The first is that, meeting with Northumberland and others prior to vacating Conway Castle, Richard had agreed to step down. The second is that, visited by the duke and the archbishop and their party at the tower on 29 September and presented by them with a written statement of resignation, he read it aloud and freely signed it. The two stories are conjoined in the previously mentioned "Record & Proces del Renunciation." In its account of the 29 September visit to the tower, the Julius B II translation of the "Record and Process" has Northumberland and others reminding the king that "at Coneway in north Walys, beyng there at his luste and liberte [*RP*: *in sua libertate existens*], behiht . . . that he wold leve off and renounce to the crovne . . . in the beste manere and ffourme that he myht, as the counseyll

---

[4] "Sed hoc omnino prohibuit Dominus Willelmus Thernyng, Justiciarius; quia tali occasione commovisset bilem totius populi contra eum; eo quod visum fuisset populo, si sic vendicasset regnum, quot potuisset quemlibet exhaeredasse pro votis, leges mutasse, condidisse novas, et veteres annullasse" (*Annales*, 282).

off wyse men and lernyd wolde ordeyne" (20). The fabricated nature of the "promise" may be indicated most simply by the fact that Creton, the best single authority for the discussions at Conway and Flint, reports nothing of it, confining his accounts to the suasions employed by Northumberland to induce the king to leave the security of the former castle. The "Record and Process" nevertheless represents the promise as fondly remembered by the king, who "louyngly [*RP: benigne*] answeryng seyd, that he wolde perfourme with effecte that he hadde byfore byhiht" (20). The king's voluntary compliance is emphasized throughout. We are told that, presented with a previously drafted instrument of resignation, he read it aloud "with a gladde chere [*RP: ac hillari vultu*]."

So obviously fabricated are these assertions of Richard's good cheer that one must finally prefer the almost equally outrageous counterfabrication of the *Chronicque de la Traïson*, in which a chivalric Richard is so angered as to accuse his visitors of treason and to challenge any four of their best to combat: "Je diz que vous faitez encontre moy come faulses gens . . . Ce vueil je prouuer et combatre contre quatre des meilleurs de vous trestous et veez la mon gaige" (67). (Each account is undoubtedly fabricated, the "Record and Process" out of Lancastrian expediency and the *Traïson* out of a sense of how a monarch might plausibly be expected to behave. Yet the French account concludes, however coincidentally, with a characteristically peevish and pathetic gesture, in which Richard throws down his hat as gage.) Even discounting the historicity of the French accounts, common sense leads inevitably to the conclusion that Richard's signature was undoubtedly obtained, not with his cheerful concurrence, but under duress.[5] So, too, can we suppose that duress was involved in other purportedly voluntary gestures, as when Richard "toke off his ffyngir a Ryng off golde, his Signet, and putt hit on the ffyngir off the Duk" (Julius B II, 23).

With this ring, and this resignation, Henry's supporters went to the meeting at Westminster Hall the next day, taking care to display the ring and to read the resignation to those gathered "ffirst in latyn as yt was wretyn, and affterward in Englyssh" (Julius B II, 23). Those estates present accepted [*RP: admiserunt*] the resignation. At this point in the process, however, a new wrinkle was introduced. Adam of Usk, describing the activities of his committee of *doctores*, noted that, although Richard was ready to cede the crown, it was determined that the process would be more secure if he were deposed by the authority of the clergy and people: "Licet cedere paratus fuerat . . . tamen . . . ipsum fore deponendum cleri et populi autoritate . . . pro majori securritate fuit determinatum" (30). In fact, the

---

[5] As John Hardyng claims to have learned at first hand from the earl of Northumberland: "I herde the seide erle saie, that . . . Henry made kynge Richarde vnder dures of prisoun in the Toure of London in fere of his life to make a resignatioun of his right to hym" (353).

committee followed through; the "Record and Process" continues that, Richard's resignation having been accepted, "yt were nedefull and spedefull vnto the Rewme in voydyng off mysconceytes and evyll suspecions, That dyuers Crymes and defautes by the same kyng . . . shulde be opynly redde and declared to the peple" (24). A lengthy series of *gravamina* or crimes was read into the record, in the general form of an appeal, except that Richard himself was neither present nor permitted to respond. Having heard the *gravamina*, "Alle the States, with oon accorde and wille, assentyd and consentyd, that it shulde be procedid fforth to the kyngis deposicion" [*RP: ad Depositionem*] (41).

Those gathered in Westminster Hall were probably not overly concerned with the nice issue of their parliamentary standing, which has mainly occupied modern commentators on the deposition.[6] They cannot, however, be considered a casual group, for they show an exceptional concern that no loophole be left unplugged, "that no thing shulde lak ne ffayle, that ouht to be done or requyred in the fforseyd thinges (Julius B II, 43). For the real concern of this primarily Lancastrian gathering was that the throne be found unquestionably void, so that the way to Henry's accession would lie open.

Collaudatio. Adam of Usk imagines the clergy and the people lending their *auctoritas* to the deposition; the "Record and Process" has the estates admitting or accepting the resignation; the same document claims their consent [*RP: unanimiter consenserunt*] to Henry's claim. Yet, *prior to Henry's accession on 30 September*, the whole matter of election seems to have carried much less weight than modern, parliamentarily oriented, historians like Stubbs have given it. The most that seems to have been imagined by the August-September theorists of succession is some form of ratification or *collaudatio*, in which assembled representatives of the estates would accept or endorse proposals placed before them. Only after Henry's coronation was the idea of election to gain much currency, and then less among Henry's immediate circle than others.

Divine grace. In a document that appears to have been considered for use by the Lancastrian propaganda machine, and then withdrawn, Richard agreed to renounce the guidance of the realm or *regimen regni* as well as to designate Henry his successor, but he then sought in a separate *protestacio* to retain the distinctive, sacral qualities conferred upon him by divine unction: "noluit nec intendebat renunciare carecteribus anime sue impressis a sacra unccione" (Stowe MS 66, quoted in Sayles, "Deposition," p. 266). That this passage, one of the few credible utterances produced by the Lan-

---

[6] With Stubbs (2:549) finding them parliamentary, Lapsley (431) finding them deliberately nonparliamentary, and Wilkinson (with whom I would tend to agree) finding them simply a convenient gathering, the precise standing of which did not trouble the Lancastrians (230–39).

castrians in the months following Henry's accession, was soon withdrawn is no surprise; the puzzle is how or why it was produced in the first place. The answer is probably that members of the Lancastrian party other than Henry himself had relatively little concern about matters of unction; their concern was with the *regimen regni* rather than with sacral or thaumaturgic kingship, and some of them evidently found Richard's proposal reasonable enough. Henry's ambitions were, on the other hand, dynastic, and issues relating to God's grace were of the utmost importance to him—as the most cursory consideration of his coronation arrangements will reveal (Wright, 151–65). Even Henry's fervent supporters, however, appear to have been less than captivated by his various attempts to claim for himself and his heirs the perquisites of sacral kingship, and claims for divine unction move to the fore only at and around (rather than prior to) the actual accession and coronation, when Henry's direct personal involvement was most in evidence.

This, then, is the larger controversial environment in which Henry advanced to the throne. It is an environment embracing real facts (such as Henry's overwhelming political power), symbolic gestures (such as the transfer of Richard's signet), rumor and disputation (among, for example, the members of Henry's committee), and, eventually, texts. This environment would, in fact, provide a generative matrix within which a variety of texts representing a broad spectrum of approaches to Henry's kingship would be produced and consumed. Within these texts, particular *causae* could be embraced or excluded, new argumentative combinations could be devised according to the vantage points of their authors. Moving to a consideration of these texts, in all their recombinant variety, we will be reminded of things that the Lancastrians evidently knew all along: an argument can accomplish its purpose without necessarily being plausible, and a text can be powerful without being true.

THE TEXTUALIZATION OF HENRY'S CLAIM

Whether or not John of Gaunt really tried to plant forged chronicles, the story captures at least one indisputable truth about the Lancastrians: their keen and precocious awareness of the value of textualization, of the sense in which a written account placed in the right kind of circulation can generate its own kind of historical truth. Who knows what words Henry spoke in laying his 30 September claim to the vacant English throne? The crucial point is that sometime in the several months after Henry became king, a written version of his claim was placed in circulation by the Lancastrians, to be subsequently incorporated in the Rolls of Parliament, in Walsingham's *Historia*, in the *Annales Ricardi*, in the Evesham chronicle, and in a host of derivative documents.[7]

At that meeting of 30 September, Richard's resignation having been accepted and the throne standing visibly vacant, Henry stepped forward to "chalange"—that is, to assert title to or to lay claim to—the realm of England.[8] Speaking for broadest effect "in Englyssh tunge" (Julius B II, 43), he is said to have pronounced the closest thing we will ever have to a "Lancastrian claim":

> In the name of the Father, of the Sone and the Holy Gost I Henry of Lancastre chalange this reme of Inglond . . . as that I am descendit be right line of the blod comyng fro the good lord kyng Henry thrid and thorowgh the rizt that God of His grace ath send me with the help of my kin and my frendes to recover it, the whych reme was in poynt to ben undoo for defaute of governance and undoying of the good lawes. (Stowe MS 66, quoted in Sayles, "Deposition")

Were these "really" Henry's words? When Gertrude Stein objected to the likeness Picasso was painting of her, protesting that she didn't look like that, the artist is reputed to have replied, "You will." To the question of whether or not this was really Henry's speech, one could reply that, from the standpoint of five hundred years of subsequent history, it might as well have been. Two considerations argue, however, for the fidelity of this widely circulated version. The first is the agreement by several authorities, including eyewitness Adam of Usk, that a written copy existed, that Henry *read* his remarks: "Quandam protestacionem in scriptis redactam . . . legit" (33), and that they existed in the form of a *schedulum* or written document (*Eulogium*, 384). The second is that this claim shows a consistent tilt toward arguments more likely to have been appealing to Henry than to his advisers; it reveals a stubborn tendency to walk off some of the very cliffs against which apologists like Adam of Usk had sought assiduously to warn him.

Contained within this *chalange* or *protestacio* (Adam of Usk, 33) or *vendicatio* (*Eulogium*, 384) are three arguments for Henry's kingship (though not the same three that tradition would encourage us to expect). Although

---

[7] Lapsley observed that "the new government seems to have taken great pains to circulate copies of the official documents recording the steps by which it came into being, and in consequence practically all writers had access to them either directly or indirectly" (432–33). See also Sayles, "Deposition," and Kingsford, *English Historical Literature*, 20. As Sherborne justly observes, "It is hard to think of another moment of comparable importance in medieval English history when the supply of information was so effectively manipulated as it was by Henry on this occasion" ("Perjury," 218).

[8] *MED*: "the act of laying claim to something." See Alford, *chalengen*, definition 2.

each appears in a highly distinctive form, the three arguments are founded upon descent, grace, and "recovery" or reclamation.

The first of Henry's arguments revives, though in modified terms, the discredited argument for descent through Henry III. ("Oh, no," one can imagine his advisers saying, "not that Edmund thing!") Henry's modification, undoubtedly adopted as a result of the cautions of his own committee, is to omit the specific contention that Edmund Crouchback, and not Edward I, was Henry's older son. Yet, that contention is still implied in Henry's claim of "right" or direct descent from Henry III, rather than, for example, Edward III. For Richard had an equal claim on descent from Henry III, through Edward I, and the mere fact of relationship to Henry III would do nothing to unsettle Richard's superior claim. Henry's reference to Henry III makes sense only to an informed audience that supplies the information he has suppressed: that *his* relation to Henry III, enhanced by his relation to his ill-used Lancastrian great-great-grandfather Crouchback, is superior to Richard's more obvious claim through Edward I. What we have here is a rather obstinate reintroduction, by Henry, of a slightly blurred or cosmetized version of a *causa* that even his best friends could not believe.

So, too, would Henry's second argument, for divine grace, appear not to have held much attraction for his advisers. The "Record and Process" reports that, before speaking, Henry marked "hym mekely with the signe off the crosse in his ffor heede, and in his breste, nempnyng the name off Crist" (Julius B II, 43), and his challenge proceeded "in the name of" the trinity. Beyond these routinely pious claims, however, lay a bolder assertion, that "God of His grace ath send me." Henry, according to this formulation, presents himself less as the active champion of good rule than as the passive recipient of God's grace. This is a point that, incidentally, Henry was to underscore repeatedly in his coronation ceremonials, of which a brief example may be given here. Around the time of the coronation the Lancastrians resurrected a hoary legend about the rediscovery of a vial of celestial unguent, originally given by the Virgin to St. Thomas of Canterbury. The unguent, they said, had resurfaced after the coronation of Richard and therefore too late for his use, but it was now conveniently available for Henry's anointment (Walsingham, *Historia*, 2:239–40; *Annales*, 297–300; Wright, *Protestation*, 159–62). This brazen fabrication—accompanied in one manuscript by the marginal notation "unguentum fictitum" (Walsingham, *Historia*, 2:239)—in turn set the stage for a particular emphasis on anointment within the coronation ceremony. The traditional coronation ceremony, as recorded in the "Liber Regalis," had provided for the anointment of the king with holy oil but treated that part of the ceremony as a private matter, to occur behind a *pallium* or covering (92). Yet, as described (or imagined) in the "Record and Process," the anointment is a good deal more public: "Kyng Herry lay vpon a cloth off golde before the hyh awter in Westm' Chirche. And there in ffoure parties off his body his clothes were opyn, and there he was anoynted, with *Veni Creator Spiritus* y-songyn. And affter this anoyntyng his body was leffte vp into another place" (Julius B II, 49). Furthermore, in the "Liber Regalis," the monarch transports himself from place to place. Here, Henry is literally lifted and carried about, presented not as conqueror but as passive vehicle of God's will.

Finally, the concept of recovery or reclamation of a kingdom about to be lost by bad governance and disrespect for law effects a reintroduction of Henry's discredited argument for conquest, in terms most likely to appeal to the assembled estates. The parliamentary estates were precisely those that had most to gain by due process and rule of law, and the articles drawn against Richard repeatedly emphasize his arbitrariness: "He seyd opynly, with a sterne chere and ouertwert, that his lawes weren in his mouthe, and other while in his breste, And that he allone myht chaunge the Lawes off his Rewme" (Julius B II, 31). Here then is conquest, but in a form designed to allay the fears attributed to Thirning in the *Annales Ricardi*. Henry would, in fact, allude to his "conquest" immediately after his advancement, but as part of a further reassurance, that no one should think that "be way of conquest I wald disherite any man of his heritage . . . ne put him out of that he hath and hath had be the good lawes and customes of the reme" (Stowe MS 66, quoted in Sayles, "Deposition," 266). Only subsequent to the accession is the bare claim of conquest to gain independent force as one of the Lancastrian *causae*.

Even this cursory discussion reveals the eccentric and contradictory nature of Henry's three claims. Nobody seems to have believed the argument from descent, or to have cared much about the motions of God's grace; only the final, pragmatic argument—bearing on the "regimen regni" and a reinstitution of respect for law—seems directly addressed to actual concerns of the parliamentary commons. Why then the trumped-up arguments for descent and unction? Rather evidently because Henry's concerns were more dynastic than those of his subjects. The predictable payoff of his argumentative exertions was to come early in his first parliament, when the Archbishop of Canterbury spoke on Henry's behalf, reminding the estates "Coment Dieu . . . ad envoiez le Roy" to recover the realm, how the estates of the realm "luy ont acceptez en leur droiturel Roy," and how precedents had been established by the king's "Progenitours," and asking for confirmation of the king's oldest son as Prince of Wales and as "droit heriter a les Roialme & Corone" (*RP*, 3:426). Accomplishment of this aim undoubtedly meant more to Henry than any consideration of argumentative consistency.[9]

[9] On the quality of Henry's arguments, the final word might appropriately be given to Richard, duke of York. Speaking in this case against the title of Henry VI, and challenging

Henry's *chalange* of the throne, developed into a narrative *proces* in the period between December 1399 and December 1400 and circulated broadly by the Lancastrians, enjoyed wide adoption, not only in the after-the-fact rolls of Henry's first parliament, but in the *Annales Ricardi*, Walsingham, Evesham, and other influential chronicles (Sayles, "Deposition," 257–264). Other accounts were concurrently being generated as well. Chaucer's "To His Purse," probably completed in the winter of 1399–1400 (*Minor Poems*, 121–22) was among the earliest. So, too, was Gower's *Cronica Tripertita*, probably completed fairly soon after Richard's death in February 1400 (Fisher, 112). Adam of Usk, a member of Henry's committee of *doctores* and an eyewitness of some of the events he describes, wrote from memory, perhaps as late as 1415 (Lapsley, 436). Among the French chroniclers, Froissart treated the events of the deposition in his final redaction, after 1400. Creton wrote his *Metrical History*, partially from firsthand evidence of the events of August 1399, in the winter of 1401–1402, and the derivative and less reliable *Traïson* was composed slightly later (Palmer, 154, 170). Of less interest here than chronology or genealogy, however, is the sheer range of narrative and explanatory materials generated around Henry's highly controversial assumption of the crown, and the variety of ways in which writers drew upon different elements of pre- and postaccession Lancastrian theory.

Henry's *chalange* (repeated practially verbatim in Walsingham and the *Annales*, as well as in other versions depending on the "Record and Process") hinged on direct descent and recovery of the crown by God's will; the Archbishop of Canterbury speaking on his behalf at his first parliament claimed recovery by God's will and the "acord & assent" of the estates of the realm (*RP*, 3:426); Adam of Usk, writing after the fact, attributed to Henry an argument of which he personally disapproved, that of *successio* or descent (33). The continuator or compiler of the *Eulogium* emphasized descent from Henry III, with the lords assenting and the commons acclaiming (*Eulogium*, 384).

Froissart, writing a year or two after the fact from "thin and garbled" information reaching him abroad (Sherborne, "Charles VI," 63), comes up with a slightly different version, though a version still woven from argumentative strands we have already encountered. He bases the *calenga* or challenge on three arguments. The first, in which Froissart strips away the rhetoric of "recovery," is conquest; the second is descent or heredity; the third consists of what Henry and the states would have considered a prior condition, the voidance of the throne through Richard's resignation and

---

Henry IV's claim to have been "right enheriter to Kyng Herry the third," Richard commented that "his said saying was oonly to shadowe and colour fradulently his . . . unrightwise and violent usurpation" (*RP*, 5:377).

Richard's own (probably bogus) wish that Henry should succeed him: "Premièrement par conquest, secondement pour tant que il se disoit estre droit hoir de la couronne, et tierchement par ce que le roy Richart de Bourdeaulx luy avoit résigné le royaulme en sa main" (16:204). Although none of the French chronicles was particularly authoritative for events after Creton's departure from England in late August 1399, an alternative interpretative line is advanced both in Creton and in the *Traïson*. Each, in its way, places a good deal of emphasis on election and not only after-the-fact acclamation as the vehicle of Henry's advancement. I am not, of course, suggesting that the idea of election originated with them. It was always lurking at the fringes of the different English explanations, with texts about after-the-fact acclamation or *collaudatio* inclining toward the concept of election, just as texts about recovery tended to incline toward the excluded admission of conquest.[10] But Creton, for example, has an extended account of the canvassing of popular will prior to Henry's elevation, in which a resounding "ouil" of the common people propels Henry to the throne:

Se leverent tous deux ensemble
Les archevesques, ce me semble,
Et alerent au duc tout droit,
Qui Ja roy eslu estoit
De par tout le peuple commun

. . . .

Apres tous les interroga
Ly mesmes, et leur demanda
Si cestoit ainsi leur vouloir:
Ilz respondirent, ouil, voir,
Si hault, que ce fut grant merveille.
Ce ly mist la pusse en oreille
Telement, que sans plus atendre,
Il volt acepter et entendre
A la couronne dengleterre.

(pp. 390–91)

It seemed to me that the two archbishops rose together and went directly to the duke, who was now elected king by all the common people. . . . Afterward, he questioned them, and asked them if it was their will. They responded, "yes," with a wonderously loud voice. This "put such a flea in his ear" that, without waiting any longer, he accepted and took possession of the crown of England. (translation compared with that of J. Webb)

[10] Both tendencies are present in the first version of Henry's challenge, when, "post eleccionem," he adds a speech of reassurance that his "conquest" will not lead to disrespect for laws and customs (Stowe MS 66, quoted in Sayles, "Deposition," p. 266).

The *Traïson* also emphasizes a process of assent leading to Henry's selection, with all the lords and prelates and commons of England and London crying, "Ouy ouy nous voulons que Henry duc de Lencastre soit nostre Roy et nul autre," prior to Henry's ascent to the throne and pronouncement of his reasons—that he had come to claim his "droit heritaige," and that Richard "auoit forfait sa vie et sa couronne" by his murder of Gloucester and exile of Arundel (68–69).

What, in the light of these varied possibilities for rationalization or explanation of Henry's kingship, are we then to make of the particular Lancastrian argument offered by Chaucer in the last stanza of "To His Purse?" With the economy of a poet, Chaucer weaves his argument into a bit over two lines, shaped not as exposition at all but as discreetly elegant, vocatively couched address to his new monarch:

> O conquerour of Brutes Albyon,
> Which that by lyne and free eleccion
> Been verray kyng. . . .

This passage contains nothing wholly original—that is, no single element not otherwise available within the broad tradition of Lancastrian argumentation. It is nevertheless distinctive, in that its selection and arrangement and weighting of arguments differ from any other rendering we have seen.

With his reference to Henry as conqueror, Chaucer cuts through more frequent and authorized reference to "recovery" with a starker formulation, but he then mitigates any severity by displacing the conquest to the legendary Britain of the chronicles.[11] This subtle instatement of the idea of conquest, transposed into a register that passes over local perturbation to associate Henry with England's largest destinies, would undoubtedly have been to the liking of a king who had himself, as we have noted, evidently already proposed an argument based on conquest to his *doctores* and only papered over this bold claim with talk of recovery after receiving cautionary advice.

Chaucer's references to "lyne" and to "verray" kingship seem a rough equivalent to Henry's own "right line of the blod," though with the implied circumstances—that awkwardly concocted and inherently unpersuasive business about Edmund Crouchback—tacitly pushed even farther to the background than in Henry's own challenge.

Most surprising is probably Chaucer's reference to "free eleccion"—a notion present only at the margins of English commentary,[12] and fully embraced only by the anti-Lancastrian Creton and his follower, the author of

---

[11] A point made to me in conversation by Alfred David. M. Dominica Legge offers a similar observation (21), in an article erroneous in almost every other particular.

[12] Though see Lapsley's brilliant (and partially convincing) attempt to construct a proelection party from hints in Adam of Usk and other texts (585–89).

the *Traïson*, as a way of showing the instability of claims resting on a foundation as untrustworthy as that of general acclaim. Yet, if presentation of a garland of arguments supportive of Henry's claim may be supposed Chaucer's purpose, free election is certainly better suited to his situation and temperament than other arguments made available to him by tradition. Strong emphasis on Richard's crimes or on his voluntary resignation would, for one thing, have been of dubious propriety. For Chaucer, loyal Ricardian for some twenty-two years of his maturity, suddenly to embrace extensive accounts of malfeasance or outrageous fabrications about Richard's resignation "hillari vultu" while his former monarch yet lived would have demonstrated a degree of opportunism and inconsistency foreign to his nature as we otherwise know it.[13] Nor would strong iteration of the sacramental or thaumaturgic elements of Henry's kingship have been consistent with the emphases revealed generally in Chaucer's poetry.

I do not mean to suggest that Chaucer has forged a seamless argument. If Henry is of the right "lyne," why did he need to conquer the kingdom? If he conquered it, why did he require "free eleccion?" Still, in this three-fold justification, Chaucer advances a line of argument that appropriately mediates his own position and Henry's rather urgent and continuing interest in bolstering his own legitimacy by asserting a series of accomplished and agreed-upon facts: whether or not Richard did resign, Henry *did* conquer the kingdom; whatever Henry's lineage, he *does* possess royal blood; the estates of the realm certainly *did* seem to want him.

Although lost alternatives can certainly be imagined, Chaucer's appears to be the first among extant texts to present this particular argumentative configuration. The same configuration will appear in the *Cronica Tripertita* of fellow poet John Gower—though, interestingly, as one of two different treatments of the subject, one close in spirit to the account of the "Record and Process" and the other close to Chaucer's own three-part formulation.

Close to the "Record and Process" is Gower's address to Henry in what may be his last poem, "In Praise of Peace." There, Gower closely tracks the "official" Lancastrian arguments for God's grace ("God hath the chose") and assistance in recovery of a kingdom in decline ("The worschipe of this lond . . . / Now stant upriht"), and of right descent ("Thi title is knowe uppon thin ancestrie"), coupled with the after-the-fact endorsement of the estates of the realm ("The londes folk hath ek thy riht affermed"). Downplaying conquest, underscoring grace, deftly introducing practical considerations about the state of the realm, mentioning descent, and reminding his reader of *collaudatio* or affirmation by the estates, Gower would seem

---

[13] Chaucer's response to critical episodes by modifying his Ricardian ties, without actually forswearing them, is discussed in my "Politics and Poetics," esp. 90–97. See also S. Sanderlin, esp. 171–75.

here to have woven together the different strands present in the parliamentary account, itself an uneasy amalgam of the Lancastrian apologies of Thirning and Arundel on the one hand and Henry's supposed words on the other (Fisher, 132).

Yet, in the *Cronica*, Gower takes a slightly different line, and one almost identical to Chaucer's own. The *Cronica* concludes with Henry's accession and consolidation of rule (and the death of Richard, supposedly by self-starvation), and it includes a defense of Henry's threefold right or *trino de jure*:

> Regnum conquestat, que per hoc sibi ius manifestat;
> Regno succedit heres, nec ab inde recedit;
> Insuper eligitur a plebe que sic stabilitur.
>
> (3, ll. 333–35)

> He conquered the realm, and because of this, right is clearly on his side; he succeeded as heir to the kingdom and thus has not abdicated from it; in addition, he was chosen by the people and thus firmly established. (trans. Eric Stockton, 321)

Or, in Gower's more succinct and reordered marginal summary: "successione . . . eleccione . . . conquestu sine sanguinis effusione." In a sense, the less said the better; Gower's prose summary is probably more persuasive than his metrical version, in which he gets into argumentative absurdities like "succedit . . . nec . . . recedit."

Although both Chaucer's poem, written between October 1399 and February 1400, and the "Record and Process" of 1400 were probably available when Gower wrote the *Cronica*, after February 1400, and "In Praise of Peace," between 1401 and 1404, any attempt to construct a clear genealogy would probably be vain. The point is that the rich environment of texts and theories surrounding Henry's accession permitted a variety of acceptably Lancastrian arguments, and Gower employed them selectively, according to circumstance. In the heavily anti-Ricardian and almost jingoistic *Cronica* he had no reason, for example, to withhold mention of conquest; the more conciliatory "Praise of Peace" aspires to surmount conflict and hence relies upon the blurred and contradictory but ultimately reassuring formulations of the "Record and Process."

Despite the inner variety of Gower's arguments, and their subtle differences from those of Chaucer, the sentiments of all three texts may be construed as broadly "Lancastrian." These texts in turn remind us that hegemonic interests—or in this case the interests of a Lancastrian proto-hegemony—can be advanced by varied utterances that need not be strictly consistent one with another, so long as all are produced and received within a matrix of generally consistent sentiments and ideas.

THE EXCHANGE-VALUE OF CHAUCER'S POEM

Henry's assumption of control upon landing in England in July 1399 was so rapid that one can easily forget how many unassimilated pockets of potential resistance remained.[14] As early as December 1399, Richard's disaffected former dukes—together with supporters like Thomas Merke, the former bishop of Carlisle and John Montagu, the earl of Salisbury—were meeting to plot the murder of Henry and his sons, in what would become their failed uprising of January 1400. Intermittent struggles with the Welsh, and with Northumberland and Percy and other disaffected northern lords who claimed that Henry had broken his promise made at Doncaster not to seek the crown, began almost immediately and persisted through most of the first decade of the century. Principled resistance to the usurpation continued among the Franciscans, some of whom professed to believe Richard still alive (see *Eulogium*, 389–94). This is not the place to attempt a summary of Henry's military and diplomatic counterstrategies, save in one regard: his apparent attempt to enlist littérateurs in his dynastic cause. One incident suggests the presence of programmatic elements behind Henry's relations with writers of the day.

Christine de Pisan, writing in her partly allegorical, quasi-autobiographical *Lavision*, narrates a surprising commingling of literary activity and personal and dynastic ambition, involving herself, the poet and Ricardian adherent John Montagu, and England's new king (165–66). In 1397, John Montagu, formerly Ricardian chamber knight and now Earl of Salisbury, came to France in connection with negotiations for Richard's marriage to the young Isabella. Although his writings, evidently in French, are now lost, Christine describes him as a lover of poetry and a "gracieux ditteur." After acquaintence with her poems, she tells us, he proposed an arrangement by which her son Jean would join the earl's household, to be raised with his son. No sooner, she laments, was this advantageous arrangement concluded, than the "pestilence" of rebellion broke out, leading to the deaths of Richard and Salisbury. At this point Henry, becoming acquainted with the "dittiez et livres" she had already sent in order to please the earl, took the boy into his own household and sent two "notables hommes" to gain her assent and to invite her to come to England herself. Doubting that such disloyalty could turn out well, she played along with the heralds, asked to see her son briefly in France, and then kept him in France once he had returned. Christine, understandably enough, portrays Henry as stirred to action by his admiration for her poems. Yet we may

[14] Evidence against Richard's unpopularity (and evidence for the continuing influence of Lancastrian propaganda) is adduced by Caroline Barron in "The Deposition of Richard II."

imagine another motive as well, springing from Henry's desire for legitimacy, for the adherence of established figures, for the celebration of poets.

If Christine, possessed at this early point in her career only of a modest reputation as an author of short lyric poems, seemed a suitable object of Henry's courtship, how much more was to be gained by Chaucer's adherence? Evidence of manuscript circulation and public reference suggests that Chaucer was relatively little known throughout most of his career, except among a circle of courtly civil servants and London intelligensia. But his sudden emergence to prominence, with broadened circulation of his poems soon after his death in February 1400, would lead to his instatement as "the noble rethor Poete of breteine" during the first years of Henry's reign, and something of this imminent emergence must have been evident to his contemporaries in 1399 and 1400.[15] Furthermore, in his initial clemency even to those *duketti* and others who had profited most from Richard, Henry had shown interest in solidifying his relations with known Ricardians while their former king yet lived, and Chaucer's own career in Richard's service would have added significance to his acceptance of Henry's claims.

Exploring the implications of Petrarch's acceptance of Visconti patronage, David Wallace has anatomized the senses in which each "exchange" with a tyrant typically magnifies the tyrant's worth. Chaucer's poem, hailing Henry's accession even as it requests his assistance, invites a form of exchange with his sovereign. Although Henry's backdated confirmation and expansion of Chaucer's grants may have occurred without the stimulus of the poem, we may reasonably assume them to result from the exchange Chaucer invites.[16] If so, we may say with confidence that Henry enjoyed the tyrant's prerogative, gaining far more from this exchange than the relative pittance of which Chaucer was belatedly assured.

Postscript: The Power of Theory and the Theory of the "Source"

Production of pseudo-Lancastrian documents has not, by the way, ceased—though the motives and circumstances have changed. A recent instance involves a document, the existence of which rests secure in the estimation of most Chaucerians: the "proclamation" to the people of England by which Henry is supposed to have claimed the throne by conquest, hereditary right, and election. This proclamation is believed, in turn, to have

[15] The quotation is from Lydgate, "The Life of Our Lady," in Spurgeon, 1:19; for the flood of tributes after 1400, see ibid., 14–19.

[16] On the initial delay and eventual backdating of Henry's confirmation, see Ferris.

been Chaucer's "source." Yet this "proclamation" nowhere exists. The idea of such a proclamation may have originated with Henry's September 30 *chalange*. But, as we have already seen, that statement makes no mention whatever of election, and elides the idea of conquest in favor of a claim based on divine grace. The supposed "proclamation" was, effectively, devised by Robert Bell in his 1854 edition of Chaucer's works, in which he appended to "To His Purse" the comment that "In Henry IV's proclamation to the people of England he founds his title on *conquest, hereditary right*, and *election*; and from this inconsistent and absurd document Chaucer no doubt took his cue" (8:142). Bell's comment was quoted by Skeat in his 1894 edition, and from there it entered the mainstream of twentieth-century Chaucer criticism, where—supported by our own preference for secondary opinion over documentary evidence and by powerful critical presuppositions—it has persisted substantially unchallenged.[17]

The imagined "proclamation" may be seen as a byproduct of assumptions about authorship current between the mid-ninteenth and mid-twentieth centuries. These assumptions hold that the choices (or preoccupations) of a sovereign "author" can be traced in a firmly bounded oeuvre or body of work, and within individual components of that oeuvre. So much about the genesis of the literary work and its relation to tradition is, however, left unexplained by the idea of virtually unlimited authorial initiative that this idea necessitated a secondary, apparently contradictory formulation, involving the author's purposive selection and manipulation of a pre-existing "source." The point of reconciliation between the sovereignty of the author and the source upon which he or she was required to depend, a reconcilation ultimately in the author's favor, is that his or her choices can be traced in the modifications (or occasional decisions not to modify) a known original. According to this theory, Chaucer as author purposefully adopts the rationale of Henry's own proclamation—in this case, verbatim and slavishly or halfheartedly, as befits a begging poem.[18]

Not only does such source-hunting encourage invention of a bogus lineage, but it actually devalues the very authorial role it sets out to defend. For Chaucer's poem is, in actuality, not passive or halfhearted at all. Not that it is wholly "original" or solely author-generated: I have sought to show that it is a product of complicated immersion within its textual environment. But it remains a fresh and conceptually energetic refashioning of elements chosen from within that environment. The way to an appreciation of those qualities we attribute to authorial initiative is confrontation

[17] See, for example, Galbraith, 234, Legge, 19, and *Minor Poems*, 131.
[18] Scattergood, for example, describes Chaucer's poem as "not markedly enthusiastic" (116).

rather than avoidance of the complexities that attend the realization of a particular text within an array of competing alternatives.

Nineteenth-century and earlier twentieth-century scholarship drifted into this devotion to the bounded "source" out of a misdirected desire to professionalize humanistic inquiry. Eager to establish literary discussion as an endeavor to be learned, taught, defended, and verified, early scholars turned to the prestigious model of later nineteenth-century science, drawing from it a distaste for fuzzy boundaries, and a wish for clear delination of persons, interests, choices, texts, sources, and oeuvres. But any approach to the problem of textual origins must accept facts of reliance on preexisting and often contradictory traditions, of multiple determinations, of limits to authorial control. I too wish to imagine an "author," but one less bounded and more open to the multiple voices of the time, to a number of sources rather than just one, to the inscription of a text within a matrix of diverse and sometimes contradictory pronouncements.[19]

[19] I am grateful to Clifford Flanigan for advice bearing on this section of my argument.

Chapter 5

QUEENS AS INTERCESSORS

P ROGRESSIVELY excluded from affairs of state, later medieval queens were compensated in sumptuous but highly inflated symbolic coin. The European zenith of queenly authority occurred in the twelfth century, its apogee marked by full involvement in the affairs of a merged household, employment of a *signum*, and mention of the queen's name and regnal year in royal charters (Facinger, 29–33). The queen's role declined thereafter, with the separation of her household from that of the king and her exclusion from affairs of state. Yet, checked in the exercise of power, queens were showered with symbolic recognition. In coronation ritual, in the size and independence of their households, in every ceremonial way, thirteenth- and fourteenth-century queens were celebrated as passive contributors to royal dignity. Despite this symbolic resplendence, their role was actually increasingly dependent upon royal sponsorship. No longer enjoying "partnership" in government, the thirteenth-century queen could now exert her will only through "influence" upon her king (Facinger, 45–46).

Underpinning and guaranteeing the reconception of queens as passive contributors rather than active participants was a reassertion of their familial roles as wives and mothers. Available for celebration in the high pomp of coronation and other rituals, these roles were also adaptable to more humble expressive circumstances. If chronicles and other records are to be believed, even the most ceremonially lavish queens were prone to cast aside the trappings of dignity and rank in order to stake a domestically grounded claim, saturated with humble imagery drawn from their activities as servitors of their husbands, bearers of children, and nurses of the young. This new form of queenly influence was *petitionary*, in the sense that it cast the queen as one seeking redress rather than one able to institute redress in her own right, and *intercessory*, in that it limited its objectives to the modification of a previously determined male resolve.

The intercessory model had, of course, been available during that period of more actively efficacious queenship stretching from the ninth century to the middle of the twelfth century. But during those centuries it was mainly latent and consistently overshadowed by such alternative roles as mistress of the household, royal counselor, and property holder in her own right (Stafford, 123, 191–92). With the decline and deinstitutionalization of queenly power in the later twelfth and thirteenth centuries, the new model of intercessory queenship came increasingly to the fore.[1] This regrounded role promised women a particular kind of power, but power premised on exceptional vulnerability. It credited women with special spiritual faculties but conditioned these faculties on an exclusion from the centers of mundane authority. It countenanced female challenge to male authority, but only challenges mounted from the margins of the discussion, from a place somewhere outside the bounds of institutions within which decisions are normally made. It invited women to correct male judgment, so long as that judgment was modified or supplemented rather than overturned.

I must admit to considerable personal skepticism about whether intercessory queenship, exercised from the margins and conditioned upon exclusion from worldly office, represented a genuinely alternative feminine power. As a formation, it would seem more likely to dupe women than to empower them, more likely to accommodate itself to later medieval ideas of theocratic and patriarchical kingship (Ullmann, 181–85) than to seek their overthrow. The very warmth of its acceptance and breadth of its promulgation by clerics, chroniclers, and other ideological agents of late medieval kingship is itself cause for added suspicion. In the thirteenth and especially the fourteenth centuries, a flood of commentaries, sermons, meditations, chronicles, ceremonials, and poems modeled and celebrated female subordination and self-marginalization as a source of characteristically feminine power.

If the texts, and the range of nontextual gestures, produced within this discursive environment were as uniform in thrust and as monologic in voice as I am permitting them to sound, this chapter could come to a speedy end. But this body of texts and gestures is synthesized from too many different sources, contains within itself the sedimented attitudes of too many different historical moments, embraces too many points of view to enforce uniformity. Because of the mixed nature of the environment of ideas and actions that sustained it, the ideal of queenly intercession remained perpetually open to reconsideration and modification from within.

Even the most venerable precedents for intercessory queenship contain high—even flagrant—degrees of internal contradiction. Consider, for example, the cases of Mary and Esther, the two most influental exemplars of all. The crucial texts bearing on each case emphasize a range of virtues regarded as "feminine" in their emphasis on queenly access to mercy or

---

[1] A persuasive argument for the expansion of the mediatory role of thirteenth-century English queens has been made by John Carmi Parsons, on the basis of evidence from chancery rolls, letters, and legal records. Noting the sparseness of earlier evidence, he refrains from claiming a dramatic extension of this role in the late twelfth and thirteenth centuries, though I believe his evidence supports such a conclusion. See "Esther's Eclipse? The Queen's Intercession in Thirteenth-Century England. "A valuable related study is "Ritual and Symbol in the English Queenship to 1500," to appear in *Cosmos*, 1991 or 1992.

compassion, personal experience of abjection or sorrow, and deference to established authority. Yet Mary and Esther also possess undeniable trappings of regality, not only symbolic power as epitomized through ceremony and splendid array, but access to practical wisdom and the worldly authority to enforce its dictates.

Marian texts almost invariably exist in complicated dialogue (either internally or with adjacent texts) over the conflicting ideas of *Maria Regina*, or Mary as victorious queen, and Mary as *mediatrix*, or humble intercessor with the divine.[2] This dialogue remains apparent within the works of Chaucer. In his "ABC," he offers an intercessory Mary, portraying her as an infinite well of mercy. In fact, in a rather disturbing image of near-total availability, she is portrayed as "the open welle" wherein the sinful soul may be cleansed of guilt (ll. 177–78). Her mercy is rooted in her helpless abjection, in the "sorwe" she suffered "under the cros" (ll. 81–82). Yet a complementary countertradition emphasizes the more majestic Mary, elevated to the queenship of heaven, competent for rule. The "ABC," attributing Mary's initial selection as mother of God to her humbleness, then stakes out a subsequent role of considerably greater authority:

> Thee whom God ches to mooder for humblesse!
> From his ancille he made the maistresse
> Of hevene and erthe, oure bille up for to beede.
>
> (ll. 108–10)

Once a humble serving maid, she is transformed to mistress of heaven and earth, well suited not just to beg or sue for errant humankind, but to "beede"—to urge, if not to command—attention to their suits. A merciable petitioner, she is simultanously seen as "vicaire" (l. 140) of all the world, a figure not just of derivative power but of considerable power in her own right.

Esther presents us with the precisely opposite case of a queen known primarily for her sage counsel, but who nevertheless knows the full syntax of self-abasement.[3] Esther first appears as a shrewd counselor to the king

[2] In her "Stabat Mater," Julia Kristeva observes that "on the side of 'power,' *Maria Regina* appears in imagery as early as the sixth century. . . . Nevertheless, besides that ideal totality that no individual woman could possibly embody, the Virgin also became the fulcrum of the humanization of the West in general and of love in particular. It is again about the thirteenth century, with Francis of Assisi, that this tendency takes shape with the representation of Mary as poor, modest, and humble—madonna of humility at the same time as a devoted, fond mother" (244–46). Marina Warner finds in the contending representations of the Virgin a constant "counterpoint of victory and subjection." On this counterpoint see Warner, esp. 103–17 (Mary as regal authority) and 285–98 (Mary as intercessor).

[3] My discussion of the mixed example of Esther and its influence on intercessory queenship has, I have learned since composing it, been anticipated in part by a splendid paper by Lois L. Huneycutt, "Intercession and the High-Medieval Queen: The *Esther* Topos." Taking

on her people's behalf, one who sets the stage with art, who brings a *petitio* or petition rather than a *deprecatio* or prayer (Esther 7:1–7). Broad four-teenth-century acceptance of this depiction of Esther as a good counselor is evident from such Chaucerian allusions as her citation in the *Tale of Melibee* as a purveyor of *good conseil* to her husband (VII.1100). (This quality is again jestingly affirmed in the *Merchant's Tale* when she is cited among good wives for having "By good conseil delyvered out of wo / The peple of God" [VII.1370–74]—the jest revolving not around her status as ad-vice-giver, but around the fact that her people rather than her husband ultimately benefit.) Yet, a contrary propensity for timorous self-abasement is also apparent throughout Esther's textual tradition. The vulgate Book of Esther makes a new beginning after 10:3, embracing an alternate account not present in the Hebrew Bible and omitted in some medieval Latin Bi-bles and commentaries as well, in which Esther prepares for her conference with the king by fasting and smearing herself with ashes and dung and then appears fearfully (*nimio timore*) to present her *deprecatio* or prayer (Esther 14–15). Chaucer invokes Esther as an example of *meknesse* in the *Legend of Good Women* (l. 250), and these qualities are backhandedly but tellingly reaffirmed in the *Merchant's Tale*, when May gives January so submissive a look that "Queen Ester looked nevere with swich an ye / On Assuer" (IV. 1744–46).

So even the founding texts of the discourse of queenly intercession con-tain alternative possibilities: the abject Mary and the sage Esther coexist with timorous Esther and Mary magistrate of heaven. In fact, this com-plexity doubles and redoubles. Esther the good counselor nevertheless pe-titions the king by falling at his feet and breaking into tears (Esther 8:3), and Esther the abject intercessor nevertheless removes her mourning gar-ments and rearrays herself in royal robes before visiting the king (Esther 15:4–5). No wonder subsequent texts and actions produced within so complicated a matrix are subject to differing inflection, liable either (in the most common thirteenth- and fourteenth-century versions) to express queenly authority as humility, deference, and unfamiliarity with the ratio-nal exercise of power or (in a recurring countertradition) to express it as practical insight and shrewd persuasion.

The invention of gendered behavior, out of available models and for particular purposes, is manifestly the property of no single kind of text but crosses the divisions between social gestures and actions and written ac-counts, and between one kind of account and another. In this essay I will consider several different acts of queenly intercession, produced at a variety

Mathilda as her case in point, Huneycutt shows how this twelfth-century queen was shaped by, and extended her own limited power by shaping herself in accordance with, the broadly available topos of Esther.

of expressive levels: a quasi-historical action by Queen Philippa as reported by le Bel and Froissart; a pageant or performance scripted by the citizens of London for Queen Anne at a crucial turning point in their own civic history; and the intervention of Chaucer's Alceste—overtly invented, but within a historically defined matrix of ideas about intercession and queenship. As I am implying, each of these texts, however it defines itself, is the product of ideas at once imaginary and historically defined—flagrantly invented on the one hand but invented within historically and socially specific structures on the other. Each, that is, operates in the ill-defined zone between imagination and social practice, that zone in which texts stand the best chance of changing the way people actually behave.

QUEEN PHILIPPA AND THE BURGHERS OF CALAIS

Jean le Bel's account of Queen Philippa's intercession gained broad circulation and considerable currency through its incorporation (with some elaborations) in the principal manuscripts of Froissart. Sorely lacking in factual authority, his account nevertheless provides a peerless historical resource of another sort, as an archive of the major presuppositions of intercessory queenship.[4]

Froissart (who gives us le Bel's account at its fullest fourteenth-century elaboration) describes Edward III as so irate over the unexpectedly stubborn resistance of the city of Calais that he demands the unconditional surrender of its residents, whether for ransom or death. Then, persuaded by the practical reservations of his advisers (who fear retaliation from the French), he modifies his demand to insist only that six prominent burghers, bearing keys of the city and castle, be delivered to his justice. The six burghers are delivered to the king and seek his mercy. Despite the pleas of his lieutenant Gautier de Mauni, Edward angrily insists on their beheading in retribution for the English deaths they have caused.

---

[4] The nineteenth- and early twentieth-century French editors of le Bel and Froissart had an enormous commitment to this narrative "si noble et si touchant" (le Bel, 164), and to its historicity. Luce brushes aside evidence that Eustache de Saint-Pierre, named by Froissart as principal among the six burghers, was on the English payroll (*Chroniques*, 4:xxv), and Viard and Déprez rely on mention of the episode in the subsequent *Chronique normande* and the fifteenth-century *Chonographia Regum Francorum* to establish historicity (le Bel, 164). In fact, the invention of a scene of completely illustrative of the assumptions and practices of queenly intercession (in the register of abjection, rather than that of good counsel) might have been realized *either* in performance, in the text of a social drama in which Philippa demonstrates complete mastery of her idiom, *or* in the quasi-historical narratives of le Bel and Froissart. Although the historicity of the account is unverifiable, it nevertheless plays a fully historical role in the history of sentiment, and of those shared structures by which real or imaginary social actors produce actions and interpreters make sense of them.

Froissart has thus far held Philippa on the periphery of his account. When the six burghers are first brought to the king's *hostel*, Edward awaits them in his chamber well accompanied by his barons, and the queen is also present, though, according to the Amiens manuscript, she evidently joins the king's party belatedly: "mais ce ne fu pas si tos." Then, when the king's party comes out of the *hostel* to view the prisoners, Edward is followed (rather than accompanied) by his queen, who is described as being in an advanced state of pregnancy: "et la roine d'Engleterre, qui moult ençainte estoit, sievi le roi son signeur" (*Oeuvres*, 5:214). Silent until the intervention of her countryman de Mauni has proven unsuccessful, Philippa now supplicates the king in these terms:

> Adonc fist grant humelité la noble roine d'Engleterre, qui estoit durement en-chainte, et ploroit si tendrement de pité que on ne le pooit soustenir. La vail-lans et bonne dame se jetta en genouls par devant le roi son signour et dist: "Ha! très-chiers sires, puis que je apassai par deçà la mer en grant péril, ensi que vous savés, je ne vous ai requis, ne don demandet. Or vous prie-je humle-ment et requier en propre don que pour le Fil à sainte Marie et pour l'amour de mi, vous voelliés avoir de ces sys hommes merchi." Li rois atendi un petit à parler et regarda la bonne dame sa femme qui moult estoit enchainte et ploroit devant lui en genouls moult tenrement. Se li amolia li coers, car envis l'euist courouchiet ens ou point là où elle estoit; et quant il parla, il dist: "Ha! dame, je amaisse trop mieuls que vous fuissiés d'aultre part que chi. Vous priés si acertes que je ne vous ose escondire le don que vous me demandés." (*Oeuvres*, 5:215)

> Then the noble queen of England, who was extremely pregnant, humbled her-self and besought his pity so tenderly that she could not be withstood. The valiant and good woman threw herself on her knees before the king her lord and said, "Ah, my dear lord, since I passed over the sea in great peril, as you well know, I have asked nothing of you, nor demanded any favor. Now I pray you humbly and ask of you a favor for the son of the blessed Mary and for your love of me, that you show a merciful disposition to these six men. The king waited a moment before speaking and looked at the good woman his queen who was so very pregnant and besought him so tenderly on her knees. And he softened his heart, and his anger abated, and when he spoke he said, "Ah, my lady, I would have much preferred that you be anywhere than here. You have prayed so forcefully that I would not dare to refuse the favor which you ask of me."

Present here are a number of elements commonly encountered in interces-sory narrative, including the queen's adventitious appearance, her intercession as the last avenue of redress, and the extreme feminization of her public role and relation to the king.

The point is repeatedly made that Philippa has no designated role in this process, that she just *happens* to be on the scene. She has only recently arrived in France, she comes late to the gathering of Edward's retinue, and she follows a step behind when they step out to view the hostages. Edward himself emphasizes this point when he exclaims that he wishes she had been somewhere else ("que vous fuissiés d'autre part que chi"), that her surprising appearance at this juncture is bad luck for him and the vengeful designs to which he is inclined. The queen is not part of his regular retinue, is not normally even on hand.[5] This queen is placed so far outside the normal processes of consultation and the production of power that her appearances have become remarkable; her interventions, once she makes them, seem so removed from ordinary process or predictability as to become nearly miraculous, or at any rate to possess a supervenient authority that even a powerful monarch hardly "dares" to deny.

Froissart deliberately and dramatically holds Philippa on the periphery of the action until all other remedies have been exhausted. Just prior to Philippa's intervention Gautier de Mauni has launched a perfectly cogent plea, urging that the king not destroy his reputation for "soverainne gentillèce" by failing to take pity on these men, and he has only further stirred royal annoyance: " 'Mauni, Mauni, soufrés-vous. Il ne sera aultrement' " (*Oeuvres*, 5:215). The message of this unsuccessful initiative is clear: the time for redress within the established processes of royal consultation, such as occurred when the king first agreed to modify his demand for unconditional surrender, is at an end. Only a differently grounded appeal, invoking a different sort of authority, has a chance of succeeding now.

Excluded from the "power of office" (Bynum, *Holy Feast*, 22), the female supplicant regrounds her authority on the very fact of exclusion. In this scene, Philippa's dutiful self-marginalization is what gives a certain torque to her intervention when it occurs. Her sudden movement from outside to inside enables her to speak from a position of exclusion, on behalf of those merciful considerations that the king has determinedly denied; it gives her, in short, some of the authority of the prophetic outsider. Moreover, the rationale for her exclusion—the equation of weakness with femininity involved in the formulation "feminei sexus fragilitas" ("Liber Regalis," 109)—is brought forward in the most emphatic terms. We are, for example, reminded three times that Philippa is far along in pregnancy and are

---

[5] With this assumption that the queen is normally absent, removed in her own *hostel*, may be contrasted the active involvement of her Capetian predecessors, as Marion Facinger has described them: "Where the king was, there too was the queen; his every act and decision was approved or assisted or contended by the queen *because she was there*, and because custom and tradition allowed that the queen was an ally and partner in governing" (27).

once again reminded of this fact when she mentions the peril of her sea-crossing.[6] The centrality of femininity, and the implications of humility and weakness that attend it, are additionally emphasized by such elements as the kneeling posture that reveals Philippa's sympathetic self-identification with the threatened and oppressed. The central themes of this passage are, in fact, brought together when Edward pauses before speaking and we are told what he sees: his wife, very pregnant, pleading, on her knees, tenderly. No wonder the sight of such abjection, so confirmatory of his own powers, moved the king: "his" wife, her pregnancy guaranteeing "his" dynasty, recognizing his superior authority in the very form of her pleas, and further recognizing it by sinking to her knees, and exhibiting diffuse tenderness all the while.

Of course, we are not simply talking about particular characteristics of Edward III and Philippa, but a widely shared idea of how fourteenth-century queens were supposed to behave. Official ideologists like le Bel and Froissart, and a host of other chroniclers and petitioners and poets, joined enthusiastically in producing representations of queenly mediation, and no fourteenth-century queen could have failed to understand that mediatory activities would comprise a large part of her job description. Queenly mediation was, in other words, a "sponsored" activity, an activity that—for all its tacitly corrective and admonitory content—seems to have been entirely congenial to male monarchs and to the whole system of relations that maintained them on their thrones.[7]

Confronted with such evidence of male zest for female intercession, we

[6] Philippa's pregnancy, mentioned once by le Bel, receives considerably more attention in Froissart's more affective account. Parsons has observed to me in correspondence that Philippa's pregnancy is exaggerated for effect, if not invented outright: "Calais surrendered on 5 August 1347. If Philippa bore William in May 1348, she may well not even have known she was pregnant at the time. She cannot possibly have been pregnant when she crossed the channel." This emphasis on fecundity may seem to suggest an incomplete assimilation of the idea of the intercessor-queen into the influential precedent of the Virgin Mary as mediatrix between God and erring humankind. Yet, on reflection, virginity and fecundity are intimately related opposites, each serving in its own way as a reminder of the distinctive femininity of the supplicant. In "Esther's Eclipse," Parsons discusses the relationship between virginity and intercession, though to different purpose, suggesting that emphasis on the queen's maidenhood was a way of camouflaging her sexual nature and thus limiting or tempering her intimate relationship with the king.

[7] Viard and Déprez argue for the historical accuracy of le Bel's depiction, on the ground that, though a partisan of Edward III, he has been willing in this instance to reveal Edward in an unfavorable light: "Sa conscience d'historien l'oblige à raconter exactement ce qui se passa. . . . Il nous montre le roi, la rage au coeur, voulant, malgré toutes ces supplications, faire venir le bourreau pour leur couper le tête. Il céda enfin devant les prières de la reine" (xxv). I would argue that, far from depicting Edward with warts-and-all historicity, le Bel has given us a monarch behaving exactly as dictated by a widely popular and heavily gendered script: adamant in his rage, but giving way before the spiritually prestigious suasions of his properly humble queen.

might reasonably pause to ask what makes the portrayal of physically weak but spiritually elevated women so very satisfying to men. Several answers suggest themselves:

Supplying a "male lack." In his study of the relations between thirteenth-century friars and the holy women with whom they worked, John Coakley has noted a tendency on the part of the friars to direct women toward otherworldly spirituality while retaining control of lay religious life in their own hands. This "division of labor," he observes, defined friars' work as saving souls, and women's work as praying for the friars' work. This system assigned women the roles of auxiliaries, beholders, refiners, and intercessors, while affirming male authority of office; women were, indeed, encouraged to cultivate a separate domain of superior spiritual refinement, but noncompetitively, in order to supply a "male lack."[8]

Coakley's shrewd analysis has several obvious points of application to the equally gendered division of labor between judgmental kings and merciful queens, in which the queens' mild intercessions may be viewed as essential course-corrections in the navigation of a male-piloted ship of state. Edward III is doing what a king is supposed to do, judgmentally and legislatively; many lives have been lost as a result of the stubborn resistance at Calais, and a price must be paid. But Philippa, with her more spontaneous emotional identification with the disempowered, alerts him to a dimension of the situation that judgment untempered by mercy could not achieve. For all his blustery wishes that his wife had been elsewhere, we must imagine the Edward of this account well pleased, for, without any disrespect to the force of his male ire, his wife has contributed a supplementary perspective that will enhance the repute of his kingship.

Permitting royal reconsideration. Philippa's intercessory activity permits the king to do something a late medieval monarch cast in the mold of "imago dei" needed on most occasions to avoid: change his mind. Prior to Philippa's intervention, we have already seen Edward modify his initial insistence on unconditional surrender upon the advice of his council. Gautier de Mauni, arguing for an additional modification in the case of the six hostages, finds the king irritably bent against further change. The king's intransigence would seem to have little to do with the merits of the case, for his lieutenant's argument is not only compassionate but grounded on excellent statecraft: execution of the six hostages will destroy Edward's reputation for *gentilèce* and give all the world cause to reprove him. Philippa's plea thus permits Edward to take a step, the wisdom of which has already been persuasively shown. Her plea is launched from regions emphatically

[8] Coakley's phrase, in conversation. Coakley's paper on "Female Sanctity as a Male Concern among Thirteenth-Century Friars," delivered at the 1990 Fordham conference on "Gender and Society, II," was a major stimulus to my treatment of this subject, and I am grateful to him both for subsequent conversation and for sharing his unpublished typescript with me.

outside the realm of conventional governance and the authority of male office, at once "higher" in spiritual refinement and "lower" in the spontaneous emotionality attributed to the state of powerless abjection (Bynum, *Jesus as Mother*, 137). As *femina ex machina*, entering from beyond the boundaries of systematized male power, she serves a welcome faciliating role exempted by its special properties from any longer-term impact on the male conduct of affairs.

Affirming "maleness." An idea of "the female" is, of course, necessary for the construction of "the male." Froissart's depiction of Philippa as hyperfemale—as marginal, maternal, abject, emotional—provides an essential counterpart to his depiction of Edward as hyper-male—obtrusive, paternal, proud, legalistic.

Seeming to attribute considerable prestige to queens as possessors of unpredictable but forceful spirituality, the system of relations involved in queenly intercession may actually be seen to support, rather than contradict, the foundations of patriarchical autocracy. Mary Douglas has commented that "beliefs which attribute spiritual power to individuals are never neutral or free of the dominant patterns of social structure. If some beliefs seem to attribute free-floating spiritual powers in a haphazard manner, closer inspection shows consistency" (112). In this case, an idea of erratically powerful female spirituality actually functions as a vehicle for subordination. The admirable but hectic traits that disqualify women from the everyday exercise of power are shown to qualify them as ideal subjects, ever ready to supply male shortcomings and humanize male rule.

The construction of a sharply defined alternative based on subordination potentially opens the way to a critique of domination. Coakley's women do not challenge the authority of their friars, but they serve as reminders of its limits and judges of its motives (9). So, too, might the existence of an alternative code of behavior exemplified in Philippa's intervention lead to a critique of Edward's headstrong behavior. In this particular text, though, such a critique is neither spelled out nor even implied. Rather than directing the reader's attention to an excluded array of compassionate values, Philippa's mediatory intervention serves mainly as an occasion for the further demonstration of Edward's triumphant regality.

A female stance so closely configured to male needs and desires threatens to be subsumed within a universal male posture that comprehends all meaningful experience. The possibility arises, in other words, that what appears to be a prescription for female conduct might not be about women at all, but only a way of saying something further about men. Susan Crane has mentioned this possibility to me, astutely suggesting that the interceding queen finally serves as a virtual "allegorical figure for mercy, a figure in a psychomachia of male decision making."[9] I want finally to stop just short

---

[9] Crane additionally suggests, in correspondence, that "locating merciful impulses in

of this reading, however, on extratextual grounds. I do not mean to suggest that anything about intercession is distinctively or essentially female. Nevertheless, ideas about intercession functioned as a socially constructed prescription for femininity, a guide (or, looking ahead to the case of Queen Anne, a *script*) for actual as well as imagined female behavior. Female intercession is gratifying to men and answers the dictates of male desire, but it remains less than completely subsumed so long as it continues actively to specify the coordinates of actual female behavior in the world.

QUEEN ANNE INTERCEDES FOR LONDON

Anne of Bohemia's thirteen-year reign was quite literally framed within previously established expectations of her mediatory activity. She arrived in England in December 1381, and during her passage through the city either on the day of her reception by the citizens of London (18 January 1382) or the day of her marriage to Richard in Westminster (20 January 1382), she was handed a bill by the citizens, soliciting her support for the city's liberties. This reminder seeks to mobilize expectations of queenly performance and the authority of past precedent to array her in the role of compassionate negotiator between Richard's two roles as husband and king.

> Cum . . . ad vestram benignissimam pietatem . . . pertineat mediatricis personam inter illustrissimum principem ac prepotentissimum dominum vestrum atque nostrum dominum nostrum Regem pietatis visceribus induere . . . sicud alie nostre domine Regine que vestram precellentissimam dignitatem in vestro regno Anglie precesserunt placeat vestre clementissime ac prestatissime nobilitati erga dominum nostrum Regem factis et verbis gratiosis taliter mediare. (Plea and Memoranda Rolls, A25 mem. 3b)

> Since it pertains to your most benign piety to assume in the innermost parts of piety the role of mediatrix between your most illustrious prince and most powerful lord and our lord the king, just as [did] our other lady Queens who preceded your most excellent highness in your realm of England, may it be pleasing to your most clement and preeminent nobility to mediate with our lord the King in such wise with gracious words and deeds.[10]

---

women is a way of describing the subordinate place of mercy in the all-encompassing masculine response. . . . The impulse to mercy is subordinate to the impulse to justice, but both are fully masculine, that is, fully 'human' in that traditional gendering that conflates maleness and humanity as the universal experience."

[10] I am indebted to Sheila Lindenbaum for her transcription of this passage, and for her advice on matters of translation. Here, as elsewhere, she has been my intrepid guide through the thickets of the Corporation Library and the PRO.

As their own words suggest, the Londoners have no personal knowledge of Anne. Nor need they know her to cast her in a mediatory role.[11] So, too, in an epitaph probably composed at the time of Richard's reburial by Henry V, was she seen to have lived out an intercessory paradigm:

> Pauperibus prona—semper sua reddere dona. Jurgia sedavit—et pregnantes relevavit. . . . Prebens solamen viduis, egris medicamen. (*Inventory*, 31)

> Always inclined to give offerings to the poor, she settled quarrels and relieved pregnant women . . . , offering solace to widows, medicine to the ill.

These texts tell us a good deal about contemporary expectations of queenship, and little about Anne herself. In point of fact, rather than hailing Anne as a promised mediatrix, Londoners and others in England showed considerable dismay at the time of her arrival over the excessive dowry that Richard was thought to have paid "pro tantilla carnis porcione" or for this tiny piece of flesh (*West.*, 24) and over the political implications of a tie with Bohemia and the remains of the old Holy Roman Empire (*Pleas*, 3–4). So, too, does evidence of dissatisfaction penetrate her eulogies. Even as it praises her for aiding those who had fallen into difficulties, the *Historia Ricardi* takes her to task for introducing an unfortunate style, shoes with long "beaks" (134).

Yet the authority and imaginative centrality of an established interpretative scheme can overrule a good deal of contrary evidence, and so does Anne take her place with such celebrated intercessors as Queen Philippa and Richard's mother Joan of Kent (see, for example, *West.*, 114). Whatever her inclinations, she seems to have sought earnestly not to disappoint the accompanying political and ethical expectations. In 1382, she is said to have interceded for one of the unlikeliest rebels, disappointed heir Thomas Farndon (or Farrington), who sought to detain Richard with an account of his grievances on the way to Mile End (*CPR*, [1381–1385], 103). In 1384, "casualiter" on the scene at Reading like Philippa at Calais, she was on her knees for John Northampton (*West.*, 92). In 1388 she was thought to have interceded, unsuccessfully, with Arundel for the life of Simon Burley (*Traïson*, 9), and, successfully, with the Archbishop of Canterbury for the lives of six justices and sergeants-at-law (Knighton, 295). It was un-

---

[11] As a matter of fact, so developed were her new subjects' expectations of her mediatory role that they were bruiting her compassion even prior to her arrival. At the Parliament of November and December 1381, which adjourned prior to Anne's arrival in England, a mixed approach was taken, repealing Richard's grants of manumission but pardoning most of the rebels. Authorities for the latter step were God, the Virgin Mary, and the special request of the noble lady Anne, soon, God willing, to arrive as Queen of England: "a l'especiale requeste de noblee Dame, Dame Anne . . . Roigne d'Engleterre, si Dieux plest, proscheinement a venir" (*RP*, 3:103).

doubtedly in recognition of such actions that the citizens of London gave her, as a gift for her second-to-last Christmas in 1392–1393, a large and remarkable bird with a very wide throat, "unam magnam avem et mirabilem, habentem guttur latissimum" (*West.*, 510)—that is, a pelican, a bird known in the Middle Ages for its self-sacrificing habit of feeding its young with blood drawn from its own breast.

The Londoners' gratitude is traceable to a more immediate cause: her role as intercessor with Richard, during that month-long period in the summer of 1392 in which, professing anger with the city, he withdrew its customary privileges, replaced its elected officials, levied an immense fine, and withdrew the royal judiciary to York. Anne was generally supposed to have played an intercessory role throughout those crucial July and August weeks. The Westminster chronicler says that she again and again, indeed repeatedly, prostrated herself at the feet of the king, at Windsor and at Nottingham, interceding submissively and sedulously for the city and for the plight of its citizens: "que iteratis vicibus, immo multociens, prostravit se ad pedes domini regis tam ibi quam aput Notyngham, obnixe et sedule deprecando pro dicta civitate London' et pro statu civium ejusdem" (502).

Even more revealing of contemporary expectations are accounts of the carefully choreographed (and partially "scripted") occasion celebrating the reconcilation itself, Richard's and Anne's 21 August procession through the city of London. This procession is treated in several chronicles and in a contempory Anglo-Norman letter (Suggett, 209–13), but the most detailed account is the *Concordia*, a 548-line Latin poem by Carmelite friar Richard Maidstone. Although floridly embellished with classical paraphrase, allusion, and moralization of dubious reportorial status, Maidstone's after-the-fact account does stand in referential relation to the events he describes, events that he must either have observed or discussed in detail with observers.

The underlying movement of Maidstone's profoundly gendered account is toward the consummation of a marriage, with Richard as *sponsus* or bridegroom, driven by perfidious tongues to desert his *thalamus* or bridal-chamber, and now returning to his chastened bride, the citizenry of London. Appropriately to this scenario, Richard is hailed as more handsome than Paris, "formosior Paride" (l. 26), as becoming as Troylus or Absolon himself, "iste velud Troylus vel ut Absolon ipse decorum" (l. 113), nearly handsome enough to warrant Venus's own envy—or, in a last minute re-masculinization of his looks, worthy to sojourn in her chambers: "Larga decoris ei si plus natura dedisset, / Clauderet hunc thalamis invida forte Venus" (ll. 117–18). About Anne's beauty less is said, in part because the city as a whole is Richard's intended companion, and it is the city that artfully grooms and bedecks itself:

> . . . tota cohors sociatur,
> Preparat et cultu se meliore suo,
> Ornat et interea se pulcre queque platea;
> Vestibus auratis urbs micat innumeris.
> Floris odoriferi specie fragrante platea,
> Pendula perque domos purpura nulla deest.

The entire city unites and the people bedeck themselves with their finest attire. Meanwhile, each street is beautifully decorated; and soon the city gleams with countless vestments ornamented with gold. The street is fragrant with a kind of sweet-smelling flowers, and from the houses no purple hanging is lacking. (ll. 55-60, trans. Charles Smith, 171)

Eroticization of the relation of king to subjects gives a new meaning to the phrase "royal entry," and Maidstone shows himself well aware of this imagistic tendency. The humbled city, prostrate ("provoluti") at Richard's feet, prays with tears in its eyes that the king return to his chamber, that he not hate that bridal chamber he has previously loved, but it also prays that he refrain from rape, that he not take by force what already belongs to him:

> Non laceret, non dilaniet pulcherrima regni
> Menia, nam sua sunt, quicquid et exstat in hiis.

Let not the most beautiful walls in the kingdom be rent nor torn, for they are the king's own and whatever is within them.[12]

Anne's role in this scenario is becoming clear and, lest it be overlooked, the citizens spell it out to her. Giving her a gift of a palfrey which will carry her tender limbs smoothly, "qui teneros vestros leniter ferat artus" (l. 237), the spokesperson for the city says,

> Flectere regales poterit regina rigores,
> Mitis ut in gentem rex velit esse suam.
> Mollit amore virum mulier: Deus huic dedit illam;
> Tendat ad hoc vester, O pia, dulcis amor.

Let the queen soften royal severity that the king may be forbearing to his people. A woman mellows a man with love: for this God gave her; for this, O blessed woman, may your sweet love aspire. (ll. 229–32, trans. Smith, 191)

---

[12] Ll. 145–46, trans. Smith, 181. The idea of female subjection saturates this narrative so completely that it surfaces even in many of its most incidental details. Maidstone tells, for example, of a *bonum prodigium* or good omen that occurred as the procession entered the bridge gate of the city, in which one of the *currus* carrying the queen's attendants overturned, and that, one of the women thereupon baring her most womanly thighs, the watching commoners were hardly able to restrain their laughter: "Femina feminea sua dum sic femina nudat, / Vix poterate risum plebs retinere suum" (ll. 253–54). Maidstone finds in this an image of *luxuria* about to be overthrown, but I would read its inclusion somewhat differently, as evidence of the saturation of this poem by heavily eroticized images of female abjection.

Linked to the king by marriage and the city by sympathy (*corde*), Anne mediates between them by enacting the city's eroticized abjection in a form that will mollify Richard's manly anger. This speech implies that the arena of the queen's acts of *dulcis amor* will be the king's own marriage chamber, and that the queen's sexual concessions will parallel those symbolic and financial concessions to be made within the *thamalus* of the city as a whole. Yet Anne's act of intercession also requires a more public embodiment, and it is toward that embodiment that this whole day of pageantry is bent.

Anne finally goes down on her knees before her sovereign not in the course of the procession through London itself, but at the end of the day, back in great hall at Westminster. This postponement is not intended to deny Londoners the sight of her abjection (for representatives were explicitly invited [ll. 429–30], but rather to underscore its symbolic centrality to the reconciliation. As with Philippa's intervention, Anne's plea is to be the determining event; as Anne herself says to the citizens just before taking her leave of the city at Temple Bar, whatever is to be brought to pass will be brought to pass through her: " 'In me, si quid erit, perficietur,' ait" (l. 454). Further, Richard, having spent the day in Anne's company, now withdraws from her, arraying himself in a long gown and seating himself on a throne specially designed for the occasion: "se vesti en une longe gowne, . . . Et puis s'en ala en la sale et s'asist en une see en haut qe fuist fait devant le grant see" (Suggett, 212). Anne's intervention, as she separately enters the hall with her own retinue and collapses before the feet of the king, "Ingreditur regina suis comitata puellis, / Pronaque regales corruit ante pedes" (ll. 465–66), thus gains some of that adventitiousness accruing to other queenly interventions, a sense that she speaks from or for a region of authority not normally represented in regal deliberations.

Invited by Richard to speak, she emphasizes his manly sway, "michi vir, michi vis, michi vita" (l. 469), and her own suffering, "intime condoleo" (l. 488), which, as in other examples of female intercession, depends upon a superior capacity for suffering with the travails of others (*condoleo*, in this sense, carries an implication of joint suffering, of actual participation in the sorrows of others). Anne enjoins Richard in the most respectful of subjunctive utterances to condescend to pardon the people who readily tendered such great gifts: "Parcere dignemini plebibus qui tanta dedere / Munera tam prompte nobis ad obsequia" (ll. 491–92).

Anne here plays to perfection the part of a Marian virgo mediatrix, whose own ties to human suffering permit her to enact a state of sorrow before a more detached tribunal.[13] This role is, in turn, underscored by the eroticization of her compliant role as Richard's actual spouse. But this sub-

---

[13] Anne's aspect as virgo mediatrix in the Reconciliation is admirably described by Gordon Kipling, in a forthcoming study from which he has kindly shown me an excerpt.

missive role does not exhaust the significance of Anne's words and actions in the course of this day of pageantry. The Virgin is indeed the authoritative reference point for those self-effacing interventions that depend for their effectiveness on their manifestation of suffering humanity. Yet, if the Virgin is the model for intercession in its submissive aspect, the alternative model of Esther, as good counselor, is also at large within this scripting of the ideal queenly role.

Anne's own coronation ceremony had emphasized the particular strength given by God to frail women to overthrow the strong, "qui infirma mundi eligendo forcia queque confundere decreuisti" ("Liber Regalis," 109), with examples including Judith's slaying of Holofernes, and, later, Esther, brought to the marital chamber of Ahasuerus as his consort for the good of the Jewish people: "reginam hester causa iudaice salutis . . . ad regis assueri thalamum regnique sui consorcium transire fecisti" (110). Judith serves clearly enough as an example of a masculinized femininity, a woman who appropriates certain restricted elements of maleness in order to accomplish a temporarily demanding task. As we have already seen, Esther is a much less consistent signifier of any one trait; known as hesitant and timorous on the one hand, she also possesses a considerable reputation as a spokesperson for sound if unpopular views.

The *Concordia* associates Anne with Esther in a way that draws upon both traditions:

> Grata loqui pro gente sua regina valebit:
> Quod vir non audet, sola potest mulier.
> Hester ut Assueri trepidans stetis ante tribunal,
> Irritat dicta que prius ipse tulit.
> Nec dubium quin ob hoc vos omnipotens dedit huius
> Participem regni—sitis ut Hester ei.

> The queen will be able to speak in behalf of her grateful people: What a man does not dare, the woman alone can. As Esther stood fearfully before the judgement seat of Ahasuerus, she made void the proclamations which he himself first ordained. There is no doubt that the Almighty gave you as the companion of this kingdom for this: may you be like Esther for your people. (ll. 441–46, trans. Smith, 213–15)

In deference to the tradition of her meekness, Esther is described as *trepidans*, standing fearfully before the tribunal of her lord. Yet she is also described as a potentially effective and forthright counselor, accomplishing what a man could not. If her outer manner is imagined to embrace fearfulness and abjection, her message is imagined as substantive, including the people's views and possessing the power to overturn dictates of the king.

As portrayed in the *Concordia*, Anne's actual moment of intercession with Richard on behalf of the city draws upon both aspects of Esther's legacy, though with a decided tilt toward her value as a purveyor of substantive counsel. To be sure, she touches a number of necessary intercessory bases, prostrating herself before the king and emphasizing that he is her strength and her intervention is based on condolence or sympathetic sorrow (as opposed to reason or any cooler calculation). Yet the actual thrust of her speech is practical and advisory. She notes the value of the gifts given by the city to the king: "What refinement! What honor! What extravagance!" ("Quis cultus! quis honor! quis sumptus" [l. 473]). And from this observation she draws a down-to-earth, even salty, conclusion. "Whoever," she says, "assumes a greater honor, is and will be the more humble, if he be wise," "Quo maiorem sumit honorem quisquis, eo plus / Est humilis et erit, si sapiens fuerit" (ll. 477–78).

Anything but abject, this speaker draws on sage apothegm as a vehicle for important advice. At this moment, she decisively parts company with those Marian mediatrices whose actions are grounded in a capacity for condolence and joins those apt counselors like Lady Philosophy and Dame Prudence who speak from a reservoir of experience, sharp analysis, and sturdy good sense.[14] Here we may return to Coakley's suggestion that female authority, usually complementary, may also possess a more critical relation toward male authority, as "a powerful reminder of its limits and judge of its motives." Anne, functioning as Richard's counselor, reminds him in effect that "enough is enough." In the process, she briefly but suggestively opens the possibility that the intercessory tradition might be assimilated to less supplicatory and more energetic forms of critique.

ALCESTE, ESTHER, ANNE

From elements at large in the discursive and practical environment, the scriptwriter and Maidstone produced a practical model of efficacious queenship. This model was, first of all, textual, both in the script for the pageant and in its reenactment in Maidstone's poem. But it was also conveyed within a tangible performance, given not just by actors or impersonators but by an actual queen. This entire situation reminds us that the "actions" produced within a discursive environment may be registered as texts or events or (in the mixed case of a scripted pageant described in an after-the-fact poem) as a combination of the two. A more exclusively textual realization of efficacious queenship is to be found in Chaucer's character-

---

[14] This group stretches beyond queenship to include the whole body of what Sharon Farmer has called "persuasive wives" (521)—wives who, in the opinions of male clerics of the eleventh through thirteenth centuries, were well positioned to correct the views of their more headstrong husbands through the exercise of persuasive speech.

ization of Alceste in the prologue to his *Legend of Good Women*, on which he worked intermittently in the years before and after 1392. But even Chaucer's textual rendition possesses implications for the world of practical events.

We might suppose Chaucer a sponsor of queenly abjection, if we were to think first of that moment in the *Knight's Tale* when ex-Amazon Hippolyta together with Emily and the other ladies of her company intercede with Theseus on behalf of Palamon and Arcite: "And on hir bare knees adoun they falle / And wolde have kist his feet ther as he stood" (I.1758–59). Their *pitee* for the young knights is spontaneous and freely given, in the tradition of Marian condolence or mutual association with the plight of another sufferer. Its effect, moreover, is to magnify Theseus's regality—much as Philippa's abjection finally enhanced rather than detracted from the manly prowess of the Edward III of le Bel and Froissart. Yet, not so much in his representation of Hippolyta and Emily as in that of Theseus, Chaucer shows his discontent with the whole system of female abjection and male concession. For, unlike the Edward who gives ground only reluctantly and with stubborn reiteration of his original wish, Chaucer's Theseus is permitted to change his mind. In fact, to the considerable extent that pity and mercy are marked in this discourse as distinctively feminine attributes (as opposed, for example, to anger and adamancy), Chaucer may be said to have partially feminized Theseus: "At the laste aslaked was his mood, / For pitee renneth soone in gentil herte" (I.1760–61). Beginning with simple compassion for the sorrowing women, Theseus takes an additional step, adopting a new and more merciful standard of lordship that embraces merciful as well as angry actions:

> And eek his herte hadde compassioun
> Of wommen, for they wepen evere in oon,
> And in his gentil herte he thoughte anon,
> And softe unto hymself he seyde, "Fy
> Upon a lord that wol have no mercy,
> But been a leon, bothe in word and dede,
> To hem that been in repentaunce and drede."
>
> (I.1770–76)

Compassionate (as opposed to harsh or leonine) lordship is here explicitly promulgated as a new standard.[15]

---

[15] This moment has elements in common with a rather incidental moment in Maidstone's *Concordia*, when Richard pauses at the foot of London Bridge to pardon a supplicant who throws himself to the ground at the feet of the horses seeking pardon: "Pronus ut ante pedes iacuit prostratus equinos; / Flens rogitat veniam; rex sibi donat eam" (ll. 189–90). Richard's granting of pardon does not necessarily reflect inner reformation; the author presents it as the enactment of a gracious custom (*pius solitus*) of royal mercy. Nonetheless, it suggests a grow-

This supposed new standard might be seen less as admiring imitation than as an appropriation or annexation, in which the entire range of emotional response is asserted as the natural domain of the male. Yet the interpenetration of conventionally gendered behaviors works both ways in Chaucer, who not only attributes spontaneity and humanity to his men, but also wisdom and procedural acumen to women. His poetry abounds in strong womanly counsel—most notably, of course, that of Dame Prudence, but even in such unlikely cases as the ordinarily submissive Griselda. One of Griselda's signal virtues is her ability to temper Walter's headstrong acts with conciliatory activities:

> If gentil men or othere of hire contree
> Were wrothe, she wolde bryngen hem aton;
> So wise and rype wordes hadde she,
> And juggementz of so greet equitee.

> (IV.436–41)

Although her activities are mediatory in nature, Griselda is more a counselor than an intercessor. For all the abjection she displays elsewhere in the tale, it is plainly on her words and insights, rather than on Marian condolence, that her mediatory successes depend.

Chaucer gives us instances of piteous intercession so effective that they not only appease but convert men, and he gives us other instances in which womanly good counsel carries the day. But he less often fuses the two. Intercession and counsel usually operate separately, as in the *Wife of Bath's Tale*, where the "queene and other ladyes mo" exercise their intercessory function by praying Arthur for grace at one point in the poem (III.894–95) and the *olde wyf* delivers her most edifying speech at another (III.1109f.). In one place, however, abject intercession and robust persuasion actively vie within the construction of a single character—and the consequence of their contention is the original and enigmatic Alceste, a mediatrix for Chaucer's time!

Alceste's "doubleness" is keenly identified by Carolyn Dinshaw, who locates her enigma in a split between praiseworthy and disturbing traits, the former including her Marian associations and traditional self-sacrifice and wisdom, and the latter including her aggressive and peremptory behavior and the somewhat ominous instability of her physical being (71–72). My own wish is to endorse this reading and to advance it by pointing to an additional element of multivalence, manifested in an unusual mixing to-

---

ing receptivity to the idea of mercy as something other than an exclusively female virtue, as an emotion to which a male might independently be moved. In each case, a rather primitive split, in which all pity resides with the woman and all adamance with the man, is promisingly surmounted.

gether of praiseworthy traits drawn from different elements of intercessory discourse.

Alceste is, on the one hand, conceived within the purest of self-abnegating traditions. She is modeled on a wife who (in the God of Love's admiring condensation) "for hire housbonde chees to dye, / And eke to goon to helle, rather than he" (F, ll. 513–14). This in a poem literally crammed with intercessory imagery.[16] Alceste's physical introduction to the poem also seems imagined within the bounds of intercessory meekness. She enters silently with her king (though not, like Philippa, pacing behind him), and she is herself followed (like Anne in the *Concordia*) by a train of ladies. She is variously described by the narrator as "benigne," "meke," and "debonayre," and only the comfort of her presence rescues him from dread of Love's stern words and harsh demeanor. She likewise, as in the model of abject intercession, ends her words on the narrator's behalf with a suit for pardon: " 'Y aske yow this man . . . / That ye him never hurte in al his lyve' " (F, ll. 433–34). And, as Edward awarded the burghers to Philippa, so does Love turn the narrator over to her keeping: " 'Dooth wyth hym what yow leste' " (F, l. 449).

Yet Alceste is more or less simultaneously portrayed as a giver of practiced and sound advice to princes, a one-time ruler in her own right, a hard negotiator, and a stern commentator on the narrator's deserts. Her intercession involves no prostration or kneeling, no impetuousity, no particular condolence with the narrator's dread. Like Esther, with whom she is compared in the ballade sung in her praise (F, l. 243), rather than Mary, she intervenes in the manner of Sharon Farmer's "persuasive wives"—as a good counselor, a worthy adviser to her prince. She reminds him of his responsibility to his own dignity, "A god ne sholde nat thus be agreved" (F, l. 345), she lectures him on the unreliability of court opinion, "Envie ys lavendere of the court alway" (F, l. 358), and, in particular, delivers a potted harangue on the responsibility of a lord to avoid tyranny and to cherish the well-being of his subjects:

This shoolde a ryghtwis lord have in his thoght,
And nat be lyk tirauntz of Lumbardye,
That han no reward but at tyrannye.
For he that kynge or lord ys naturel,
Hym oghte nat be tiraunt ne crewel

---

[16] Even the flower to which Alceste is linked by sympathy and imagery, the daisy, "emperice and flour of floures alle" (F, l. 185), is couched in terms of Marian mediation, serving as a well of mercy for errant birds (F, ll. 155–62). Lisa Kiser has pointed to the daisy's intercessory role, and its saturation with Marian imagery: "His daisy performs the same intercessory role in the poetic model that Mary performs in the theological one. She intercedes on behalf of humans in the face of God; the daisy intercedes on behalf of viewers in the face of the sun" (47).

As is a fermour, to doon the harm he kan.
He moste thinke yt is his lige man,
And is his tresour and his gold in cofre.[17]

Alceste's intercession is, in fact, so tilted toward good advice that even its sympathetic recommendation—that the God of Love show mercy to the feckless poet—is presented as a general rule of good godly (read *princely*) conduct; she argues that, if a petitioner

. . . asketh mercy with a dredeful herte,
And profereth him, ryght in his bare sherte,
To ben ryght at your owen jugement,
Than oght a god by short avysement
Consydre his owne honour and hys trespas.

(F, ll. 404–8)

So fully in command of her oral performance is this competent queen that she can easily frame dually directed address—utterances that simultaneously function as reassurances to her slower-witted consort and wounding flouts to the poet-narrator's pride: "Al be hit that he kan nat wel endite" (F, ll. 414).

Her actual suit on the narrator's behalf is bolstered, not by abjection or supplication, but by the reminder that as a former ruler, "your Alceste, whilom quene of Trace," she knows what she is talking about (F, l. 432). Moreover, she does not simply ask the God of Love for an unreasoned act of mercy based on her own compassion, but constitutes herself as a canny negotiator, proposing a reasonable exchange:

Y aske yow this man, ryght of your grace,
That ye him never hurte in al his lyve;
And he shal swere to yow, and that as blyve,
He shal no more agilten in this wyse. (F, ll. 433–36)

Further, her benignity has its limits. Awarded the disposition of her supplicant, she behaves very differently from Philippa, who provided her supplicants with clothing, a good dinner in her *hostel*, and six nobles each.

---

[17] F, ll. 373–80. The larger environment of political theory within which these and subsequent observations are produced has been been admirably delineated by Margaret Schlauch, who cites twelfth- through fourteenth-century discussions of the king's responsibility to his subjects, the naturalness of the Aristotelian state, and the aberrations of tyranny, as well as the civic humanists' reexaminaton of contemporary Italian instances (esp. 135–50). Other, less formal precedents have been noted in such popular texts as the pseudo-Aristotelian *Secreta Secretorum*, which includes such observations as, "The peple and thi sugetis is the hous of thi memorie, and thi tresore by which thi reme is conformyd" (Steele, 36). At the moment, however, I am less interested in the particular features of the advice that Alceste gives than the simple fact that she is giving it.

Irked by the narrator's continuing protestations of innocence, Alceste curtly draws the line—"Lat be thyn arguynge" (F, l. 475)—and reconstitutes herself as a stern confessor, enjoining a stiff *penaunce* (F, ll. 479f). Despite the God of Love's enthusiastic endorsement of her qualities, "But pite renneth soone in gentil herte" (F, l. 503), Alceste has revealed herself as a tough and experienced woman, more than equal to her somewhat fuddled consort. Her transformation from an abject intercessor of royalty to royalty's companion and adviser and a source of irrefutable authority in her own right is complete. In the process, the audience is asked to recognize in a single character aspects of humility and strength that it has been schooled by tradition to seek in different places.

The same convergence was apparent in Queen Anne, as scripted by Maidstone and the rest. And this convergence—together with Alceste's instruction that the completed *Legend of Good Women* should be delivered to "the quene, / . . . at Eltham or at Sheene" (F, ll. 496–497)—encourages an investigation of the relation between Alceste and Anne.

Among other of his cavils at the identification of Alceste with Anne, Bertrand Bronson points out that an Alceste standing in for Anne would hardly have suggested delivery of the *Legend* to herself (55). But, in the multileveled reality of the dream vision, displaced mention of a character may encourage the reader or hearer to recognize a relation; incidental mention of Esther just before Alceste starts behaving in the most Estherly fashion, and incidental reference to Anne just as Alceste is presenting a personal example of fully mobilized queenship, may suggest identification rather than difference. Despite Bronson's objection, Alceste's allusion to Anne undoubtedly serves to sharpen our awareness of a possible relation between these literary and historical figures. We may nevertheless probe the question of a referential relation between Alceste and Anne without going to the other extreme, of assuming that Alceste "is" Anne or even directly "symbolizes" her. The key to the relationship between Alceste within the poem and the historical Anne rests less in the denial or affirmation of particular congruences than in a recognition of the environment of interpretative structures within which Alceste was invented and within which Anne seems at least partially to have invented herself.[18]

---

[18] The issue of Alceste's possible referentiality has analogies with the critical debate over "Lak of Stedfastnesse," when readers like Pollard, Brewer, and Scattergood seek to relate the poem to particular occasions and others like Cross find it a tissue of ahistorical commonplaces (see above, chapter 3, nn. 5, and 6). So in the case of Alceste have some critics developed what Donald W. Rowe calls "occasional" readings and others "formalist and structuralist readings that ignore a text's relationship with anything but other texts" (6). An example of an "occasional" reading is Norton-Smith's perceptive but simplified claim that the poem "is partially a transfiguration of real experience based on Anne of Bohemia in her intercessorial role as *advocatus clementiae* in the dispute between the king and the city of London" (63). "Formalist and structuralist" readings in Rowe's sense are harder to come by, though one

Many critics still suppose "historical" readings to consist of good literary detective work, leading to the identification of discrete events or occasions to which a work refers. Yet no less historical than such events are the larger interpretative structures within which social and literary events are produced—the queen as politically powerless but spiritually influential mediator, for example, or the queen as a persuasive counselor. The historicity of these schemes lies in their origins, and (more importantly in the present case) their transmission and the varied uses to which they are subject.

Both Anne (in the *Concordia*) and Alceste (in the *Legend*) are realized within and between contending ideas of queenship. Both function as mediatrices, seeking to exercise influence through the monarchs with whom they are allied; both function as persuasive wives and good counselors, telling their lords how best to behave in order to win general approval. Furthermore, not only did Richard Maidstone and Geoffrey Chaucer enjoy common possession of both ideas of queenship, but their respective audiences undoubtedly possessed them as well. Which is to say that versions of Anne and Alceste are not only produced but also comprehended within these schemes. The two queens would have reminded contemporary audiences of each other, less because of particular identifying details than because of certain shared protocols of queenly behavior.

Broadening our idea of history to include the development and transmission of interpretative structures can save us from embarrassing argumentative contortions likely to be generated in the course of overly narrow historical sleuthing. John Norton-Smith, rightly perceiving a similarity between Alceste's intercession for the narrator and Anne's intercession for the city of London in August 1392, wants to make the latter a source for the former and is forced to assign a very, very late date to the F version of Chaucer's prologue (63). (Borges's conceit of fictional influence on reality in "Tlön" notwithstanding, Norton-Smith would presumably have found the alternative—the poem as a source for the event—unacceptable.) But if we understand that Chaucer's poem, Maidstone's poem, and the pageantry of 21 August 1392 were *all* produced and understood within a historically created and broadly available environment of ideas of queenship, then the seeming paradox of a poem that precedes rather than follows an event to which it apparently refers is immediately resolved.

---

may note that both Frank and Kiser, while preserving a high degree of authorial intentionality, confine their attention primarily to issues of literary tradition and problems of narrativity. The problem here would seem to lie in a false dichotomy, in which Alceste either "is" or "symbolizes" Anne (or even Anne at one particular moment), or she has nothing to do with Anne and exists only as a distinctive (and rather unstable) textual construct in her own right. Rowe's own effort to avoid this dichotomy, "the god and Alceste may remind us of Richard and Anne without representing them" (181) in fact merely blurs it, by failing to propose a theory of how such reminders are textually embodied and transmitted.

Of course, the simple assertion that Chaucer, Maidstone, and the citizens of London were all operating within structures made available by tradition still begs an explanatory issue. Any or all of them might have given us an Alceste or an Anne along the lines of Froissart's Philippa, all *conscience* and no brain. Yet we are given something else: persuasive and Esther-like queens with their feet on the ground and practical advice worth hearing. These choices are not coincidental, and the explanation for them is broadly historical—historical, that is, in relation less to a particular event than to a general situation.

Soon after his resumption of sole rule in May 1389, Richard reactivated his campaign for what might (in Ullmann's vocabulary) be considered theocratic kingship according to his own will and beyond the laws of the kingdom, as opposed to feudal kingship limited by law and custom and common consent.[19] Granted that the articles of Richard's deposition were a propaganda production, they may be assumed to embrace some commonly held (or at least recognizable) views of his kingship. His tendency to autocracy is there neatly summarized: "He seyd opynly . . . that his lawes were in his mouthe . . . , And that he allone myht chaunge the Lawes off his Rewme and make newe" (*Chronicles*, 31). The particular form of his autocracy and "singular" rule was, moreover, to refuse good counsel, not just once but repeatedly: "In meny grete counceilles ffor the kyng, whan the lordes off the Rewme, Justices and other were charged that they shulde trewly counceille the kyng in alle thinges . . . , whanne they yaff trewe counceille affter hir discrecion and witte, they were bytterly blamed by the kyng" (*Chronicles*, 33). Though the king appears in 1392 to have moved against London with the tacit assent of his own council, he certainly played a close hand in his dealings with the city; summoned before him at Nottingham on 25 June and Windsor on 22 July, the aldermanic leadership might have hoped to parlay but in fact found itself under abrupt assault upon grounds predetermined, and only partially explained, by the king (C. Barron, "Quarrel," 181–89). In their unpredictability and highhandedness, Richard's moves in June to August 1392 have much to tell us about the decidedly unparliamentary character of his royal style.

I add little to the existing store of historical knowledge by saying what everybody knows, that Richard had a consultation problem. Of interest here is a related contention: that the tendency of the London scriptwriters and Maidstone and Chaucer to softpedal the imagery of queens as abject

---

[19] I am, in simple summary, unpersuaded that Richard's period of "appeasement" of his aristocratic adversaries lasted from 1388 until 1396–1397 (see, for example, Steel, 180–216). In my view, Richard's generally exhibited tendency to assert the broadest possible scope for his prerogatives is once again clearly discernable by the Smithfield tournament of October 1390, at which his brief "law and order" campaign came to an end and he announced his livery of the White Hart (see above, chapter 3).

intercessors and to prefer that of queens as good counselors may address Richard's notorious impatience with counsel. Easily available to Maidstone and Chaucer were intercessory images of proven compatibility with late medieval ideas about autocratic kingship. But their poems move beyond intercessory images pleasing to autocracy in order to produce ideas of queenship that argue for the tempering of kingly power by good advice. In their works, queenship not only supplements and confirms male power but acts, in Coakley's terms, as "a powerful reminder of its limits."

Both Maidstone and Chaucer finally move beyond the ostensible subject of queenship to address broader questions about the relation of authority and good counsel. These questions embrace the whole array of dominant and subordinate relations crucial to fourteenth-century society: those of subjects to kings, wives to husbands, children to parents, apprentices to masters. But, in creating a discursive model in which the subjected individual is encouraged to address the terms and conditions of seigneurial authority, Maidstone and Chaucer need not stray far from their starting point. Whatever their additional ramifications, the representations of Anne in the *Concordia* and Alceste in the *Legend* are conceived within a thirteenth- and fourteenth-century discussion of gender and power.

Chapter 6

TREASON IN THE HOUSEHOLD

> "You listen to me, Charley Kray. A house is a battlefield, all on
> its bloody own."
> —*The Krays* (1990)

I N THE MIDST of his account of the spring 1388 treason trials, the
Westminster chronicler pauses to describe a lurid crime:

> Item xvij. die Aprilis quedam generosa mulier rem nephariam in absen-
> cia sui mariti habuit cum quodam presbitero; unde suasu dicte mulieris virum
> suum de transmarinis partibus redeuntem prefatus presbiter insanus occidit in
> lecto suo jacentem. Illi vero incontinenti summo mane in aurora et in eodem
> lecto dormientes fuerant intercepti et de tanto facinore palam convicti presbi-
> ter in carcere fuit detrusus, ubi penas condignas sustinuit usque ad mortem,
> mulier vero die quo supra juxta Bermundesey ad furcas fuit combusta. (*West.*,
> 322)

> 17 April. While her husband was away, a woman of good family formed a
> nefarious connection with a certain priest. Upon the husband's return from
> overseas, this crazed priest—persuaded by the woman's words—killed him as
> he lay in his bed. The two were quickly seized early one morning, as the dawn
> was just breaking, sleeping in the same bed. Publicly convicted of this terrible
> crime, the priest was thrust into prison where he suffered appropriate punish-
> ment until he died, and the woman was burned at the stake near Bermondsey
> on the date mentioned above.

What, we may reasonably ask ourselves, is a salacious recital like this one
doing in the middle of a narrative about treason? This item appears in its
proper chronological place, between a 13 April entry in which the doomed
Ricardian chamber knights plead for an opportunity to answer the charges
against them and an 18 April entry in which Richard complains that Justice
Tresilian was dragged from sanctuary. But chronology alone does not explain the appearance of so seemingly discrepant an item in a chronicle that
normally sets a standard of political importance for the events it includes.
The *Westminster Chronicle* usually meets Hayden White's standard: an
"annual" arranges events by chronology alone, but a "chronicle" selects
events chronologically but also in reference to a recurrent subject or principle (17–19). Underlying the chronicle, in White's view, is an idea of a

social system sustained by law. Such a standard of narrative selectivity certainly does prevail throughout most of the Westminster chronicler's lengthy treatment of the spring treason trials. Ideas of social justice and due process underlie the chamber knights' petition to answer charges, and Tresilian's right of sanctuary depends upon ideas of civil and natural law. Few would, however, recognize a theory of society based in law in this racy micronarrative of a faithless wife and her clerical accomplice. Perhaps, I permitted myself to suppose on first encounter, it merely represents a momentary victory for vagrant impulse over grand design, a temporary (but welcome) swerve into random gossip and low scurrility?

Suppose, though, that we give gossip (and that cherished outer margin of gossip properly known as scandal) full credit for the ambitious socializing uses to which they are regularly put. The distinctive contribution of gossip, as Patricia Spacks has explained, is to mediate between public and private, to restate "public facts in private terms," and, conversely, to give "private detail general meaning" (262). Embedded in this apparently private episode of a faithless wife and her accomplice is one clue to a partially obscured public signification, a "general meaning" that might explain its place among the varied episodes of that spring's treason trials. Notice that the wife was not simply hanged, but was put to death by burning. For fourteenth-century women, burning was the exemplary punishment for a particular crime: the crime of treason.[1]

This fact alone offers a rudimentary answer to the narrative question I have posed. The chronicler has treason on his mind, moving from the treason trials of Richard's chamber knights, to the treasonous conduct of this faithless wife, to Tresilian dragged from sanctuary to answer a charge of treason. But, if a narratological question has been resolved, a good many other questions remain. The first involves the definition of "treason" itself, for little in our experience prepares us for a concept of treason sufficiently

---

[1] As noted by Hector, *West.*, 323, and W.R.J. Barron, 190. Hanawalt observes that only in the case of treason were male and female punishments differentiated: "The treasonous man was drawn and quartered and the woman was burned at the stake" ("Female Felon," 265). Barron offers an explanation, that women were burned live "to avoid the indecent exposure of their bodies in public" (190). Burning at the stake was, of course, the traditional punishment for a variety of crimes other than treason, including arson, certain instances of adultery, and—most often—witchcraft or heresy (Reinhard, 186–209). Interestingly, though, burning was seldom practiced in England prior to the fifteenth century except in the cases of treasonous women. Burning became common in the fifteenth century as a punishment for heresy, but a link between treason and heresy may underlie the practice; those Lollards burnt in the first decades of the fifteenth century with Lancastrian concurrence may also have been thought to constitute a threat to political stability. For suggestive comments see Pike, 1:256, 476; and Gibson, 30. For an ambitious study of the commingling of sedition and heresy as objects of Lancastrian attack in the first decade of the fifteenth century, with special attention to the burning of John Badby, see McNiven.

expansive to embrace court and bedchamber, state policy and personal desire, Richard's discredited advisers and a homicidal wife. Progressively elaborated throughout the fourteenth century, the concept of treason conferred real interpretative power—the power to imagine meaning narratively in chronicle episodes, to assert meaning judicially in accusations and indictments, and to dramatize meaning concretely via trips to real stakes and scaffolds. Fortuitous as the chronicler's attribution of treason to this husband-killing woman might at first seem, his account is actually produced within the strong ambit of fourteenth-century treason theory and tellingly enacts its most dire assumptions. Within treason theory rests an explanation of the challenge that the woman's apparently private and household-centered deed posed to commonly held notions of civil order and the state.

THE STATUTE OF TREASON, 1352

The definition and scope of treason was a matter of recurrent concern in the second half of the fourteenth century, attracting the repeated attention not only of the judiciary but of Parliament as well.[2] The central document in this continuing discussion was the statue of treason—often called the "great statute"—of 1352. It resulted from a petition of commons at the Westminster Parliament of 1352, alleging irregular judicial extensions of treason law and seeking clarification. This petition elicited a royal declaration, fixing in statute those actions against the king, the queen, their son and heir, or his wife, that were to be considered treasonous. These actions included war against the king, counterfeiting the king's seals or money, or killing the chancellor, treasurer, or judges in the execution of their duty. Because all such deeds derogated the majesty of the king, properties of those found guilty would be forfeit directly to him.

J. G. Bellamy, the leading historian of medieval treason-theory, offers a modest and plausible theory for the timing and thrust of this statute: since conviction for treason resulted in forfeiture of property to the crown, any extensions of the scope of treason benefitted the royal treasury at the expense of local heirs and jurisdictions. Uneasy for some years about arbitrary and irregular alterations of the scope of treason, the commons now sought to limit grounds for conviction (*Law of Treason*, 59–101). That the commons did believe some justices were expanding the boundaries of trea-

---

[2] The 1352 statute itself allows that cases of "semblable treson" will undoubtedly continue to arise in the future, and that such cases should be resolved by parliamentary means (*Stat.*, 320). Parliament did in fact subsequently extend the definition of treason to cover the case of an attack on a merchant, one Janus Imperial, sojourning in London under the protection of letters patent from the king (*KB*, 7:19–20).

son is clear from the wording of the 1352 parliamentary petition, in which clarification is sought for the practice of justices "en diverses Countees" who judge "les gentz qe sont empeschez devant eux come Treitours par diverses causes descounues a la Commune estre Treison" (*RP*, 2:239). The statute limits the definition of treason, and thus those offenses for which the crown could claim forfeiture, in several ways. For example, the new definition excludes several categories that might reasonably be thought to threaten the crown, such as the riding of armed parties for purposes of murder or robbery (*Stat.*, 320; *RP*, 2:239).

Puzzlingly, though, the statute *extends* the formal designation of treason to one category of violent homicides that does not involve the king at all:

> And in addition there is another kind of treason, that is to say when a servant kills his master, a woman kills her husband ["une femme qe tue son baron"], when a secular man or man in religious orders kills his prelate, to whom he owes faith and obedience ["a qi il doit foi & obedience"]. (*Stat.*, 320)

This second order of treason (which would come in the course of the fifteenth century to be known as "petty treason") involves deeds directed against masters, husbands, and prelates, a tier of persons thought to occupy positions of special responsibility. The last case, of prelates, includes a few words of explanation that reveal the logic behind the entire provision: one must not kill a person to whom faith and obedience are owed. When one does rebel against such ties, the concept of treason is invoked (though with the limitation that the properties of those found guilty are forfeit not to the king himself, but only to the immediate lord who holds them in fee).

The fact that the properties of those convicted are not forfeit to the king might seem to sustain Bellamy's argument for the conservative intent of the statute—but then why call these actions against lesser authorities "treasonous" at all?[3] Certainly felonious, but not self-evidently treasonous, these actions could have been clustered with those armed ridings and other acts excluded altogether from the terms of the statute, had the framers of the statute not had some other reason for mentioning them. What we actually encounter here is a deliberate extension of the concept of treason to a category of acts to which it was previously sporadically applied, with the apparent intent of lending its protective deterrence to a category of previously unprotected institutions. This category includes what I would call

---

[3] Bellamy finds this category itself to constitute a narrowing of such diffuse earlier instances of treason as a wife plotting but failing in the murder of her husband or a son killing his father (*Law of Treason*, 228). But I would argue in reply that nothing required the framers of the 1352 statute to apply the term or concept of treason to *any* cases not involving the king; the attribution of treason to crimes against master, husband, or prelate was plainly a purposeful act, to be understood in its own terms.

"intermediate" institutions—the guildmaster's workshop or merchant's salesroom, the husband's household or private chamber, the parish church or college or chantry or monastic precinct.

This extension recognizes the political character of these ostensibly non-political institutions, asserting that the master in his shop and the husband in his household and the priest in his parish participate analogically and symbolically in the regality of the king. This symbolic participation actually operates at several different levels. Most simply, if the master or husband or priest is understood to occupy a position "like" that of the king, then his position must be protected lest the king suffer analogical or derivative slights. More subtly, the heads of these intermediate institutions derive legitimacy from the analogy, and their own authority is bolstered by the right to cloak themselves in derivative and watered-down versions of royal protections. Of course, royal authority would hardly collaborate in too broad a dispersal of its intrinsic powers, were not some larger interest involved. Royal and other interests alike are ultimately served by the institution and protection of an accessible and influential model of hierarchy at a level close to the lived experience of most members of the middle strata.[4] Thus, the attempt to protect masters, husbands, and priests results not just from a sudden perception of similitude, or a sudden deference to localized interests, but from a more broadly couched defense of a cluster of sites vital to the reproduction of monarchic and patriarchal practices.

Even though the statute had been brewing before 1348–1349, its 1352 date places it at a moment when plague survivors at every social level experienced new opportunities to improve their social and economic situations by renegotiating the terms on which they offered services and skills. Protective extension of the treason umbrella to new categories of institutions may thus be associated with many other contemporary legislative and judicial moves to protect threatened hierarchies: the attempted regulation of peasant wages and obligations via the statutes of laborers; the proscrip-

---

[4] Flandrin, in fact, finds familial organization to be central in the production of early Christian ideas about God, kingship, and patriarchy in general: "The first Christians made use of the relationships of subordination to the father, to the husband and master (*dominus*) . . . to explain and win acceptance for the concept of absolute obedience to a unique God, envisaged as the universal Father and universal Lord (*Dominus*). . . . The authority of the father of the family and the authority of God not only legitimized one another: they served to legitimize all other authorities. Kings, lords, patrons and ecclesiastics have all represented themselves as fathers and the representatives of God" (119–20). See also Fraad, Resnick, and Wolff for a contemporary Marxist account of the household as crucial for production of patriarchy (though the essay's value is limited by its lack of specificity with respect to considerations of history, geography, and class; see the valuable observations of historian Stephanie Coontz, in the same volume). Louis Althusser is extremely acute in describing the household as a site of ideological state apparatuses, but he unaccountably dismisses the possibility that it played such a role in the Middle Ages (*Essays*, 24–25).

tion of urban apprentices' and journeymen's organizational efforts; the numerous attempts to hinder unattached or lightly attached men-at-arms and lesser gentry from joining retinues for short-term advantage; and the repeated gestures toward protection of status-demarcation in ornamental dress and other forms of aspiring consumption.

If the concept of treason was redeployed in the second half-century to protect husbands and others, from whom was this protection required? In the case of the household, the 1352 statute is perfectly clear: the *baron* or head of the household is potentially threatened by his *femme* or wife. The divide therefore falls not just between men of higher and lower status, but between a powerfully instated male and a less powerful female. In contrast with the workshop or the parish church, the household does not just produce hierarchy pure and simple but *gendered* hierarchy, and its tensions are gender-specific. Martha Howell has detailed the senses in which "the male-headed household was, after all, not only the consitutional, social, economic, and political unit of the urban community, it was also the foundation of male dominance" in our period.[5]

Although patriarchal domination of the household may never have been as complete in practice as in its varied imaginary productions, a good deal of evidence suggests that it reached its point of maximum consolidation in the years before 1349. Judith Bennett has shown that women in the period 1300–1348 enjoyed far more public opportunities and responsibilities as unmarried adolescents and as widows than as married women. Not that women were wholly devoid of resources, either as a result of small-scale production or of inheritance, but the definition of the domestic as a sphere of private endeavor tended to submerge the evidence of their toil (Harris, 151; Swanson, 39–40), and their husbands enjoyed legal control of their inherited properties.

By contrast, in the years after 1349, surviving women at every social level enjoyed opportunities to expand their independent economic power (see esp. Goldberg, 35). Even small economic successes could, in turn, affect the distribution of power within the household. Olivia Harris, speaking of the household in general and not just that of the Middle Ages, observes that

Shifts from household production for subsistence to household-based petty-commodity production, to an economy based on the sale of labour power,

[5] 20. Judith Bennett has shown that marriage was the primary engine of gender differentiation of the earlier fourteenth-century English countryside, with femaleness defined by the submissiveness of wives and maleness by the authority of husbands (6). See also Olivia Harris: "The domestic sphere is the site where gender subordination is produced and re-enacted" (137).

affect radically the structure of households, power relations within them, and
the resulting changes in the power to command the fruits of one's own labour.
(144)

And Howell, working with continental sources closer to the fourteenth
century, has shown how "a woman's responsibilities for economic production could lead her into market production and, as a result, could free her
from her husband's tutelage." Such women could, for example, attain the
status of *femme sole*, with its conferral of independent legal capacities (19–
20).

Developments of the later fourteenth century therefore posed a new
challenge to the household as a site for the production of gendered hierarchy. When coordinated with such contemporary challenges as that posed
by masterless journeymen and restless apprentices to the guild system, and
by underemployed ecclesiastics to parish organization, this challenge explains part of the pressure that led to an extension of the concept of treason
into domestic life. Caught between a breakdown of traditionally sanctioned relations of domination and subordination on the one hand, and a
revolution in rising female expectations on the other, husbands probably
felt they could use all the help they could get. The 1352 statute offers such
consolation as legal language and judicial process, shaped within an ideology of male domination, could afford.

But what has this macronarrative of economic emancipation to do with
the husband-killing *mulier*'s unruly erotic desires? Treasonous or not, she
seems a poor representative of the economic and personal struggles of her
half-century, and she would continue to seem so if the chronicler's narrative were all that we knew. But, fortunately, a further record exists. Treason
cases were heard before the king's bench, and the full record of her case
survives.[6] This record would be pertinent in any event, in providing a separate and material rational for the *mulier*'s domestic crime. Beyond any
details it adds to the chronicle narrative, however, it possesses significant
value simply *as* an alternative account. Moving between the details of the
trial and the chronicler's lurid rendition, we are afforded a privileged
glimpse of a largely effaced realm where ideology and textuality meet to
shape belief and direct human action. Neither the trial record nor the
chronicle account can be considered free of distortion. But the suppres-

[6] As *KB* 27/508, mem. 4. Valuable references permitting the connection of the Westminster
chronicler's account with the Wauton case are given by Hector, *West.*, 322–23. Note as well
that the Westminster chronicler's execution date of 17 April 1388 corresponds well with the
dates of the Wauton case; her final hearing prior to execution of judgment was the fortnight
after Easter or 12 April 1388. Her records (and presumably Elizabeth Wauton herself) were
summoned for the first day of Easter term—12 April—and burning at Bermondsey, near
Westminster, on 17 April accords well with this timetable.

sions and distortions that accompany the chroncler's revision illustrate tell-ingly the imaginary processes by which disturbing subject matter (in this case, women's economic assertion) was opened to restatement in exaggerated forms that invited revulsion and justified repressive control.

THE WAUTONS: PROPERTY AND TREASON

The case in question is that of Elizabeth Wauton, tried, convicted, and burned for the 24 June 1387 murder of her husband Andrew. Arrested and tried were Andrew Wauton's servants Robert Blake, *capellanus*, John Ball, and his wife Elizabeth. Their case was heard by justices Belknap and Charlton, and, according to the indictment included in the record and process of their trial:

> Robertus et Iohannes apud Henton' Daubeney insidiarunt . . . ad eundem Andream interficiendum, et ipsum ibidem felonice ac prodiciose interfecerunt, ac iidem Robertus et Iohannes diuersis vicibus per quindenam ante predictum diem lune in quadam semita vocata Godevynyepathe in quodam agro vocato Compesfeld' iacuerunt ad interficiendum dictum Andream, ac . . . ymaginauerunt interfecisse . . . et eos in quodam puteo apud Compesfeld' ymaginauerunt proiecisse, et quod sunt communes insideatores viarum ac depilatores agrorum ac viarum predictarum ac communes latrones ac proditiores populi domini regis ac dicti Andree, magistri sui, et de eo quod predicta Elizabetha ad interficiendum dictum Andream, virum suum, fuit concensiens et auxilians. (*KB*, 7:54–55)

> Robert and John . . . lay in hiding at [Andrew's manor of] Hinton Daubeney in order to kill him, and did kill him, feloniously and treasonably and the same Robert and John on various earlier occasions lay in wait at a footpath called Godwinspath in a field called Compsfield in order to kill him [and others] . . . and they planned to throw them into a well near Compsfield. They are common waylayers and despoilers in these fields and roads and common thieves and traitors to the king's people and to their master Andrew. Said Elizabeth gave consent and aid to the killing of Andrew, her husband.

Robert Blake and John Ball were charged with guilt of death and treason, "culpabilis de morte et prodiccione." Elizabeth Wauton was charged with consent and aid, "de concensu et auxilio."

The charge of aiding and consenting may be something of a surprise, considering her centrality in the chronicler's report. It would, of course, have been the proper charge if she encouraged the killing but did not take part (if, that is, she was not actually out there behind a tree with Robert and John). But it was also the customary charge. Women were usually reported to work with and through male accomplices, either by choice or because the male judicial system was unable to imagine them functioning in any other way.[7] Cases in which women enlisted male accomplices were, in fact, frequent enough to elicit a precedental decision: in 1360 the justices agreed that a woman plotting her husband's death with a servant should be found an accessory, but that nevertheless, as a participant in a treasonous crime, she should be burnt (Bellamy, *Law of Treason*, 228).

The outcome of the trial was forgone, though subject to delay. John Ball, mentioned no more, was presumably executed forthwith. Robert Blake, as *capellanus* or chaplain, pleaded benefit of clergy, thus postponing though not forstalling his fate.[8] Upon her conviction, Elizabeth Wauton

---

[7] See Hanawalt, "Female Felon," 124; *Crime*, 117; and Bynum, *Holy Feast*, 86). Wives are invariably indicted with accomplices in other extant cases of the later fourteenth century. In addition to reiterating the Wauton case, Mary Hamel cites a 1377 Yorkshire killing in which a chaplain and a merchant's wife were indicted (but not convicted) for feloniously slaying her husband and a 1379 Middlesex case in which a servant and wife were convicted (he drawn and hanged and she burnt) for slaying her cordwainer husband (134–35). In a London case circa 1390, a "goode man" was said to have been murdered in his bed by his wife—later burnt—assisted by no less than three men of his household—all later hanged ("Gregory's Chronicle," 93; see n. 13 below). Jail delivery rolls of II Richard 13–14 (1389–1391) contain three relevant cases, cited by Garay (101–2) and kindly transcribed at the Public Record Office by my colleague Sheila Lindenbaum. Agnes Milner with three servants (some, according to their names, members of her husband's family) feloniously and treacherously slew her husband in the heart of his domicile, as he was sitting in his chair by the fire in his own house ("sedebat per ignem in propria domo in vna Cathedra"); they were drawn and hanged and she was burnt (PRO JUST 3/177 mem. 27a). Juliana Danker was burnt for slaying her husband Thomas with the help and advice of others, wounding him in the stomach with a knife and breaking his neck with a club (PRO JUST 3/180, mem. 30a). Alice Pyrye was convicted of killing her husband John by night, with two accomplices, they hanged and she burnt (PRO JUST 3/180, mem. 30a). To these instances may be added a 1359 case mentioned by Bellamy in which a woman conspired with a servant to kill her husband (*Law of Treason*, 228), and a 1375 case in which Maud de Cauntelo was suspected of conspiring with servants in the death of her husband, a knight (*KB*, 6:174–75). Failure to mention the accomplices' names in the Danker case may, as Sheila Lindenbaum has observed to me, suggest that their presence was presumed rather than documented. I know of no instances in the second half of the fourteenth century in which a woman was reported to have killed her husband while acting alone, although Hamel mentions the 1400 case of Agnes Cran, who was burnt for killing her husband, unassisted, with an axe-blow to the skull while he was asleep in bed (134).

[8] Robert's clerical status is by no means unprecedented. He is called *capellanus*, or chaplain, and when he claims benefit of clergy he describes himself as *clericus* or clerk. He was, evidently, one of the growing number of later fourteenth-century clerics without fulltime ecclesiastical employment (see Gabel, 76–85). His actual capacity seems to have been a rather modest one, that of chaplain to the marginally gentle household of the Wautons, and his status would more likely have been that of subdeacon or deacon than fully ordained priest. In any event, he seems to have found considerable time to lurk in fields and byways and develop his reputation as a common waylayer. Such chaplains might have seemed particularly eligible for suspect involvements, like chauffeurs or gamekeepers in modern fiction, and a case of 1377 also links a wife and a chaplain in a husband-killing (*KB*, 7:5–7). Nevertheless, Robert's clerical

declared herself *pregnans*, and a panel of examining matrons upheld her claim. In consequence, her sentencing was postponed until the next jail delivery. She was sentenced five months later and executed seven months later, by burning at the stake, on or about 17 April. Asked prior to her death if she knew any reason or could say why judgment should not be performed against her, she said no:

> Quesitum est ab ea si quid pro se habeat vel dicere sciat quare execucio iudicii . . . iuxta consideracionem predictam prius redditi fieri non debeat, que dicit quod non. (56)

Given Elizabeth Wauton silent or silenced, we must return to the coram rege roll for evidence bearing on her actions. For, although the roll stops short of ascribing a "motive" for her deed, it does construe it within a material and ideological context that offers a good deal of insight into domestic restlessness and why it needed to be curbed. This context concerns the relation of fourteenth-century women to property, and it associates Elizabeth Wauton with the deprivations and frustrations of other women of her time. But let me approach it by way of the Wauton estate, Hinton Daubeney.

The manor had been held by the Daubeney family, from the king, since the time of Henry III.[9] It provided the income of half a knight's fee— twelve marks in 1387—enabling its proprieter to maintain himself in gentle estate, close to but not quite at the level of knighthood. Ellis, the last to bear the Daubeney name, had a single daughter, Elizabeth, in 1357. She did in fact marry a knight, one Gilbert Giffard. By the time of Ellis's death in 1383, however, Gilbert had died, and she had married Andrew Wauton, not a knight but a man with a reasonably high economic profile in his own right (*CCR* [1381–1385], 106). Elizabeth's position as heir secured by the fact that her second marriage had already produced a child (*CCR* [1381–

---

standing permitted him to refuse cooperation with the civil court, calling for a bishop's representative or ordinary to assert jurisdiction. A parson of Winchester did in fact appear, fortified with appropriate letters, to ask that Robert be handed over to him. If his hope was to avoid trial, he was, however, disappointed, for the civil judges followed the custom of the day by going ahead with the trial, in order to know in what capacity ("pro quali") Robert should be handed over. And he was finally handed over as a "clericus conuictus," under the burden of his assessed guilt. The sequence of actions in Robert's case follows exactly that cited by Gabel as a typical fourteenth-century pattern: a chaplain accused of murder identified himself as a clerk and called for his ordinary, who claimed him forthwith. "Before handing him over, however, the court ordered that the truth of the charge be investigated by a jury of the 'country' in order that it might be ascertained in what capacity (*pro quali*) the prisoner should be delivered. The jury returned a verdict of guilty of murder and the clerk was then delivered to his Ordinary as a *clericus convictus* to be transferred to the bishop's court for canonical trial" (32–33).

[9] Except as otherwise noted, this paragraph is based on *Calendar of Inquisitions*, vol. 15, no. 974, and *VH*, Hampshire, 96.

1385], 459), she and Andrew received livery of the manor at the time of Ellis's death. The close rolls note that "the king has taken the homage and fealty of the said Andrew, who has taken the said Elizabeth to wife" (*CCR* [1381–1385], 459).

This detail—that Andrew does homage for Elizabeth's inheritance— would not have fallen strangely on a fourteenth-century ear, for most women of the time possessed the right neither to own property, nor to enter into contracts, nor to write wills, nor to enjoy any control of goods they happened to inherit. Kay E. Lacey notes that married women or *femmes coverts* could not even buy goods without their husbands' consent (41), and that their hold on their own property was so tenuous that a husband sometimes bequeathed his wife her own clothes: "In the 1417 will of Walter Rede, he left his wife Emma £100 sterling as dower, utensils, and her clothes and ornaments" (40). We need hardly be surprised that "women who did hold land, through inheritance, gift, or purchase, en- countered many obstacles to their free control and use. . . . Any real prop- erties held by wives were administered by their husbands" (Bennett, 33; see also Lacey, 26–27).

By the jury's reasoning, the law of the land entitled Elizabeth Wauton to possess no chattels while her husband was living. After his death, the absence of a will, together with her crime, precluded any sort of inheri- tance:

> Iuratores dicunt quod non intendunt ipsam Elizabetham aliqua catalla tem- pore mortis predicti Andree, viri sui, per legem terre habuisse debere et cum hoc dicunt quod nulla catalla eidem Elizabethe post mortem predicti Andree. (55)

The one possible exception involved the manor, of which the jurors were obliged to admit that she was seised, or enjoyed possession, in her own right, "seisita est vt de iure suo proprio" (55). Even in this case, however, the jurors found her *status* or legal position to be unclear. Her possession was not unconditional—not in "fee simple"—in a way that permitted her to do with it as she wished, but was rather held by her conditionally—in "fee tail," or *feodum talliatum*—to be passed on to her rightful heir (see Simpson, 85–89). Part of the jurors' hesitation might have derived from tact, or fear. For, though the land was rightfully to be passed to Elizabeth's heir, and we know that she had one and would soon have another, the lord to whom the lands would otherwise revert was the king, who did in fact reclaim them, for later reassignment to members of his household (*VH*, 96). Elizabeth Wauton, in short, never enjoyed control of her own lands.

A few married women of the towns in the later fourteenth century were able to attain the status of *femme sole* in order to control wealth they actu- ally produced or to engage in trade (Lacey, 40–42), but this status was

virtually unknown in the countryside and would at any rate have been unthinkable for a gentlewoman not engaged in production or trade. Only one
status would have permitted Elizabeth Wauton a measure of control of her
land: the status of widowhood. For, in her case, Judith Bennett's description of the relation of women to property in the first half of the century
undoubtedly still applied:

> Wives, of course, could not independently control personal properties. . . .
> Widows, however, often enjoyed extensive control over extensive proper-
> ties. . . . A woman who independently acquired land (through purchase, gift,
> or inheritance) forfeited control of that land to her husband during her mar-
> riage, but regained full ownership when widowed. (163)

Suppose they had really managed to stuff Andrew down into that well.
Elizabeth, as a widow, would have once in her life enjoyed control of her
family lands. Subject only to the restrictions on inheritance accompanying
the status of "fee tail," she would have held the land as an effective life
tenant, enjoying control of her family estate. She would, for the first time,
have been able to possess her own chattels, to make necessary purchases,
to set her own priorities in the disbursement of her twelve marks annual
income.

I do not mean to suggest that control of her own property was the only
possible motive of Elizabeth Wauton's crime; to do so would clearly be to
overread the evidence of the trial record, by placing the entire burden of
explanation on the few elements of the case that are known in distinction
from the many that are not known. Nevertheless, I would connect her
property dilemma with a broadly relevant fourteenth-century state of affairs and argue that this state of affairs itself constitutes an articulation of
her situation. Feminist historians have partially raised the curtain of "the
domestic" to reveal the previously unrecognized extent of female production and trade in the later Middle Ages and the modestly successful efforts
of some women to emancipate themselves from the legal restrictions of
coverture.[10] Even though Elizabeth Wauton was an heiress and member of
a property-owning family that enjoyed gentle status and was situated at the
boundaries of knighthood (and was thus far removed from household

[10] Judith Bennett points out that the economic activities of women before 1348 "never
conferred upon them the basic privileges of males" (195), and she doubts that even the improved economic possiblities of the post-plague years led to significant amelioration (197–
98). A somewhat more optimistic reading, based on increased numbers of early fifteenth-
century York women admitted to the franchise and writing wills, is that of P.J.P. Goldberg
(esp. 35–36). My own argument is not, however, that later fourteenth-century women actually expanded their legal rights in any very dramatic way, but simply that their improved
economic expectations generated a *pressure* for expansion that may be read in the *counter-
pressure* of disenfranchising gestures like the 1352 statute on treason.

brewers, spinners, and other women of peasant or petty bourgeois status), her insecure relation to her own inherited estate may be analogized to the difficulties of female small producers in gaining access to wealth produced by their own efforts. In each case, we find powerful mechanisms rolled into place in order to prevent the woman's control of her own wealth. One such mechanism is the 1352 statute, with its expansion of the definition of treason to protect the claims of the *baron*. Whatever its immediate motive, her crime may be better understood against a larger backdrop of women's economic strivings and the household as the institution within which those strivings were most effectively controlled.

The Wauton case underscores the effectiveness of the household for purposes of social control. The main elements of this control have been usefully specified in Howell's discussion of women's work, in her description of a *sex-gender* system that specifies women's roles and dictates gender relations and an *economic system* that organizes the production of goods and services and sets a value on different kinds of work (5), and her distinction may be usefully applied here. The fourteenth-century system for control of property continued the medieval English practice of exposing everyone— male or female—to a degree of insecurity, denying absolute ownership in favor of a system of seisin or temporary interest which might be supplanted by an older title or superior claim. Within the sex-gender system, the wife's claims were further defined as different from, and self-evidently inferior to, those of her *baron* or lord in marriage (Simpson, 88–89). Thus, like any fourteenth-century property holder, she was liable to supplantation, and as a fourteenth-century woman her claims were virtually bound to be supplanted. Further, the economic and gender systems were joined and effectuated in common law, with its codification of the husband's superior claims to inherit and control property and the wife's absence of standing (Lacey, 26–27). Women were inserted into the law—just as Elizabeth Wauton is here inserted as one possessing "catalla . . . nulla . . . per legem terre"—only in order to evacuate their category, to create a void that a husband, son, or (ultimately, in this case) the king could fill.

For all its dedication to the "real," embodied in witnesses, oaths, and testimony, the trial record is something other than a trove of pure facts. It realizes its account of Elizabeth Wauton as a woman caught between a material or economic system designed to adjudicate the right to enjoy and inherit property and an imaginary or sex-gender system that denies women equal access or standing. Between these two systems, she is (if I may use a domestic metaphor) hung out there helpless as laundry to dry. Despite its apparent factuality and materiality, this record gives us a woman already partially captive to cultural and imaginary constraint.[11] The difference be-

---

[11] Although the sex-gender system can be written into law, it remains an essentially imagi-

tween the trial record and the Westminster chronicler's still less factually fettered account is that the trial record permits us to map at least a few of the material coordinates of Elizabeth's predicament, while the chronicler's reimagining of her crime comes very close to an unfettered illustration of the process by which gender is socially imagined.

GOSSIP AS SOCIAL CONTROL

Compared with the legal record and process, the Westminster chronicler's racy account may be considered a species of gossip. Perhaps he composed it directly from a record or firsthand report of the trial; Elizabeth Wauton's records as well as her person were summoned to the king's bench at Westminster, and the final judgment was made there. Or perhaps report of the trial reached him already partially processed by intermediaries, as gossip often does. Either way, his account fulfills one of the principal responsibilities of gossip, mediating—as Patricia Spacks has shown us good gossip must—between the particular and general, the individual and the social. As a written account, it is stabilized in ways that more oral and exploratory forms of gossip never are. It nevertheless performs that vital function of unifying an already intimate circle of hearers or readers in shared belief about appropriate and inappropriate behavior (see Spacks, 15, 21–22). Although gossip, and in fact scandal, it is *virtuous* scandal, in the sense that "scandal is . . . virtuous if its aims be to demonstrate some kind of social unity" (Gluckman, 314). In this case, the unifying factor is disapprobation,

---

native system, through which people explain their material reality to themselves. Thus, for all their dedication to the verifiable and the "real," these records give us imaginary women, conceived within the frames and suppositions employed by male writers to make positive or negative sense of female behavior. An a priori idea of women as schemers and unworthy daughters of Eve working through gullible male accomplices seems to underlie many of the household treason-narratives. Consider, for example, the remarkable case in which Maud, widow of William de Cauntelo, appealed Richard Gyse and Robert Cook of treasonously slaying their master (and cauterizing his wounds with boiling water, re-dressing him in clean garments with spurs and belt, and throwing his body in a distant field in order to avert suspicion). Like other women raising a hue (see Hanawalt, "Female Felon," 263), she then found herself under suspicion and indictment for complicity, forced to withdraw from the case and to sue the king for her own freedom (*KB*, 6:174–75). Just as the records suggest ingrained suspicions of women, so do they contain the opposite, idealizations of women as the most steadfast and self-effacing of mourners. When Richard Pope and William del Idle slew their master John Coventry, his wife Elena set a standard of spousal rectitude that is singled out for approving mention, promptly pursuing the fleeing murderers through four neighboring villages and beyond ("Elena ipsos recenter insecuta fuit de villa in villam vsque ad quatour villatas propinquiores et vlterius") in order to bring them to trial (*KB*, 6:154–56).

shared among the small circle of Benedictine monks and selected others who had access to the sole manuscript of the *Westminster Chronicle*.[12]

Such a readership would probably have had no difficulty in condemning Elizabeth Wauton's conduct as depicted in the trial record alone, but the chronicler is taking no chances. As part of this communicative and norm-setting project, he eradicates certain local and adventitious details in his characterizations, reinscribing them with a new set of heightened social resonances. Elizabeth, for example, simply becomes any *mulier*. But her social position at the lower borders of gentility is simultaneously pumped up to "generosa"—implying gentility at the least, and possibly even some aristocratic connection. Andrew is cast simply as a *vir* or husband, but his social position is subtly raised a notch too: he has not merely been away for a fortnight but has been overseas, "de transmarinis partibus," presumably on business of some import. Our clerical murderer has now been stripped of his male accomplice in order to sharpen his implied relation with Elizabeth, and he receives a small heightening too: no longer a part-time *capellanus* to a small household, he is elevated to the position of *presbiter*, or priest. The function of such generalization is, of course, to state the case in a form against which opinion can be fully mobilized, to sketch motivation so broadly that it can plead for no excuse in the name of indeterminacy or the cross-purposes of human action. And what of the motivation these characters are designed so transparently to signify?

Simply hearing of these personae—a socially prominent but lonely *mulier*, a husband or *vir* across the sea on business, an out-of-control priest or *presbiter insanus*—most modern readers know enough about the fourteenth-century horizon of narrative expectations to suppose that a sexual transgression will be involved. Many of these same materials are, as Frank Grady pointed out after hearing a paper based on this chapter, at large in Chaucer's *Miller's Tale*, in which domestic hierarchy is threatened by a sexual machination against husband John (out of town at Osenay) by a frisky wife and two co-conspirators including parish clerk Absolon (probably occupying a place in the ecclesiastical hierarchy roughly equivalent to that of Robert Blake, *capellanus*). I do not mean to suggest that the chronicler's account has been reconceived within the framework of the fabliau. With the exception of Chaucer's acts of affectionate homage the fabliau was no longer current in the later fourteenth century anyway. This narrative is very much in its own mode, a scandalized anecdote, moralizing in its tendencies, with more affinities to the *exemplum* than any other narrative form.

---

[12] John Taylor observes that "despite the undoubted importance of their work, neither at St Albans nor at Westminster did their chronicles circulate widely. The Monk of Westminster's chronicle survives only in a single manuscript" (74).

But this narrative *does* go to the same imaginative sources that once fostered the fabliau at its most rudimentary, replacing the primarily economic details in which the legal record is arrayed with an explanatory framework depending entirely on runaway sexual passions.

Now that passion prevails, and irrationality, and the whole set of unruly impulses and strivings that follow in passion's train, the entire motivational structure of the episode can be reconfigured. Whether because of actual features of the crime, or because of the dominant assumption that a woman could not possibily be more than an accomplice in a crime requiring initiative and physical courage, Blake and Ball are treated in the indictment as plotters and instigators, with Elizabeth ("concensiens et auxilians") relegated to the role of an abettor. Now suddenly propelled into an area of passionate agency, the *mulier* of the account becomes an even more disturbing exemplification of perverse female volition. No longer simply seduced (like Eve by the serpent) this already fallen daughter of Eve becomes seducer (like Eve in relation to Adam). It is now she who enlists the priest, already himself *insanus* by virtue of her sexual advances, by her persuasive words ("suasu dicte mulieris") to join her intrigue. This woman's monstrous passions now unleashed, the physical scene of the crime reconfigured around them. The location of the crime shifts from an outdoor ambuscade near a footpath in an open field to the symbolically charged confines of the nuptial bed. The legal record's indefiniteness about the circumstances of arrest (which it describes as occurring *alias*, at another time) gives way to a discovery of the amorous couple in the most transgressive of locations: in that same marriage bed ("in eodem lecto"), early in the morning, presumably in exhausted slumber as a result of the amours of the previous night. Our earlier narrative veered between circumstantial realism and economic background; aside from its telltale detail about the woman's burning, this one is reconfigured on almost exclusively sexual grounds, presenting its monastic readers with the disturbing spectacle of a woman propelled by her desires into an initiatory and insurrectionary role.

As in all good gossip, we are not simply given sexual information and innuendo but also a perspective on that information (Spacks, 21–22). The most apparent thing about the chronicler's perspective is its extreme antifeminism: women are creatures of appetite, rage out of control, seduce men, act out their antagonism and rebellion within the relations and at the sites of greatest trust, gratify themselves unrepentently (and slumber untroubled) at the very locations they have desecrated. This passage may, in other words, be associated with a persistent discourse of antifeminism with a long life and inner history of its own. Recall, for example, that the Wife of Bath's last husband, Jankyn the clerk, had a book founded on authorities like Theophrastus and Jerome, from which he used to read accounts of wicked wives aloud to her, and one of his allegations is that some have done just what the Westminster chronicler hints that his *mulier* might have done:

> . . . slayn hir housbondes in hir bed,
> And lete hir lecchour dighte hire al the nyght,
> Whan that the corps lay in the floor upright.

(D.766–68)

So powerful is this lurid fantasy that it is realized in a number of accounts, fervent in their narration but uncertain in their particular historicity.[13]

Seen in this enlarged perspective, the crime of the Westminster chronicler's *mulier* might seem so deliberately sensationalized, so conventionally atrocious, as to soar over its immediate circumstances and to invite reassimilation into a discourse unbound to any one moment in history. To be, in the currently fashionable term, "transhistorical." But history cannot finally be transcended, even in the case of those recurrent propositions and fantasies that seem, or aspire, to transcend it. Each realization of a recurrent pattern finally possesses its own, inescapable, history. Of any particular realization of a familiar narrative one is still obliged to ask: Why here? Why at this moment? Who sponsors it? Whom does it serve? What is its particular historicity?

The answer I have previously given—that the imaginative turbulence of the Westminster chronicler's account registers contemporary concern over women's modestly increased margin of economic freedom—remains unchanged, but the evidence of the Wauton case enables me to press it with more confidence. To be sure, the economic particulars of the trial record and the inquisition post mortem are absent in the chronicler's recital. But Elizabeth Wauton's economic predicament constitutes an absent cause that is neatly excised from the chronicler's narrative but still registered in the intensity with which it perturbs his imaginary recreation. In other words, her and other women's economic threat is restated, with the threat reposed in sexual terms.

This reposing of economic issues in sexual terms is a familiar strategy of

---

[13] A story very much like Elizabeth Wauton's, for example, resurfaces in a fifteenth-century London chronicle in a form that may be true, that may be wholly imaginary, or that may even be a recasting of our 1387 event, stripped of all its localizing details. This account involves the 1390 killing by his wife and servants of a "goode man at the sygne at the Cocke in Chepe at the Lytyll Condyte . . . mortheryd in hys bedde be nyght" by his wife and servants. In this case, the chronicler arrays his narrative with details about the particular dwelling in which the crime occurred but cannot produce the names of any participants ("Gregory's Chronicle," 93). These disturbing details—the "goode man," the insurrectionary spouse, the enlistment of servants, the violation of the marriage bed—seem to be generated from within a whole culture's project of female subordination and its accompanying guilt and not to belong to any one historical moment or locale.

late medieval and early modern urban literature, which, as Howell has suggested,

> seems . . . to express unusual hostility toward aggressive women, women whose aggressiveness in some measure attends their positions in market production, and it seems to equate such aggressiveness with sexual aggressiveness, even sexual misconduct. (182–83)

Misconduct indeed, up to and including sexually motivated husband-killing! Elizabeth Wauton had no position in market production, but she was nevertheless a woman who had title to wealth and position she could not control, and in this she had something in common with her more productive sisters. Like her distant cousins in the fabliaux, she is held up to mockery, her motivations recorded as sex-driven, out of control, beneath reason. For hers is a threat that needed defusing, a deep disturbance of patriarchy that required redress by a narratively refashioned community of disapproval.

But if women's economic situations do stand in the relation of an absent or erased cause of unease, one mark of their erasure remains. Whether we think specifically of Elizabeth Wauton's inability as an heiress to enjoy her paternal estate of Hinton Daubeney or think more generally of the inability of "covered" women in trade or small production to enjoy the fruits of their labor, the critical issue remains one of property and its control. So, too, does the sex crime of the chronicler's *mulier* revolve around issues of property and control, with her own body offered as a powerful and irreducible figure for her property, and with her crime consisting in seizing the right to bestow that property according to her desires. In this sense, I would suggest that the chronicler's narrative of sexual aggressiveness is something other than an arbitrary figment or outer husk to be discarded in order to reach the real economic foundations of Elizabeth Wauton's act. For the chronicler's sex crime, while invented, possesses its own quantity of historical truth, in its uneasy perception that women's anger derives from issues of property and control. A woman's claim to enjoy her property at the expense of her *baron* is a frightening thing, whether the property in question is topographical or physiological. The legal process is, in one sense, the "source" of the chronicler's account, either directly or through intermediate versions. But, in another and more pertinent sense, each of these texts is produced within a larger, shared environment—an environment that registers the extent to which, and the form in which, women were found threatening at the end of the fourteenth century.[14]

[14] Timely advice from my colleague Linda Charnes aided me in shaping this discussion of women's bodies as figure for property and women's control of their own bodies as a form of property right. Amplifying this same point with regard to medieval practices of seisin, Kay Harris of the University of Texas has pointed out to me in correspondence that "since the

The actual frequency of spouse-murder in the fourteenth century is difficult to determine. Pursuing a variety of sources, I have been able to identify only one case in the first half-century and eight or nine (depending on whether the case mentioned in "Gregory's Chronicle" repeats one from the 1389–1391 Gaol Delivery Rolls) in the second half-century.[15] Yet the occurrence of four or five recorded cases in the four years between 1387 and 1391 would seem to argue for recurrence. Whether rare or relatively common, however, these crimes appear to have possessed an enormous symbolic importance. More than just isolated acts, these crimes threatened hierarchy and, in threatening hierarchy, threatened social order. This is why Elizabeth Wauton is condemned in the legal arena, in that wild mix of devotion to pure fact and to culturally created fancy known as the common law. This is also why the anonymous *mulier* is haled out and condemned in another tribunal in which norms are no less seriously set, the Westminster chronicler's rumor mill. The chronicler takes a "low" road to a "high" purpose, and the burning of his *mulier* reaffirms his vision of the social system as a gendered hierarchy of male property-owners, a hierarchy ratified by custom and sustained by law.

CHAUCER'S TREASONOUS WYF

Moving from Elizabeth Wauton's trial record to the chronicler's scandalous relation, we move from a woman placed in a particular economic situation to a woman driven by lascivious desires. Interestingly, the movement from Chaucer's Wife of Bath as portrayed in the General Prologue to her self-portrayal in the prologue to her own tale traces a very similar trajectory, but with a telling difference: Chaucer fuses the categories of economic and sexual assertiveness into a single epitome of contemporary male dread.

We are told early in the General Prologue that Alice of Bath is a cloth-

---

laws regulating seisin were also extended to such things as conjugal relations, the chronicler's anti-feminist slant on Elizabeth's trial makes sense in terms of property law. As a matter of seisin, the conjugal relation was treated as a piece of land. With such an interpretation, the husband would, so to speak, hold the marriage in his possession. To disturb the conjugal relationship could be seen as a challenge to or a trespass of the husband's seisin."

[15] Pike records a lurid case from the first half-century, in which the wife of a baker strangled him in his bed and disposed of the body in the ovens, although the formal charge and the woman's penalty are omitted (1:256). For the second half-century may be added the Wauton case, and the eight (or nine) additional cases detailed in n. 7, above. I am reluctant to generalize from these few instances, although one might reasonably conclude that the statute did anticipate (as well as facilitate) an increased number of occurrences as we move from the first half of the century, when Bellamy himself notes a "small" number of cases brought (*Law of Treason*, 226), to the second.

maker: a vocation at once deeply traditional in its associations with the woman's task of spinning and very much of the moment in its association with a British cloth trade involving independent women jobbers in the second half of the fourteenth century. As to the Wife of Bath's precise responsibilities as a cloth-maker, we are not given enough information to judge. The cloth-making process was a complicated one, and a Bruges manual of the end of the fourteenth century assigns three of its elements (combing, spinning, and knotting) to women and five (beating, weaving, fulling, shearing, and dyeing) to men (van Uytven, 175); Alice might possibly have involved herself in one of these lesser, feminized functions. (Read against this background, Chaucer's comparison of her skills to those of the male weavers of Ypres and Ghent [I.447–48] is even more likely to be, as J. M. Manly thought [229], an exaggerated jest.) On the other hand, the whole process of cloth manufacture was diversifying in later fourteenth-century England, with a correponding increase in possibilities for entrepreneurship.[16] Alice's vocation may in fact be, as Mary Carruthers suggests, that of "capitalist clothier," on a substantial and highly lucrative scale (210).

Nevertheless, unlike the massed categories of women in the tax rolls who simply constitute a mixed estate all their own, Alice of Bath is assigned a vocation.[17] Consequently, her widely recognized assertiveness is given a material basis in the exercise of a stipulated, income-producing activity. But, her vocation once mentioned, it is then in effect withdrawn and never mentioned again.[18]

The fact that the Wife's vocation is ignored once introduced does not render it unimportant. Her portrait in the General Prologue may well have been written after the prologue to her tale, and we have no reason to believe Chaucer's reference to her cloth-making anything but purposeful. The point is simply that, as with Elizabeth Wauton, her possible economic independence is briefly asserted and then extensively reworked in sexual terms. Alice's sexual energies are, of course, epic in scope:

> I ne loved nevere by no discrecioun,
> But evere folwede myn appetit,

[16] Entrepreneurial possibilities for women in the cloth trade are described by E. Lipson, 68–73.

[17] Jill Mann argues, citing *Canterbury Tales*, III.401–2, that the Wife's vocation of weaver amplifies her membership in the largest of estates, the "estate of women" (121–22). I would, however, additionally propose that her cloth-making functions importantly if briefly to establish her relation to a general, later fourteenth-century economic tendency, submerged in her prologue only to be restated in primarily sexual terms.

[18] We never, as Beryl Rowland points out, see her practice any aspect of her vocation; on the contrary, she seems noteworthy in her secure possession of an enormous amount of leisure time ("Chaucer's Working Wyf," 137–41).

> Al were he short, or long, or blak, or whit;
> I took no kep, so that he liked me,
> How poore he was, ne eek of what degree. (D.622–26)

But, for all their apparent indirection, they are rarely left unattached to economic endeavor; specifically, the endeavor of inveigling gifts and inheritances from her numerous husbands. This virtuosity is quickly established. In usual terms of inheritance she would be entitled to a third of her husbands' estates in any event, and—her husbands evidently being childless—she seems actually to have gained reversion of "al hir lond."[19] For all the apparent generosity with which she bestows her sexuality outside marriage, she is quite clear about the fact that within the contested ground of her first three marriages her sexual favors are strictly for sale:

> I wolde no lenger in the bed abyde,
> If that I felte his arm over my syde,
> Til he had maad his raunson unto me.
>
> (D.409–11)

The philosophy that supports her sexual economy in marriage is external and explicit: "Wynne whoso may, for al is for to selle" (D. 414). And, even in the speech of brave fortitute in which she determines to persevere in spite of time's ravages, her perseverance is finally as much mercantile as sexual: "The flour is goon; ther is namoore to telle; / The bren, as I best kan, now moste I selle" (D.477–78). In fact, her downfall with her fifth husband is a matter of economics, of pricing her goods too cheaply and thus allowing him to hold them in little regard. She observes that "Greet prees at market maketh deere ware, / And to greet cheep is holde at litel prys" (D.522–23). Misjudgment, and the declining value of her own stock, have rendered this skilled sexual entrepreneur temporarily vulnerable in a struggle that she is conducting by every available means.

Alice's overt "sexual economics" are, of course, central to her characterization and have been discussed more searchingly and with greater insight than I can muster in this brief excursus.[20] The point is that, in linking her

---

[19] D.211. Under normal circumstances, the Wife of Bath would have received one-third of a deceased husband's estate, and she was eligible to receive more, both because of the absence of competition by an heir and because a husband might elect to grant sums to her out of the last third normally reserved for charity (Lacey, 34–35). That the extent of her ultimate inheritance was a matter of negotiation is suggested by her ongoing arguments for common property and access to her husbands' chests (D.308–10). That her husbands made such voluntary concessions is suggested by the fact that she later gives Jankyn "al the lond and fee / That evere was me yeven therbifoore" (D.630–31).

[20] The phrase "sexual economics" is itself derived from Sheila Delany's ground-breaking "Sexual Economics, Chaucer's Wife of Bath, and *The Book of Margery Kempe*." Of Alice's tactics, Delany proposes that we "recognize the degree to which such internalization of capitalist

sexual strivings with economic and ultimately political strivings, Chaucer has made explicit and brought to the textual foreground a maneuver that usually remains implicit and textually concealed. Those partriarchally inclined commentators who employ sexual assertiveness as a restatement of women's emancipatory strivings have found a representational way to mock those strivings without alluding to their origins and hence acknowledging their possible legitimacy. But Chaucer's Alice is rather obviously conducting a struggle for dominion in marriage, with sexuality only as an instrument of struggle and with dominion ultimately figured in terms of property, the most tangible of scales. Her mistake with Jankyn is that of yielding her accumulated "lond and fee" (D.630), and her victory is registered in his concession, if not of ownership, at least of "governance of hous and lond" (D.814). Throughout the prologue, though, the struggle has raged, with a clear understanding that this is a zero-sum game and that one must bow to the other: "Oon of us two moste bowen," she asserts to her first three husbands (D.440), and ultimate governance under her law is her aim (D.219). Alice is striving to overturn male domination in marriage, with the household the battleground, with sexuality the weapon, and with control of property the prize by which success is to be reckoned. She is, in other words, a treasonous wife.[21]

Alice's attitudes and behavior simply teem with insurrectionary implications, and, far from removing her from the fray, her chosen arena of the domestic places her at its charged contemporary center. In her character, Chaucer raises to discursive knowledge what he and all his audience already knew practically, and what the framers of the 1352 statute knew as well: that the household models the state, that the *baron* of the household occupies a position analogous to that of the king on his throne, and that, if husband-killing is a form of regicide, extreme husband-abuse must be rebellious at the very least. Alice's quest for dominion in marriage thus becomes something other than a quest for personal fulfillment and bears the historical marks of more general female strivings.[22]

---

method is a defensive strategy against the special oppression of women in a society whose sex and marriage mores were thoroughly inhumane" (105). And which, I would add, were important agents of social and political, as well as economic, control, focused and implemented within the institution of the household. On the Wife's economic rebellion, see Alfred David, 143–44. See also Mark Amsler's ambitious extension of the terrain of Alice's rebellion to embrace property, sexuality, *and* textuality, in "The Wife of Bath and Women's Power," esp. 78.

[21] I do not, I hasten to add, mean to subscribe to the hyperextended and utterly unwarranted reading that would indict Alice as a literal husband-killer and plotter with male accomplice Jankyn to eliminate number four (Rowland, "Timely Death," 273–282). But I do mean to suggest that she is treasonous through and through, that the household as a protected site for the production of legally sponsored images of male dominion is precisely the object of her unceasing attack.

[22] This is yet one more sense in which, as Mary Carruthers has so well shown, Alice is not

I thus draw the opposite conclusion from that of Lee Patterson, who finds Chaucer's creation of the Wife of Bath "politically timid," in its deflection of a class-determined opposition to seigneurial and mercantile dominance into the more neutral "claims of a socially undetermined subjectivity" (466). Patterson finds that the portrayal of the Wife represents Chaucer's retreat into a privileged category of "subjectivity per se," and that the Wife herself is "the free-floating individual whose needs and satisfactions stand outside any social structure"(466). The Wife is therefore "the transhistorical being that criticism has traditionally taken Chaucer himself to be" (466), and her "independent selfhood" and "marital happiness" can be comfortably accommodated within "the traditional order" (483–84). I would argue in reply that the fourteenth-century household is extensively identified as a critical site of struggle within which the assumptions of hierarchy and the privileges of patriarchy were subjected to sore trials, and that struggle within the household is not necessarily less historical than struggle in the streets or the fulling-mill.[23]

Even the Wife's unruly imagination is, in a sense, presented to us as socially constructed, in its deployment of the current imagery of domestic struggle. Rosemarie McGerr has, for example, drawn my attention to the content of the inventions with which Alice seeks to manipulate Jankyn, such as her dream—"He wolde han slayn me as I lay upright, / And al my bed was ful of verray blood; / But . . . blood bitokeneth gold" (III.578–81)—and her improvised reproach to his blow—" 'And for my land thus hastow mordred me?' " (III.801). In these fabrications Alice reconfigures motives of property and power that underpin marital relations: violence and mayhem as figures for insurrectionary impulses, the marriage bed as a place where relations of domination and subordination are both evoked and transgressed, and the vulnerability of women's modest economic gains

---

just presented as a unique sensibility, but as a character acting "within the context of her class and station" (211). I differ with Mary Carruthers in just one respect. Drawing largely on fifteenth-century examples, she sees women of this class as having already achieved effective control of their own property; I am more inclined to see such matters as objects of aspiration, barely conceivable in the later fourteenth century, occasionally realized in the first three quarters of the fifteenth century, and receding thereafter.

[23] An argument with close affinities to Patterson's is that of Louise Fradenburg, in "The Wife of Bath's Passing Fancy." She, too, argues for a shift from the General Prologue, in which the Wife is a "productive participant" in the world of work, to the prologue, in which her desire is confined to the sphere of "private" relations, to the tale, in which desire is expressed as pure fantasy. Yet she also notes a general countertendency, in which the *Canterbury Tales* as a whole embraces a "resistance to individual fantasy." This resistance, as she characterizes it, may be found in the broad, moralizing categories of the Parson and others of his ilk. It may, as I argue here, likewise be found in those respects in which private experience is presented as consequence and epitome of a general historical tendency. Chaucer's "resistance to individual fantasy" is thus expressed within his accounts of fantasy itself, as when he associates the Wife's insurrectionary domestic desires with larger social currents very specific to the later fourteenth century.

to male counterinsurgency. In other words, her imagination, far from being individual or private, is highly public, furnished with the same sorts of lurid fictions that agitate the Westminster chronicler. And much of the excitement of these fictions is precisely their status as "fictions of truth"— as epitomizations of tensions current within the later fourteenth-century English household.

Scourge of her old husbands, Alice of Bath is less a dreamer in search of personal fulfillment than an antagonist in a struggle that involved other fourteenth-century women across the middle strata of society who opposed male domination and who sought control of their own land and property. She is, to be sure, an extreme statement of the case, and elements of her struggle are expressed as a dangerous and unruly sexuality that exposes her to opprobrium or ridicule. But, precisely *because* her arena of struggle is the household, she remains a fully historical embodiment of resistance to masculine control.

Chapter 7

THE TEXTUAL VICISSITUDES OF
USK'S "APPEAL"

THOMAS USK had a remarkable and touching faith in the power of the written word to reorganize social reality. At critical junctures of his life, he repeatedly created texts that asserted his personal control over vagrant and uncertain circumstances. Working within existing genres, he not only cast himself as the subject of their discourse, but as an availing subject, a person capable of decisive actions and principled choices.

His most ambitious effort at textual self-assertion was, of course, the *Testament of Love* (1385–1387), in which he emphasizes his loyalty to the Brembre cause and his readiness for continued service (Strohm, "Politics and Poetics," 97–106). But he had previously attempted to create a role for himself by textual means, on the occasion of his notorious switch of allegiance from the Northampton to the Brembre factions. This switch occurred in August 1384 when, under arrest in the custody of Mayor Brembre in London, he agreed to testify against former associate John Northampton before king and council at Reading. Shortly before the 18 August meeting at Reading, he gave testimony to London coroner John Charney—not in the usual form of an oral deposition but in the extraordinary form of a personal accusation, or *appellum*, written with his own hand.[1] Drawing upon varied legal and expository traditions, this remarkable English document instates Usk as a central—in fact, indispensable—

---

[1] Northampton having been in custody since late winter, Usk's arrest is said by the Westminster chronicler to have occurred on 20 July 1384 (90). In any event, letters patent for the arrest of Usk and others to be brought "to London, to be there imprisoned at the disposal of the mayor" are dated 6 August 1384 (*CPR* [1381–1385], 500). The chronicler says that Usk was originally imprisoned, and that then, seeing no alternative, he switched sides, whereupon he was released from prison and lodged in the mayor's own house: "liberatusque de carcere in domo majoris manebat" (90). There, according to the chronicler, he prepared his "Appeal," reciting Northampton's crimes in various articles, appealing him, and then setting the whole in writing: "contra J. Northampton' multa enormia et sinistra in diversis articulis recitavit et eum super hujusmodi appellavit ac in scriptis redegit" (90; see also *Testament*, 30). Whatever the precise sequence of events, Usk evidently appeared before king and council on 18 August; the chronicler says that there he proclaimed ("publicavit") these articles and formally appealed ("appellavit") Northampton upon them (92), and an order dated 20 August notes that Usk, having appeared at Reading, should now be returned to Brembre's custody (*CCR* [1381–1385], 476).

actor in an important and highly conspicuous legal process. It was, more-over, briefly and dazzlingly successful, temporarily propelling him into the visible role of chief accuser of a man whom Richard II and Mayor Brembre were determined to destroy.

Although a textually created identity can (and in this case did) propel its subject to prominence on a real stage, it remains vulnerable to the vicissi-tudes of textuality itself—to revision, resistant reading, capricious treat-ment by those upon whose encouragement it depends, or loss of place to an alternative textual tradition or generic rival. Tracing the history of Usk's text, we trace its author's history too. His text enjoyed momentary sway and then, failing to gain institutional support, was revised and dropped from view. Usk wielded his text creatively, transformatively; but texts nev-ertheless stand in contingent relation to political institutions, and that con-tingency finally limits their transformative power.

The Genre of Usk's "Appeal"

Once Usk had agreed to appeal Northampton and his immediate followers of conspiracy to seize the city, legal tradition obliged him to appear before city coroner John Charney.[2] Charney's duties would normally have in-cluded swearing Usk (as he evidently did) and taking his verbatim deposi-tion (which he surprisingly did not). The novelty of Charney's failure to take a verbatim deposition was marked, since the London coroner's central duty was to hear and record confessions and accusations or appeals with-out variation of form or detail (Hunnisett, *Medieval Coroner*, 73; Kellaway, 80, 85). Nevertheless, rather than *dictating* his text, Usk *supplied* it— "knowleched thes wordes & wrote hem with myn owne [honde]" (Cham-bers and Daunt, 22). This departure, in turn, requires several different sorts of explanation, touching on such matters as how Usk gained his re-markable authorial competence in the first place, how he gained a general or "generic" awareness of the sort of document he set about to produce, and how he adapted this document to serve his own urgent needs.

---

[2] Although Charney had recently resumed office after an absence and was about to request another leave on the basis of infirmity, he was apparently able to exercise his duties between February 1383 and November 1384 (*CCR* [1381–1385], 255, 506). The heading of Usk's document, oddly omitted by Chambers and Daunt in their edition, is "Appell[um] . . . Vsk f[a]c[tu]m coram Joh[ann]e Charn[eye] . . . London' " (PRO E163/5/28, no. 9). Chambers and Daunt transcribe the damaged citation in the body of the "Appeal" as "in the presence of John . . . co . . . of london' " and note that a likely reading is "John Charney coronatore" (22). The external details of Charney's coronership are summarized in Kellaway, 90. Char-ney's title was technically that of deputy coroner, the actual coronership belonging to the king's butler, but deputy coroners of London were normally known simply as *coronator* (Kel-laway, 78).

Son of a hurer or capmaker,[3] Usk might ordinarily have had some rudimentary education at St. Paul's or Greyfriars and possessed himself of the kind of "pragmatic" literacy that M. B. Parkes describes as common among freemen and citizens of London engaged in commerce (557–59). In any event, his command of written Latin, French, and English was to be extended in his practice as an "escryveyn de court lettre," or practitioner of the scrivener's trade.[4] In fact, his first significant step into the swirl of London factional politics depended on his trade: Usk was originally hired by Northampton and his group in the summer or fall of 1383 to serve as their secretary, attending meetings at the tavern of John Willyngham in the Bowe "to write thair billes" (23). Of course, Usk promptly showed himself ready for more responsible employment, first for some six months as a deputy with increasing responsibility to the Northampton faction, and later as undersheriff of Middlesex after his switch to the Brembre party. We might say that, once through the door in 1383, he never looked back. Yet the skills he had gained as a scrivener, including the fundamental skill of producing finished texts in his "owne honde," were not to desert him.

Another of Usk's vocational areas shows him building on the basics he learned as a scrivener, and particularly his knowledge of legal formalities. The scrivener's trade demanded an acquaintence with "testamentz, chartres, et toutz autres choses touchantz la dite mystier" (LBG, fol. cccvii), and Usk evidently put this knowledge to work in a sideline career as an attorney. A case of 1376 has him as the attorney of record, in the prosecution of a plea of trespass, winning for his client John Bere less than the £200 he had sought in compensation for an assault on Bere in his Milk Street home, but gaining a successful verdict and an award of £23.[5] Finally, a "shadow career" is evoked by several references to Usk as *clericus* or clerk. He is so identified in the Plea and Memoranda Rolls (2:204), and also in Malvern's continuation of Higden's *Polychronicon* (see Chambers and Daunt, 237). Despite evidence of considerable familiarity with the liturgy in his last hours (*West.*, 314), Usk is unlikely to have been in clerical

---

[3] As established by Caroline Barron, with reference to Hustings Rolls 91/186, 187; 103/38, 39, 279. See also Ramona Bressie, 517.

[4] Usk is described as *skriveyn* in the coram rege roll that represents the ultimate adaption of his "Appeal," and also in CCR (1381–1385, 476). His initial employment with the Northampton faction was, as he tells us, "to write thair billes" ("Appeal," 23).

[5] *Pleas*, 2:221. Bere's subsequent political history offers an interesting contrast. Bere is cited in the same coram rege roll that includes the latest Latin version of Usk's testimony—but as a singularly obstinate Northampton partisan. He is cited, among other things, for claiming that Northampton's 1384 imprisonment was as unjust as the murder of St. Thomas of Canterbury, and he intended to maintain this view to the death: "hoc advocare volebat et manutenere usque ad mortem" (Powell and Trevelyan, 35; see also *Pleas*, 59). He was, in other words, to prove as steadfast as his advocate Usk was to prove mercurial.

orders as such, yet the term *clericus* may be taken as a further compliment to the degree of literacy he had attained.

Those legal forms and documents familiar to Usk as scribe and attorney provided the matrix within which he composed his "Appeal." This is not to suggest that his "Appeal" was simply executed within existing models or according to legal formularies, for to do so would vastly underrate its originality, reflected especially in its composition in English and in its cross-generic mix. Yet it is clearly fabricated within an environment of pre-existing legal utterance, even as it draws upon different components in extraordinarily supple ways. It is, in various respects, a simple confession of an apprehended felon, a piece of testimony taken from an informed witness as a preliminary to a process of jury inquisition, and an appeal—or accusation—of treason by a concerned citizen. Even in this final aspect, it draws upon several subvarieties of appeal, including the formal appeal of treason by a past confederate.

Each of these overlapping kinds or "genres" of legal document bore its own formal expectations, as well as its own prescriptions for the role and conduct of its speaking subject. Usk's "Appeal" possesses elements of a confession and plea for mercy, though its speaker is for the most part anything but abject, suggesting constantly that his perceptions and analyses have a great deal of value in their own right. It has the descriptive detail of a disinterested testimony taken for presentation to an inquest, but it continually reminds us that its speaker was himself an aider and abettor. It contains elements of a public-spirited and even rather self-righteous accusation or appeal of treason by a citizen concerned for the good of the realm. Some features of such an appeal include its conventional division into separate articles (each prefaced by "also," the English equivalent of the customary item); its reiteration of Usk's personal role as appellant (each item ending with a variant of "her-of I appele John Norhampton"); and its iteration of the time, place, and circumstances of the Northampton group's actions ("the night to-for the day of the eleccion of the mair"). Yet, for all the assurance with which he inhabits the role of a public-spirited citizen, Usk would have been legally hampered in that role by the fact that he was himself a conspirator and thus technically unfit to testify on a matter of treason.[6] In addition to its participation in these varied legal genres, Usk's testimony reveals his awareness of the structures and precedents of the special category of appeal that recognizes the complicity of the speaker in the misconduct he exposes but that converts complicity into a source of authority if not a virtue in its own right: the form of the approver's appeal.

---

[6] Bracton emphasizes the responsibility of anyone ("quilibet de populo") to offer an accusation of lese-majesty or treason, though he limits the accusation-rights of those who have personally conspired in the crime (2:334–35).

The approver's appeal originated in the twelfth century, when crimes were normally brought to trial by personal appeal and the system of jury inquest and presentment was not yet in full effect. Its virtue was that, felonies and treasons being crimes against the king, a confessed felon might be elevated to the position of an officer of justice in a desperate—and rarely successful—attempt to save his own life (Hamil, 239; Pike, 286–89; Rörkasten, 14–22). The appeal proceeded, according to Hamil, by these steps:

> A person who wished to turn approver had first . . . to confess the crimes for which he was indicted, and make his appeals against his accomplices, whom he bound himself to convict. The court assigned him a coroner to take his confession and appeals, and requested a writ of approvement from the king. The approver was then delivered to the custody of the keeper of the king's prison. (240)

The appeal dictated by the approver to the coroner was expected to include a high degree of specificity, with the approver (both in his dictated appeal and in oral testimony upon his later appearance in court) describing a particular event and all its circumstances without any variation or alteration ("oportebit probatorem certam rem exprimere, et omnes circumstantias sine variatione et mutatione alique"). Approvers' appeals often embraced several persons found confederate on a particular occasion ("sic poterit plures appellare eodem die de societate"). Somewhat anachronistically, and rarely, the fourteenth-century approver might be expected to defend his charges in a duel, offering the defendent recourse to "proof by body" ("per corpus suum").[7]

Several of these elements, including the approver's confession of personal involvement, his specificity with respect to time and place, and his inclusion of several persons in his charge of confederacy, may be illustrated by this extract from a late thirteenth-century coroner's roll:

> Willelmus de Insula . . . cognovit se esse latronem et se fuisse ad quamdam roberiam factam super Walterum de Codestone in parochia de Weckensted de Lune prox' ante festum Sancti Edmundi Regis prox' preteritum ut de pannis lineis et laneis, equis, jocalibus et aliis bonis et catallis unde pro parte sua j. marcam, etc. Et devenit probator et appellat Thomam de Alderbecke, Alexandrum filium Alani Matfrey, Ricardum le Bonde et quemdam Petit Jak' conversantem apud Edelbrigge in comitatu Kancie de societate et de roberia ad domum.

> William de Lisle . . . confessed that he was a thief, and that he took part in robbing Walter of Codeston in the parish of Wheathampstead on Monday

---

[7] All Bracton, 2:431. Convenient protocols of the form to be followed in an appeal by an approver or "fiz le Roy" are given in the late thirteenth-century *Placita Corone*, esp. 20–21.

next before the feast of St. Edmund the King last past, namely, of linen and woollen cloths, horses, jewels, and other goods and chattels whereof he received one mark as his share, etc. And he turns approver, and appeals Thomas of Alderbeck, Alexander son of Alan Matfrey, Richard Bond, and a certain Little Jack, who lives at Edenbridge in Kent, of confederacy in the robbery of the house. (*Select Coroners' Rolls*, trans. Gross, 131)

This is the coroner's transcription, prior to the trial itself; the trial presumably ended either with the defendant seeking the judgment of the county or challenging William de Lisle to prove his accusation by duel.

I do not mean to suggest that Usk's "Appeal" possesses the technical standing of an "approver's appeal." Even this brief characterization reveals that it lacks several elements essential to approvership. Although held in custody, Usk seems not to have been formally charged, either with felony or treason. He seems never formally to have become a king's approver, or "fiz le Roy," and no writ appears to have been issued to any such effect. Nevertheless, in his drafting process and in his appearance before the king and his council at Reading, Usk appears to have constituted himself not only within the general understanding of appellancy, but within some of the more particular expectations accompanying approvership.

This reliance on approvership may be seen in the extent to which Usk goes out of his way to acknowledge, rather than to deny or ignore, certain elements of his own complicity. An approver's appeal normally follows upon a confession of felony, and Usk registers this understanding by amalgamating his appeal with a hedged acknowledgement of responsibility. Although careful to attest only to a marginal role for himself ("atte some tymes wer' ther' more pryuier than I" [24]), he nevertheless repeatedly places himself near the center of events ("than sente he Richard Norbury, Robert Rysby, & me, Thomas Vsk, to the Neyte, to the duk of lancastre" [28]), and he does not refrain from a confession of general responsibility ("to which euel menyng I wa a ful helpere & promotour in al that euer I myght & koude" [29–30]). These admissions naturally serve to make Usk a more credible witness but also to establish the standing of former participant required for the approver's role. Also, as when William de Lisle accuses Little Jack and the rest, Usk recognizes the approver's common responsibility to convict more than one felon, and to achieve the conviction by demonstrating the presence of a *societas* or illicit conspiracy. Northampton and More and Northbury and Essex operate "be confederacie, congregacioun, & couyne" (29), and Usk's intent is to bring an entire band to justice.

Cast in the framework of an appeal, and the more particular framework of an approver's appeal, Usk's document dictates for its speaker the active role of an accuser bent on establishing the guilt of the accused and securing his own exoneration in the process. As with all effective appeals, Usk's is highly circumstantial, building its case in fourteen articles dealing with Northampton's conspiracy to win reelection against Brembre and then, having lost the election, to overthrow its result. Embodied in these articles is, by the way, a virtual account of the invention of electoral politics in London, with strategems that now seem wholly unexceptional presented alongside more flagrant abuses. According to Usk, Northampton conspired to give special weight to the opinions of crafts that agreed with him; to promote election of the common council by crafts rather than wards; to replace hostile officials with sympathetic ones; to make former mayor and opponent John Philipot pay money he had borrowed; to gain reelection in order to secure the gains of his first term; to raise ill-will against the fishmongers; to impeach worthy citizens; to indict enemies for misconduct during the disturbances of 1381; to electioneer among the goldsmiths and other sympathetic crafts; to arm his followers prior to the election at the Guildhall; to seek the duke of Lancaster's support for a new election in the wake of Brembre's victory; to organize demonstrations for a new election; and variously to promote insurrection. Along the way, Usk plays on fears of disorder, summoning the specter of class warfare: "Yt was seide thus to the poeple that euer the grete men wolden haue the poeple be oppression in lowe degre, for whiche wordes, & be thair meigtenance, the dissension ys arrise betwene the worthy persones & the smale people of the town" (25). This same point is fostered by sharply idiomatic phrasing, as when Northampton is said to have been ready to maintain his ordinances "or elles haue sette al the town in a rore" (27), or when Northampton's desire to overthrow the election is judged likely to promote a situation in which "eueri man sholde haue be in others top." (28) Despite his former complicity, Usk now portrays himself as an advocate of civic order, against the disorder that Northampton might yet bring: "The cite hath stonde in grete doute & yet doth."

Effectively as it accomplishes its ends, the written document is relegated in medieval judicial process to a secondary role. The coroner's notes— or, in this case, Usk's articles of "Appeal"—are strictly preliminary to the judicial occasion itself, to that moment when the approver moves center-stage to confront his former confederates at their trial, repeat his accusations in detail, and offer to sustain their veracity.[8] According to the Westminster chronicler Usk did indeed play out his role, confronting Northampton unblushingly and spelling out his accusations in a series of articles evidently parallel to those of his written "Appeal." The chronicler captures the dramatic moment in which Usk, ushered into the trial by Brembre himself (90), did what was expected of him:

[8] An observation offered by Jens Rörkasten, during discussion of a paper based on this chapter, at the Institute of Historical Research, May 1991.

Sicque ibidem seriatim in diversis articulis mala non pauca et odiosa contra J. Northampton' et suos complices sine erubescencia publicavit ac eum super eisdem articulis appellavit; et ad quemlibet articulum sic incepit: "Ego, T.H., proditor, etc." (92)

And thus, serially, in diverse articles, he publically and unblushingly attributed numerous and detestable misdeeds to John Northampton and his accomplices, introducing each article with, "I, Thomas Usk, traitor, etc."

At this moment of face-to-face confrontation many approvers broke down, confessing the falsity of their claims (Rörkasten, n. 8). Usk evidently saw his through to the end, at this critical moment and thenceforward, including even a reiteration of his charges from the scaffold in March 1388.[9]

Usk's self-portrayal at Reading appears to have drawn on the idea of approvership in several respects and extended it in at least one: at Reading he surpassed his own earlier admission of complicity, branding himself *proditor* in each article of his accusation. And, if he portrayed himself as an approver, he was perceived as approver to no less a degree. According to the chronicle account, Northampton responded to Usk's accusation as one was expected to respond to an approver—first (naturally enough) by denying the charges (see Bracton, 2:431), then by accusing Usk of false rascality (Bracton, 2:433), and finally by offering proof by his body or "per corpus suum" (Bracton, 2:431).[10] For that matter, in his 1385–1386 *Testament of Love* Usk would even mount an after-the-fact claim that he had stood ready for combat, like the good approver he had sought to be:

"Sothely," quod I, "it is wel wist, bothe amonges the greetest and other of the realme, that I profered my body so largely in-to provinge of tho thinges, that mars shulde have juged the ende; but, for the sothnesse of my wordes, they durste not to thilke juge truste." (31)

Moreover, with all this talk of a *duellum* designed to elicit the judgment of Mars surfaces a final element of Usk's many-faceted self-portrayal. For, as Andrew Prescott points out in his discussion of the accusations against Thomas Austin, Northampton's response may also have drawn upon the treatment of treasonous appeals in the court of chivalry (appendix 1, 168). Northampton, himself a draper, might have known and understood little

---

[9] "Semper usque ad mortem numquam fatebatur se deliquisse contra Johannem Northampton' set erant omnia vera que de eo predicaverat coram rege in quodam consilio habito apud Radynggum anno elapso" (*West.*, 314–16). ("Until the point of his death he never admitted that he had erred [in his accusations] against John Northampton, but [insisted that] everything he had said about him before the king in a council held at Reading in a previous year was true.")

[10] "Et econtra J. Northampton' constanter negavit ea que sibi obiciebat, vocansque eum in presencia regis falsum ribaldum morteque dignum; et quod falsum sibi imposuit manu propria optulit se probare duello" (*West.*, 92).

about the forms of chivalric appeal and self-exoneration; the Westminster chronicler reproves him for failing to couch his retort in a form that displayed proper reverence for the presence and role of the king (92). Yet, to the extent that chivalric imagery was invoked, supple code-switcher Usk was undoubtedly equal to the occasion!

Of course, no combat (either the bloody and gritty sort common to approvership or the more stylized performance appropriate to the court of chivalry) was to occur. The outcome of the trial had been preordained by the Brembre faction. Enjoying full control of the process, they had no cause to risk their verdict by permitting a martial encounter between Usk and an aroused and combative Northampton. Far from fighting a gaudy *duellum* with Northampton, Usk delivered his charges and was then swept promptly off the stage. Despite his brave talk in the *Testament*, his post-Reading allies gave him the arms-length treatment an approver might expect, perhaps even consenting to his further imprisonment (Bressie, 517–22) and in any event letting him wait three years for the preferment he anticipated and desired.

That Usk sought through his text and textually dictated behavior to constitute himself as an appellant and an approver-without-royal-writ is no surprise, for the role permitted him to claim the very centrality he had consistently sought. Usk's whole career may be viewed as an attempt to move from outside to inside, from a scrivener and jack-of-all-legal-trades to the personal secretary of the then-mayor; from mere transcriber of Northampton's bills to a full-fledged member of the covin; from an unemployed outcast to undersheriff of Middlesex and a preferred member of the royal faction; and—in this case—from a turncoat witness to a triumphant appellant, lodged in the quarters of London's powerful mayor and escorted by him and influential members of the city government into the presence of king and council. Yet, also characteristically, Usk got ahead of himself: claiming a more considerable role for himself than he was thought even by his new associates to deserve, he was shortly to be put back into his place. And appropriately, just as Usk had scripted an active role for himself in the form of a written "Appeal" constituting himself as Northampton's principal accuser, so would his rebuke occur in a textual form: the recasting of his "Appeal" into a new kind of document, an ordinary inquisition, with the effect of effacing his carefully created role.

Personal Appeal to Jury Presentment: the Effacement of Usk

Despite Northampton's sentence by the king at the end of the hearing at Reading—first to drawing and hanging and then, after the intercession of the queen, to life imprisonment—Usk's activities as approver and the evidence he provided were not ultimately to be dispositive. Jurisdictional disputes led to the scheduling of a more formal trial,[11] ultimately to be held at the Tower on 12 September 1384 before a composite panel consisting of officials of the household together with justices Tresilian and Bealknap (*West.*, 96). Although Usk appears to have been detained in the custody of Brembre through the date of this final trial (*CCR* [1381–1385], 446) and remained available to repeat his performance at Reading, nothing in the record suggests that he was present on this climatic occasion.

Although Usk was not personally present on 12 September, his evidence was—contained in a new document, a point-for-point recasting of the "Appeal" into Latin. This recasting is, however, in the form of a new kind or genre of legal document, no longer a personal appeal but now a jury presentment resulting from an inquest or inquisition. Under its new heading of "Inquisicio capta apud London' in parochia ecclesie sancte marie Bothawe coram Nicholo Brembre maiore," the opening half of this document is preserved among the miscellanea the Exchequer as PRO E163 5/ 28, number 12. This new document would appear to have been produced under the auspices of Brembre and Charney. It tracks its original in every respect save one: it ousts Usk from his role as speaking subject and appellant, pressing him back into the position of just one more participant in the conspiracy. The speaker of this new document is no longer "I, Thomas Usk," and it now issues from the jury itself—Nicholas Brandon, William Culham, Thomas Blosse, Laurence Thronesbury, and others sworn to hear testimony, "iur' presentant & dicunt super sacramentum suum." The new document embodies the collective findings of a jury, leading to an indictment, and Usk's carefully crafted stance as an appellant simply disappears without a trace. With it, since Usk no longer need establish himself as a co-conspirator, goes his self-indictment; Usk's detailed account of his

[11] Two months after his initial arrest, in a document apparently aimed at the parliament convened in April 1384, Northampton complained to king and council that he had been wrongfully impeached and imprisoned by Brembre (Bird, 142). He evidently expected a better hearing from the king than from Brembre and either chose to ignore, or did not know, that the king had witnessed the writ bidding his February arrest (*CLBH*, 229). Then, dissatisfied with the initial results of his hearing before the council, Northampton asserted that the Reading meeting was not the proper tribunal for judgment, in the absence of the Duke of Lancaster (*West.*, 92). (For an alternative account, in which Northampton is found guilty of sedition rather than treason and offered an opportunity to defend himself by combat, see Walsingham, *Historia*, 2:116.) These challenges the king brushed aside, but a more formidable objection was raised during a 7 September strategy session at Westminster, during which Justice Tresilian declared that judgment in such a case should belong only to the mayor, "dicebat enim illorum judicium majori London' tantummodo pertinere," save for the fact that *prodicio* was at stake (*West.*, 94–96). Thus, the matter ended up before a reconstituted panel at Westminster on 12 September, in which Northampton was joined in the dock by fellow conspirators More and Northbury.

own role drops away, and he is given the lesser role of an unindicted subordinate, "dictus Thomas." Naturally, other evidences of Usk's first-person vantage point and agency disappear in the transformation. The assertion that "I, . . . Thomas Vsk" was present "to write thair billes" becomes "etiam Thos. Usk skriveyn ad scribendum billas suas," and so on throughout the document.

The very fact of a second trial, its new (and unusual) venue at the Tower, and the strategy sessions that preceeded it all suggest that the members of the Brembre faction were reaching for a definitive occasion that would either quiet pro-Northampton agitation or, failing to quiet it, would at least leave no doubt about the irreversibility of its outcome. One element of this new trial's greater authority would appear to be its avoidance of any unnecessary reliance on their already unpopular star witness and stool pigeon Thomas Usk. The mechanism of this avoidance was the substitution of one judicial process for another: rejection of the rather obsolescent form of the personal appeal coupled with the even more antiquated trappings of the approver's appeal in favor of an emergent and increasingly dominant system in which testimony was furnished to a jury as part of an inquisition, with the jury then deciding which elements of testimony to accept as its own.[12]

In E163 5/28, number 12, the jury therefore embraces Usk's claims wholesale and (except for the conversion into Latin) practically verbatim, but their author has begun to disappear from view. Usk's effacement is to be extended, and virtually completed, in a third document dating from January-February 1388.

USK'S AUTHORSHIP: LOST IN A
CORAM REGE ROLL

The Latin version of Usk's "Appeal" was to have another life in a new setting. Several years later, in 1388, it would be gathered along with several other presentments dealing with civic agitation on behalf of John Northampton into a coram rege roll, or roll of the king's bench.[13] In this new,

---

[12] Pollock and Maitland, 2:642–48. This is what Hamil calls a "duplex" system of presentment, in which elements of a testimony or coroner's inquest or other prior document (in this case, Usk's "Appeal") are accepted by a jury as its own and embraced as its own findings (239). For additional discussion of the mechanism by which a jury accepts witnesses' words as its own, see Hunnisett, "Reliability," 206–35.

[13] Although the circumstances of this compliation are not entirely clear, its date—Hilary term, 11 Richard II, or between 20 January and mid-February 1388—suggests that it was commissioned in response to new pressures by Northampton partisans for redress of penalties they had endured since Northampton's arrest and trial in 1384. Varied evidence suggests that

composite document, extant as KB27/507/40a-43b, not only is Usk's voice gone, but we have even lost the sense of a particular jury. The document continues to present the evidence of Usk's "Appeal," in words that closely track the surviving sections of its Latin precursor, but its evidence is now offered on behalf of the indefinite "it," as in the recurring phrase *extitit presentatum*, "it stood presented that. . . ." The sense of a jury lurks somewhere in the background, captured in the recurring *Item presentant*, "they likewise present," or show, that . . . , but its members are no longer named.

More tellingly still, the clear textual boundaries of Usk's original "Appeal" and its first Latin recasting have now disappeared. No longer a freestanding document, its inception noted only by the offhanded tag of "alias," his text is now nearly seamlessly amalgamated with any number of other, anonymous testimonies. In this new document, many voices are offered as a single, composite testimony. Interestingly, closely as the Latin of the first jury presentment tracked the English of Usk's "Appeal," one now realizes that its smoothed-out style blends extraordinarily well with that similar documents under other authorship. And, indeed, many of Usk's more vivid figures have disappeared. His assertion that Northampton would "haue sette al the town in a rore" is omitted outright, and the colorful possibility that Northampton's machinations might put "eueri man . . . in others top" has become a bland expression of concern about "magnus rumor et insurrectio."

The ending of the first Latin jury presentment is lost, but here at any rate we know for certain that Usk's concluding plea for mercy and possible preferment is gone. "I aske grace & mercy," he says near the end of his

---

the pressure for reconsideration had been mounting since the first stirrings of the Appellants in the fall of 1387. The "loyalty oath" produced on behalf of the City of London by Brembre and Exton in October 1387 registers this pressure by reiterating a disclaimer of allegiance to Northampton (CLBH, 314–15) and the king's letter of 7 October 1387 signaling the appointment of Usk as undersheriff of Middlesex requests that the aldermen of the City cease sending petitions on behalf of Northampton and his followers (*CLBH*, 316–17). More overtly symptomatic of pro-Northampton pressure are the petitions of various guilds to the parliament that convened in January 1388, and the fact that Northampton and his followers were up for review is reflected in a blanket parliamentary pardon of those accused of treasons and felonies in the sixth to eleventh years of Richard's reign, excepting only Northampton lieutenants More and Northbury (*RP*, 3:248). Many did benefit, despite this exclusion; we have already discussed the favorable alteration of the Austin family's fortunes during the winter of 1387–1388, and numerous others were affected as well. Consider, for example, the rehabilitation of John Constantine, summarily executed in 1384 for his role in fomenting a sympathy strike over Northampton's arrest; his head was now removed from Ludgate and restored to his widow for burial in hallowed ground (*CCR* [1385–1389], 373). The new climate is particularly evident in the replacement of Richard's partisan chief justice, Tresilian, by moderate Walter Clopton by 31 January 1388 (*CPR* [1385–1389], 447). It is under Clopton's justiceship that the review of Northampton materials in KB/27/507, mems. 40a–43b was prepared.

"Appeal," "of my lyge lord the kyng; & afterward of the mair, & of al the worthy aldermen, & of al the gode comunes of the town" (30). And, though badly damaged, the conclusion contains a number of phrases suggestive of his hope for new affiliation: "euer stonde be the town & be the worthy . . . may do next my lige [lord] . . . be redy [at] al tymes" (31). By contrast, the coram rege roll simply shades off in a discussion of unrest in Westchepe on the day of Northampton's arrest. Then it moves blandly and without particular emphasis to another testimony—an adaptation of E163/5/28, number 11—that represents matters similarly ("item per quandam inquisitionem similiter presentatum extitit"). Within this next segment, Usk recedes even farther into the background, as we find him simply listed among ten conspirators who caused trouble after Brembre's victory in 1383.

Usk's testimony therefore exists in three states: the English "Appeal" preserved as E163 5/28, number 9; the jury presentment of E163 5/28, number 12; and the latter document's reappearance in Coram Rege Roll KB 27/507, mems. ff. 40a-41a, its identity now submerged within a longer compilation of jury presentments related to the subversive activities of John Northampton. Apparent as we move through these three documents is a progressive effacement of Usk's role, a process in which our would-be appellant becomes a mere witness and finally ends up as a minor participant, glancingly mentioned, far short of eligibility to stand with Northampton and his confederates in the dock there at the Tower in September 1384, so small a fish that he was not even physically present in the room!

USK AND TEXTUALITY

Despite the progressive deterioration of his position, Usk would seem to have enjoyed some temporary success in mobilizing a judicial and textual process in support of his own advancement. The mechanism of his self-advancement was, in the first instance, textual. Usk seized personal control of a process of textual production when, rather than dictating his accusation to a coroner who recorded it in the form of an objective account, he wrote it in his own hand as a first-person narrative. In the mixed process of creation and self-creation peculiar to first-person texts, he both created an accusatory narrative and was in turn created *by* that narrative as an unofficial agent of the king, a "fiz le Roy" manqué with guaranteed centrality to the trial of John Northampton. The text of the "Appeal," that is, specified and guaranteed an extratextual role for Usk, casting him at once as something like a "star witness" *and* a special prosecutor upon whom the whole trial depended. It also proposed an extratextual role for everybody else, including the king and mayor and citizens of London, as Usk's associates and confederates, waiting hopefully but passively for him to carry forward the case against Northampton. Without a preexisting textual genre (the appeal and, especially, the approver's appeal) and a set of preexisting extratextual procedures (the trial in which appellant confronts appellee and sustains all that he has claimed), Usk's masterful strategy could never have worked at all. Because it was rooted in a set of shared expectations about appeal and approvement, and because it was so brilliantly conducted in its own right, Usk's strategy briefly worked; his text and the accompanying roles it specified succeeded for a time in organizing friend and foe alike in the roles and performances it dictated for them.

Usk's success was, however, brief, and in fact the textually based terms of that success equally enabled his undoing. For writing itself, as the primary basis of Usk's self-empowerment, may just as often turn out to be a vehicle of disempowerment. Although Usk might have thought he was serving his own ends when he wrote his document, he actually ceased to be necessary to the Brembre faction *precisely at the moment when he reduced his testimony to writing*. For, Usk's testimony once existing as a written document, Brembre and Charney could arrange for it to be recast as a jury presentment, and the result of the recasting was the return of its author to the sidelines where they had always felt he belonged.[14]

Whether we imagine that Usk briefly seized the initiative through his command of textual process or conclude more despairingly that he was always in some sense manipulated by the Brembre faction, the end result is the same. His brief career as appellant demonstrates both the power of a text to organize external reality and the ultimate limitations of that power. Usk would seem to have gained temporary advantage by preempting a nearly obsolescent textual and legal tradition of personal appeal and approvement and its accompanying expectations. But the ascendant Ricardian-Brembre faction retained full control of such crucial matters as the form of textual and judicial process ultimately to be pursued. They demonstrated that control when they opted for the emergent mechanisms of inquest and jury presentment over the older and more individualistic procedures for personal appeal. Once the decision makers of the Brembre faction decided to reduce Usk's visibility, they had little difficulty in arranging to recast his personal appeal as a jury presentment and in mandating a new and definitive trial at which his presence was not even required. The terms

---

[14] I am indebted to Caroline Barron and Vanessa Harding's London medieval and Tudor history seminar at the Institute of Historical Research for a stimulating discussion of this very issue. In my May 1991 presentation I argued for Usk's writing practices as a vehicle for short-term empowerment that was subject to rewriting and eventual disempowerment. Members of the seminar contributed the darker (and hence more believable) suggestion that the act of *writing itself* might have left Usk at the mercy of his menacing new sponsors. On writing as a device of social control see R. I. Moore, *The Formation of a Persecuting Society*.

of Usk's own struggle for visibility and his ultimate defeat were textual, but the final decisions that moved him to the sidelines were taken extratextually, by Brembre, Charney, and the other London power brokers. Despite the immense power of a text like Usk's "Appeal" to create a version of reality within its own bounds and even temporarily to impose it, a text's ultimate history must finally involve questions of reception, the conditions of its entry into a field of occurrences and circumstances beyond its own bounds.[15]

READING USK

Usk's "Appeal" and his *Testament* represent two apparent attempts to mobilize literacy to overcome serious economic and political disadvantages. At the end of his life we find Usk once more attempting to reground his identity within a new textual *ordo*. Arraigned by the Appellants on 3 March 1388 as an operative of the Brembre faction, he was sentenced to be drawn and hanged and beheaded with his head to be displayed at Newgate (*West.*, 284). On his way to the scaffold later that same day, he marshalled textual materials, reciting a collection of liturgical and devotional pieces bearing on the time of death: "dicensque cum traheretur valde devote Placebo et Dirige, vij. Psalmos Penitenciales, Te Deum laudamus, Nunc dimittis, Quicumque vult, et alios in articulo mortis tangentes" (*West.*, 314). This near-professional repertoire may be the chronicler's own invention,[16] but we have come to expect a high degree of professional attainment from this remarkable man. Did he not, after all, parlay a position as scrivener into successive accomplishments as attorney, secretary, politician, littérateur, and factionalist at a national level of visibility? No wonder that now, on his way to death he revealed a remarkable liturgical virtuosity, drawing upon hymns, antiphons, and segments of the office of the dead to recreate himself once again as the devout subject of his own discourse, one whose steadfast devotion would sustain him through the trials he was about to face.[17]

Of course, no composer of a text—however artful—gets to say how it

[15] A recent and stimulating argument for the importance of confronting an entire text, its internal disarray and the complexity of its insertion in a larger environment of texts and symbolic actions, is Harold Mah's discussion of Darton's *Great Cat Massacre*. Readers of the present volume will recognize my conceptual debt to Darton, but this and other of my essays do seek to enlarge his referential frame and broaden the acknowledgement of the text itself as a site of conflict.

[16] Caroline Barron has observed to me that this repertoire may be compared with the standardized list of prayers and hymns employed by Will in his capacity as private chaplain or prayermonger, singing for the souls of those who help him (*Piers Plowman*, C Text, 4.45–47).

[17] Including execution by thirty strokes of the axe (*West.* 314).

will ultimately be read. The Appellants knew what *they* thought of this mercurial personality, fixing him with epithets "faux & malveise" in their articles of indictment (*RP*, 3:234). Even the Westminster chronicler, approving of his devout end, cannot refrain from comment on his "evil" life (314). Nor have subsequent commentators refrained from judging Usk. Some implied judgments are certainly present with earlier pages I have written about him ("Politics and Poetics," 85–90).

The temptation is to read a scrambler like Usk, living by his wits and talent one step away from the hat-maker's shop, in a superior or even supercilious way. Northampton probably read him this way, when he hired him as an aspiring factionalist in 1383, and Brembre when he half-sponsored, half-compelled Usk's opportune conversion in 1384, and Gloucester when he scapegoated him in 1388.[18] I am aware, concluding this essay and this book, of Samuel Johnson's comment on the life of Richard Savage:

> Those are no proper judges of his conduct, who have slumbered away their time on the down of affluence; nor will any wise man presume to say, "Had I been in Savage's condition, I should have lived or written better than Savage."[19]

A decent and epistemologically humble stab at comprehension, rather than judgment, is what we can offer poor Usk now.

[18] Though Northampton might have felt differently in confinement in 1384, or Brembre on the scaffold in 1388, or Gloucester as he went to his death in 1397.

[19] *Lives of the Poets*. Brought to my attention by Richard Holmes, writing in *Granta*, summer 1990.

Appendix 1

THE ACCUSATIONS AGAINST
THOMAS AUSTIN

A. J. Prescott

ITEM NUMBER six in Magdalene Weale's list of English documents at the Public Record Office, which forms an appendix to Chambers and Daunt's *Book of London English*, is a document described by Weale as an "appeal of treason" made in 1387–1388 against Thomas Austin, supposedly a confederate of John Northampton (274–75). In 1931, when Weale compiled her list, the accusation against Austin was in the large artificial class of Chancery Miscellanea and bore the reference C 47/68/12/357. During the early 1970s, a large part of the Chancery Miscellanea was rearranged and integrated with other material to reconstitute the medieval chancery files (see Hunnisett, "Chancery Records," 158–68; Barnes, 430–76; introductions to the class lists, *List and Index Society*, vol. 130 [1976]). The document relating to Austin was placed in the file of returns to writs *certiorari corpus cum causa* for 11 Richard II and given the new reference C258/24/9.[1]

This document is in poor condition. It is very badly faded and the top left-hand section has been damaged by the application of a chemical reagent intended to make the writing clearer. Chambers and Daunt were unable to obtain a consecutive reading of the text and consequently omitted it from the *Book of London English*. With the aid of ultraviolet light, it has now proved possible to read the bulk of the document, which is printed below.

The accusations against Thomas Austin rank with the other more famous English documents produced as a result of the factional disputes in London in the 1380s. A comparison that immediately springs to mind is with the "Appeal" of Thomas Usk (discussed above, chapter 7). Both are quasi-judicial documents and are full of colorful and circumstantial details about the political controversy in London at this time. Although the allegations against Austin do not, as Usk's "Appeal" does, show Northampton

---

[1] Medieval returns to writs of *certiorari super recordum et processum* and *super omnibus et singulis indictamentis* may have been kept on the chancery *recorda* files rather than the *corpus cum causa* files, but only one fragment of an original *recorda* file now surives. See the introduction to the class list for C258: *List and Index Society*, 130:166.

and his immediate associates at work, they do evoke the personal animosity and sheer rancor of London politics in the early 1380s. Usk's "Appeal" shows the London conflict from the point of view of the major protagonists; the accusations against Austin give an idea of how these disputes appeared to the second rank of Northampton's supporters. Usk and Austin neatly complement each other—one looking towards the inner circle and the other to the supporters in the street.

Like Usk's "Appeal," the form of the accusations against Austin is unusual and their precise legal character is difficult to define. An outline of the chief stages in the dispute between Austin and his former apprentice John Banham and the resulting proceedings against Austin and his family for treason and felony has been given above (chapter 1, 12, n. 3). The document printed below is a return to writ *certiorari super indictamentis* dated 9 January 1388 directed to the mayor, sheriffs, and coroner of London. The writ ordered the mayor and his colleagues to send to chancery all indictments, appeals, and other accusations of treason, felony, trespass, and other misdeeds taken by them against Thomas Austin, his wife Alice, and Roger Austin.

Writs of *certiorari* were available in a wide variety of forms for requesting from local officials every kind of information, ranging from the name of a coroner to details of those responsible for maintaining a bridge (Prescott, "Judicial Records," 212–19; Henderson, 83–93; De Smith, 45–48). *Certiorari super indictamentis* and other closely related writs such as *certiorari super causa capcionis* were apparently often issued in response to petitions from aggrieved prisoners and litigants. Links between the receipt of petitions and the dispatch of such writs have been traced in the mid-fifteenth century by analysis of chancery files (Barnes, 432–33). Some petitions requesting a writ of *certiorari* survive. For example, William Roth claimed that he had been imprisoned without good cause and asked for a *certiorari super causa capcionis* so that his case could be examined in king's bench (PRO, SC 8/303/15108). In 1421, a prisoner in Ludgate even made use of writs of *certiorari* to initiate false proceedings for homicide against his enemies (*KB*, 7:248–57).

The writ requesting copies of any indictments against the Austins was therefore probably issued in response to a petition by Thomas or Roger Austin complaining of the accusations against them. Unfortunately, no copy of this petition has been traced. How far the issue of the *certiorari* was related to the release from prison on surety of Thomas and Roger on 19 November and 3 December 1387 respectively cannot be established (*CCR* [1385–1389], 359, 362). The issue of the *certiorari* was the first stage in bringing the case against the Austins to trial. On 29 January 1388, shortly after the writ had been returned to chancery and examined there, a special commission of gaol delivery was issued ordering Robert Tresilian, the chief justice of the king's bench, and others to try Thomas and Alice Austin, Hochon of Liverpool, and other prisoners in Newgate (*CLBH*, 322). Two days later, however, Tresilian, having fled from the accusations against him by the Appellants, was replaced as chief justice by Walter Clopton, and on 1 February a new commission was issued to Clopton and four others for the delivery of the Austins (*CPR* [1385–1389], 463).

The return to the *certiorari* requesting details of any accusations against the Austins was made by Nicholas Exton, the mayor of London, John Charney, the coroner of London, and William Venour and Hugh Fastolf, the sheriffs. Fastolf himself of course figured prominently in the accusations, having narrowly avoided being shot with an arrow by one of Austin's servants. The return begins by repeating the "accusation and appeal" that provided the basis of the proceedings against the Austins. This is given in English, an unusual procedure at this time. This "bill," as it was later described, was addressed to the mayor of London and was in the name of John Banham, a former apprentice of Thomas Austin who had been in dispute with him over some accounts (*Pleas*, 146–47; *CLBH*, 317). Banham made his accusations against Austin sometime between May and September 1387, probably in early September. As will be seen in more detail later, Banham's accusations are not in any recognizable legal form and comprise a mixture of vague accusations and innuendo without any of the specific information about the nature of the offences and the time and place at which they were committed that might normally be expected in such a document.

The officials who made the return seem to have been aware of the legal shortcomings of Banham's allegations and went on in their return to declare apologetically that they did not have any other indictments relating to the people named in the writ apart from an inquest into Banham's accusations taken by Exton and Charney together with William More and William Standon, Venour and Fastolf's predecessors as sheriffs, at the Guildhall on 16 September 1387.

A jury had been summoned to the Guildhall "to inquire into the articles and accusations specified in the said bill." Again the form of this inquisition was unusual. No attempt was made to recast Banham's bill into a proper legal form or even to translate it into Latin as happened, say, when Usk's "Appeal" was called in king's bench. The jury simply stated that the bill was true, apart from the article alleging that Austin had stolen a thousand pounds from the king. This article is quoted in the original English and then repeated in Latin. The jurors declared that they knew nothing about this allegation but added that Austin had concealed custom duties worth £125. The Guildhall jury did provide one of the details normally required in an indictment, namely some form of date for the offence, but this was given only in a very rough and ready form. The jurors said that "all the indictments described in the said bill were committed and performed before the election of Sir Nicholas Brembre as mayor of the city of London, that is to say, before the feast of the Translation of St. Edward King and Confessor in the eighth year of the present king and continued until about the first of May then following and not afterwards as far as they could discover among themselves." The jurors finally added that Austin had secretly continued in his heart to plot his evil purpose against the government of the city until the present time.

The last paragraph of the return is perhaps the most remarkable in the whole document. Nicholas Exton reported that "a certain horrible accusation" had been made before him and the sheriffs against Roger Austin that touched the person of the king. The mayor was unwilling to give details of this allegation in writing or to inquire into it without a special mandate from the king himself. Exton and the sheriffs were ready to repeat the accusation before the king, who, they assured the chancery, was fully informed of the matter.

The nature of this sensational accusation against Roger Austin is a mystery. Clearly it was more serious than the kind of loose talk of which Thomas Austin was accused. Exton's reluctance to give this allegation wider currency by preparing a written copy or summoning a jury to investigate it may perhaps be explained by the great political turmoil at the time he was making his return. Shortly before, the Lords Appellant had entered the Tower with an armed company and forced the king to accede to their demands. Exton's unwillingness to forward a copy of this allegation through normal channels foreshadows the procedure that developed in the king's bench towards the end of the fifteenth century whereby documents dealing with sensitive accusations of this sort were kept separately under lock and key in a special file series known as the *baga de secretis* (Harcourt, 508–29, and the introduction to the Public Record Office class list).

The various terms applied to Banham's accusations in the documents relating to this case suggest that even contemporary officials had difficulty in categorizing them. In the writ *certiorari* by which the allegations were summoned into chancery, it was stated that the Austins had been "indicted and appealed." In the return itself, Banham's charges are variously described as "articles and accusations," a "bili," an "accusation and appeal," and an "indictment." The term used by Magdalene Weale to describe Banham's allegations, "appeal of treason," is not a helpful one. At this time, the term "appeal" was used in treason cases to describe three different methods of initiating proceedings. The common feature of all three is that they proceeded from charges made by an individual who was prepared to prosecute them in person and was willing if need be to undertake trial by battle in support of his accusations. There is no suggestion in the surviving documents that Banham was willing to substantiate his allegations against

Austin in this way, which makes it difficult to regard them as an appeal. It is worth looking more closely into the reasons why it is inappropriate to describe Banham's charges as an appeal, in order to illustrate some of the unusual features of this document from a legal point of view.

In the thirteenth century, an appeal by an individual was the most common method of initiating prosecutions for felony (Hunnisett, *Medieval Coroner*, 53–68; Bellamy, *Crime*, 125–28; Baker, 574–76). The rules governing the making of such an appeal were extremely strict. The appellant made a preliminary complaint to the coroner, who recorded the details and took sureties from the appellant to ensure that he would appear at the next county court to prosecute his case. At the county court, the appellant had to recite the appeal aloud in a carefully defined form. Material evidence such as wounds or torn clothing were also examined. The accused was summoned and was required at a later county court to repeat the appeal word for word. Any slight variation from the previous declaration invalidated the appeal. If both parties agreed or the defendant claimed that the appeal was motivated by malice, the case was put to a trial jury. Otherwise it was settled by judicial combat. Despite some improvements in appeal procedure in the fourteenth century, such as allowing the appeal to be read from a written schedule, the appeal was superseded by indictments as a means of initiating felony cases and by Richard II's reign only accounted for a small proportion of felony prosecutions.

The use of this form of appeal in treason cases seems to have been rare even in the late thirteenth century, the heyday of the private appeal (Bellamy, *Law of Treason*, 19–21, 23–58). Such an appeal of treason seems to have been little more than a theoretical possibility, and the only detailed descriptions of such prosecutions comes from legal treatises such as the late thirteenth-century *Mirror of Justices*. This gives a form of appeal of treason that the author claimed to have found "in old rolls of the time of King Alfred" (54–55), with the special explanation suggesting that such a method of proceeding was unusual, to say the least. It is extremely unlikely that Banham would have had such an archaic and exotic procedure in mind when making his accusations against Austin. In any case, Banham's allegations do not possess any of the usual features of an individual appeal. Like the appeal of felony, a private appeal of treason would have had to be made in a carefully prescribed form and repeated at every stage of the prosecution. Banham's rambling anecdotes, apparently repeated just once before the mayor, are as far removed from the formality of an individual appeal as can be imagined.

The most common sort of appeal for treason in common law courts at the end of the fourteenth century was an approver's appeal (Hamil, 238–58; see additional references in chapter 7). An approver was a medieval "king's evidence," a traitor or felon who confessed his own crimes and named those who had joined him in these acts. He was kept by the king and known as "the king's approver." If an approver defeated in judicial combat a sufficient number of those he appealed, he could hope to avoid execution and either be pardoned or have his sentence commuted to perpetual imprisonment or banishment. An approver defeated in combat immediately suffered the penalties due for the crimes previously confessed.

Approvers' appeals were usually recorded by a coroner. As has been seen, Banham's accusations were addressed to the mayor. The coroner only seems to have been involved in the subsequent inquest into Banham's claims. There was a certain amount of formality associated with becoming an approver. This does not seem to have occurred in Banham's case, and he is nowhere described in the return to the *certiorari* as being an approver. As a convicted felon, an approver remained in a suitable jail throughout the course of his appeal. Although Banham was held in the Fleet at the time of his accusation against Thomas Austin, he was kept there as a debtor, the result of his financial dispute with Austin, rather than as an approver. Some form of confession was essential in an approver's appeal. Banham does not at any point in his accusations confess to any crimes. He appears in the role of bystander or at most messenger, acting as a spy for Austin to see what was going on at the Guildhall or going on a wild goose chase to Hertford to find out what Gaunt was up to. Indeed, he is not referred to by name until halfway through the accusations and is mentioned directly only three times in the entire document.

Not only is Banham's role in the events he describes elusive, but there is even a suggestion at one point that he may have been the author of only part of the accusations against Austin. In the description of the incident in which Hochon of Liverpool threatened to shoot Hugh Fastolf, it is stated that "i Johan Hore" persuaded Hugh to spare Fastolf's life. It is clear from the entry on the Plea and Memoranda Rolls relating to the financial dispute between Banham and Thomas Austin that John Hore was not an *alias* used by Banham but a separate person, another of Austin's servants (*Pleas*, 146–47). Moreover, this entry states that both Hore and Banham had made accusations against Thomas Austin. This, taken with the reference to "i Johan Hore," raises the possibility that the English accusations sent to the chancery by Exton and his colleagues were either jointly compiled by Hore and Banham or a conflation of two separate documents. This is not an entirely satisfactory interpretation, since it contradicts the final sentence in which Banham affirms the truth of the charges against Austin and seems clearly to indicate that he was responsible for all the allegations. Perhaps, in the passage relating to the ambush of Fastolf, the phrase "i Johan Hore" should be read as "one Johan Hore" rather than "I Johan Hore," but this does not explain why a copy of Hore's allegations was not forwarded by the city officials when the chancery requested copies of all documents relating to the Austins.

Such ambiguity and uncertainty about precise authorship would be unthinkable in an approver's appeal, where it was a central requirement that the approver himself should confess to involvement in the crimes described and the approver had to prove the allegations personally in armed combat. It is instructive to compare the charges against Austin with the celebrated mole-catcher's appeal of 1440, in which a Kentish approver revealed details of a plot against Henry VI (Aston, 83–90). Although the mole-catcher's appeal was in English and, like the accusations against Austin, is full of colourful and circumstantial detail, there is no doubt about who was responsible for the accusation. The appeal begins, "Hit is to have in mynde that I Robert Goodgroome of Osprenge in the Counte of Kent, Moltaker, otherwyse called Robert Grene, late of London', Coryour, aprovour of our lord þe kynge . . . knowliche þat." The contrast with Banham's accusations could not be greater. Goodgroome is placed center stage at the very beginning of his appeal and remains there throughout. Banham sidles on only halfway through his accusations, and his relationship to the main action is never made entirely clear.

A more flexible method of bringing an appeal of treason, also available at this time, simply involved making an oral complaint or presenting a bill to the council or parliament. This procedure was particularly associated with the court of chivalry held by the constable and marshal of England (Squibb, 22–28; Bellamy, *Law of Treason*, 141–76). The jurisdiction of this civilian court was, properly speaking, limited as far as treason cases were concerned to offences occurring outside the realm, but throughout Richard II's reign the court also dealt with incidents of treason committed at home. Proceedings in the court of chivalry were begun by submitting a petition with details of the articles of complaint. The terms used to describe Banham's accusations, such as "appeal or accusation," were also frequently used in referring to appeals of treason before the court of chivalry.

A characteristic example of a bill initiating an appeal of treason was that brought by John Keighley against Sir Stephen le Scrope at the beginning of Henry IV's reign, alleging that, in December 1399 at his manor of Byngbury in Kent, Scrope plotted to restore King Richard (*CPR* [1399–1401], 401; *Foedera*, 3:193–94). Keighley's bill is a very direct and personal accusation, beginning, "I John Keighley accuse and appeal you Stephen Scrope knight," and roundly denouncing Scrope as a "false traitor." The appeal ends with a ringing declaration of Keighley's willingness to prove his charges against Scrope by armed combat: "I offer and promise with God's help to prove the foregoing according to the law and custom of arms." Despite the relative informality of this form of appeal, it was not to be undertaken lightly, as an unsuccessful appellant was himself treated as a traitor. When, following an inquiry by the court of chivalry, Keighley's appeal was found to be false, he was executed.

Attempts to ensure that the court of chivalry did not deal with cases of treason committed within the realm meant that treason prosecutions initiated by informal accusations of this sort were increasingly transferred to common law courts for trial. Thus Richard Cliveden placed before parliament a bill alleging that Sir William Coggan had supported the commons of Bridgwater in their activities during the revolt of 1381 (*RP* 3:105–6; Bellamy, *Law of Treason*, 143). Like Keighley, Cliveden declared that "if the said William contradicts this bill, the said Richard will prove it with his body before our noble lord the King and his honourable council in the manner demanded by the law of arms." William denied the allegations, and the case was adjourned from parliament and sent to the common law courts to be tried there.

Of the three types of appeal for treason used in Richard II's reign, this last form corresponds most closely to Banham's accusations, but perhaps this is only because they were both relatively informal and unstructured. Many of the most distinctive features of this procedure are not apparent in the Austin case. An appeal of treason by bill was begun by petition to parliament or the council. Banham's accusations were addressed to the mayor of London. A bill of treason usually repeatedly emphasized the gravity and nature of the offence, whereas Banham only accuses Austin of "tretorie" once in very vague terms at the beginning of his accusations. Above all, in an appeal of treason in this form the appellant offered to establish his case by judicial combat. Banham did not apparently make any such offer. An informal appeal of treason in English reminiscent of Banham's accusations was used in an interesting Sussex case of 1441, in which Thomas atte Wood rushed into a view of frankpledge and declared that Robin Seman was a "fals Traitour." The similarities between Wood's outburst and Austin's informal accusations are striking, but there is one critical difference. Wood swore that he would "make good upon [Seman's] body" and prove his charges in judicial combat (Hunnisett, "Treason by Words," 116–19).

If the influence of informal appeals can be discerned in any of the English documents generated by the factional conflicts in London, it is perhaps most apparent in the "Appeal" of Thomas Usk. There are many similarities between Usk's "Appeal" and, say, John Keighley's bill against Sir Stephen Scrope. For example, the way in which Usk concluded each article of his appeal with a declaration that he appealed Northampton, More, Northbury and so on is strongly reminiscent of bills of this kind. A preliminary hearing by the council was common procedure in dealing with an appeal in this form. Northampton clearly regarded Usk's allegations as an appeal similar to those heard by the court of chivalry and responded in the time-honored fashion by throwing down a glove to deny the appeal and offer judicial combat. An alternative to seeking the judicial roots of Usk's "Appeal" in approver's appeals is to seek them in cases such as those of Sir Stephen Scrope or William Coggan (but, on Usk as approver, see Strohm, chapter 7, above, and Bellamy, *Law of Treason*, 151).

The shortcomings of Banham's accusations as a means of initiating any conventional form of prosecution were apparently recognized by the city authorities, and their immediate reaction was to seek ratification of the allegations from a jury. This was a perfectly normal procedure. Allegations by a private individual were at this time frequently used as the basis for indictments. An aggrieved party presented a bill to the appropriate officials, who submitted it to a presenting jury. If the jury felt that there was a case to answer, they marked the bill *billa vera*. If they considered the allegations false, the bill was endorsed with the word *ignoramus* (Lambarde, 467–69; Bellamy, *Crime*, 122–23; Virgoe, 214–15). Informal accusations were probably often recast by the clerks of the court into the proper form of an indictment before they were submitted to the jury. This is suggested by the phrase often used at the beginning of such "true bills," addressed to the presenting jury: "Let it be inquired for the king whether . . ." During the fifteenth century, "true bills" came to be the most common method of making indictments, but numerous examples of indictments produced in this way survive from the reign of Richard II onwards.[2]

This was the procedure adopted with Banham's accusations. The jury summoned to the Guildhall declared that Banham had submitted a "true bill" apart from one article. So far so good, but this still did not represent a valid indictment. An indictment had to include certain basic information: the names of the jurors, the year, date, and place of the offences, a description of any chattels involved and their value, and a statement of the nature of the offence, using the adverb *felonice* if it was felony or *proditorie* if it was treason (Bellamy, *Crime*, 124). Jurors frequently supplied additional information to emphasize the gravity of the case against the defendant, but indictments were generally laconic and formulaic documents, completely different in character from Banham's colorful anecdotes. They were usually in Latin, but occasional examples of French and even English indictments are found.[3] These vernacular indictments nevertheless retained the basic form of the Latin indictments.

---

[2] Examples of early "billa vera" occur frequently in indictment files compiled by the itinerant King's Bench, e.g., PRO KB9/92 (files of presentments *coram rege* at Northampton, Michaelmas term 4 Richard II) and KB9/100 (file of presentments *coram rege* at Oxford, Easter term 21 Richard II).

[3] For an indictment partly in French taken by a commission of 1381 against rebels in Norfolk, see PRO KB9/166/1, mem. 108. For an English indictment, see Chambers and Daunt, 233–35.

As has been noted, no attempt was made to turn Banham's accusations into a proper indictment. The jury simply stated that everything Banham had said was true. The only point at which they disagreed with Banham was in his claim that Austin had stolen a thousand pounds from the king. Here they reverted to something more like normal legal language. They stated that "they knew nothing of this accusation and said that the same Thomas Austin at various times had concealed and retained customs of the lord king . . . to the sum of one hundred and twenty five pounds." Even this was still extremely vague.

The basic information required for an indictment is either omitted from both Banham's bill and the jury's confirmation of it or is given in an unsatisfactory form. Banham declared at the beginning of his accusations that Austin was "on of the principall meyntenours of tretorie touchynge to owre lyge lord the kynge," but he made no attempt to show how far any of the particular incidents described by him constituted treason. It is difficult to imagine that Banham's reconnaissance of Gaunt's household at Hertford could have been construed as treason, whereas the concealment of customs was at best felony. The presenting jury do not refer to the nature of Austin's offences at all. The date of the offences is given only in the vaguest terms by the presenting jury, while no information is given about where, for example, Austin held his treasonable conversation with "a man of Kyderminstre" or where the house from which Hochon tried to shoot Hugh Fastolf was situated.

The impression given by the surviving documents in the Austin case is of a prosecution in the course of preparation that was stopped halfway, perhaps by the change in the political situation. Presumably the next stage would have been the preparation of a formal indictment against Austin and his associates, but for some reason this was never done.

Another source may have influenced the form of Banham's accusations against Austin and should be mentioned. It was common practice to draw to the attention of the mayor of London instances of conversation which was disloyal to the city or the king. The Plea and Memoranda Rolls sometimes give the impression that late fourteenth-century London was full of potential informers. In 1383, Thomas Depham of Norfolk was imprisoned for saying that news of the war in Flanders was false, and John Filiol was committed to prison for calling John Northampton a *falsus scurro vel harelot* (*Pleas*, 36). In 1384, William Mayhew was charged with having said that the judgment of the mayor and aldermen was unjust, that the city was badly governed, and that John Constantine had been iniquitously condemned to death (*Pleas*, p. 50). It was decided by the mayor's court that "as had previously been done in like cases according to the custom of the city on many other occasions . . . the said William should have a year's imprisonment." Such accusations were doubtless frequently brought by bill addressed to the mayor. In directing his bill against Austin to the mayor of London, Banham was following this customary procedure. It was decided, however, perhaps by the mayor, that Banham's accusations went beyond the normal allegations of loose talk, and Austin and his associates were arrested for treason.

It is fruitless to try too hard to establish the legal character of the case against Austin when the record of the trial of Thomas, Roger, and Alice Austin, and Hochon of Liverpool has not survived. Perhaps when the case came to trial, a formal indictment was offered against them. Alternatively, the allegations may have been dismissed because they were not in the proper form. In a 1401 case in king's bench strongly reminiscent in some respects of the Austin case, Thomas Samford, a servant of John Inglewood, alleged on oath that Inglewood and others had plotted to kill Henry IV and take control of the kingdom (*KB*, 7:111–14). Thomas Yokflete was accused of being privy to this plot. At his trial, Yokflete said that "the aforesaid appeal or accusation establishes nothing in fact against the said Thomas Yokflete with respect to the aforesaid acts of treason but only the verbal statement of what John Inglewood said to the said Thomas Samford." The judges agreed that "none of the foregoing matters is sufficient in law, so far as the said Thomas Yokflete is concerned, to put him on trial by the law of the land of England for the aforegoing things."

Although the accusations against Austin were more direct, something similar may have happened at his trial. The allegations against him and the others may simply have been dismissed as invalid. Whatever happened, there is no doubt about the result of the trial. Thomas Austin, and presumably the others, were cleared of the charges against them. Austin went on to be elected as as a sheriff of London for 1387–1388 (*CLBH*, 332). He lived until 1391, being survived by Alice, who died in 1395 (*Index to Testamentary Records*, 1:8).

From a legal point of view, the very difficulty in defining the character of the proceedings against Austin makes them interesting. Cases rarely depart so much from accepted norms as that against Austin. Some element of improvisation in response to political pressures seems to have been usual in treason cases, but, whatever shortcuts were adopted, a concern to preserve at least the appearance of proper procedure is usually evident. In Austin's case, many of these proprieties seem to have been forgotten.

The terminology used in the official documents relating to the case seems to recognize its unusual character. For example, it is stated in their respective letters of mainprise that Thomas and Roger had been impeached (*impetitus*). Outside parliament, this term seems to have been used as a catchall phrase for any slightly odd form of prosecution. Thus the men brought before commissions in Suffolk in 1381 to answer allegations by private individuals that they had supported the rising and were traitors were also described as having been impeached.[4] Gabrielle Lambrick has argued that such extraparliamentary impeachments were initiated by communal charges and were heard before the council (250–76), but cases such as those of Austin and the Suffolk rebels suggest that the term *impeachment* was used much more loosely to describe any non-standard form of prosecution.

Despite the great legal interest of Banham's accusations, they are nevertheless of most value as a description of the London political scene. The loss of the trial record makes it difficult to interpret Banham's allegations, since the reasons why they were rejected at trial are not known. Austin was at best only on the fringes of Northampton's party and may have shown nothing like the degree of personal commitment to the cause that Banham suggests. However, regardless of how far Banham's detailed allegations against Austin were true, they do vividly capture the atmosphere of London political life at this time.

Banham's bill contains many fascinating details—not just the vignette of Fastolf relieving himself against a churchyard wall, but also Banham's secret communications with Northampton's brother in prison, the meetings of Northampton's "false common council" at night, the way in which Austin supposedly attempted to protect his goods by altering his merchant's mark, Banham's attempt to get information from Gaunt's servants about his intentions, the importance attached to Austin's alleged refusal to obey Brembre's orders "to ryden or to gon in worschippynge of our lyge lord," and so on.

Apart from such circumstantial detail, Banham's accusations add to the general picture of the factional disputes in London in three major areas. First, they emphasize the central role of personal antagonism in the conflict. This was very much focused on the leaders of the factions. Austin denounces Brembre as a "false harlot" who should be hanged and tells the mysterious man from Kidderminster that there would be a thousand men against Brembre. Such is the attention to personalities that the dispute is presented entirely in these terms, without reference to any of the underlying issues. As far as Austin was concerned, the whole matter could be settled if he could "getyn ij. men and sodeynly stekyn Brembir and gon her way."

This antagonism was directed not only towards Brembre but also towards the king, who was seen as a tool of Brembre. Austin saw no hope while Richard was on the throne, and his wife claimed that Richard could not conceivably be the Black Prince's son. The problem was that he was controlled by Brembre. This strong antiroyalist feeling perhaps supports

---

[4] PRO KB9/166/1, mems. 43–44d. Two of these cases are printed in Powell, *Rising*, 126–27, and translated in Dobson, 254–56.

Pamela Nightingale's thesis that the conflict in London was not generated by tensions between merchants and craftsmen but arose from antagonism against the staplers and the tensions produced by serendipitous royal interference in the city. Austin would have agreed with Nightingale that "the really disruptive force in the community of London was the crown" (34).

Finally, Banham's accusations add to the enigma of John of Gaunt's involvement in the dispute in the city. Austin and his household, Banham suggests, had high hopes of Gaunt. Gaunt's reaction to Brembre's election in 1383 was seen as critical: Austin dispatched Banham to try and find out what Gaunt proposed doing, and when Austin heard "þat ye Duk hadde nat his purpos a ȝens oure lige lord" he despaired. At the beginning of his accusations, Banham declares that Austin considered "that Norhamptone shulde hau had forthe his falshed touchynge to ye Duk of Lankastre þat he shulde hau had the betere in his wrong aȝens owre lyge lord ye Kynge." Despite these suggestive comments, however, Banham does not give any concrete information about Gaunt's connection with Northampton's party and does not help in understanding Gaunt's role in the dispute, other than by emphasizing yet again how he was widely seen as a figure of critical importance.

The editorial procedure adopted for the English portion of the document printed below is based on that used by Norman Davis in his edition of the *Paston Letters* (1:lxxx–lxxxv). Original spelling is used throughout, including the runes þ and ȝ. No attempt has been made to "correct" spelling. *Th*, for example, has been retained even where þ would be more appropriate. Extensions of abbreviations are in italics. Superscript letters in abbreviations have been dropped down. In such cases only the supplied letters (not the superscript letters) are printed in italics. Conjectural or doubtful readings are in angle brackets. Interlineations are in half-brackets. Capitalization and punctuation are editorial, as is the division into paragraphs. Parts of the Latin text are still illegible, despite the use of ultraviolet light. Illegible portions of text are indicated by angle brackets containing an ellipsis, with the number of lost words indicated in a footnote.

PUBLIC RECORD OFFICE C 258/24/9

In primis tenor accusacionis siue appellum vnde in breui domini regis hinc consuto fit mencio continetur inferius prout sequitur.

To myn worschipful meir of Londone bet knowyn that Thomas Austyn is and hath ben on of the principall meynteno*urs* of tretorie touchynge to owre lyge lord the Kyng*e*, that is for to seyne helpynge and meyntenynge with Johan Norh*a*mptone and hese in the same openyo*u*n that he was inne in the struxsio*u*n of the cete of London*e* and menynge and h⟨ol⟩dynge that Norh*a*mptone shulde hau had forth*e* his falshed touchynge to þe Duk of

Lankastre þat he shulde hau had ⟨the⟩ betere in his wrong aȝens owre lyge lord þe Kynge.

O poynt is this that Thomas Austyn was euere ⟨more⟩ redy ⟨with⟩ Johan Norhamptone body and good and alle hese for to hau stondyn with þe same Johan Norhamptone and hese in þe distruxsioun of owre lige lord þe Kynge in as ferthe forthe as he cowde and dorste and mythe.

A noþer poynt is this that whanne Sire Nichol Brembir was meir that at euery tyme that Thomas Austyn was warnyd be ⟨þe⟩ meir for to ryden or to gon in worschippynge of oure lyge lord and also in meyntenynge of the pees þat he þe forseyd Thomas Austyn was þat man þat hadde skorn and dispit and nat wolde don it but hedde hym owt of þe weye or ⟨ellse h⟩ad hym an arnde owt of towne.

An oþer poynt is this that which tyme þat the elexsioun was the seconde of Sire Nichol Brembir ij. dayes be foryn the same Thomas hadde owt his principall godes be nyghte in to dyuerse plasis ⟨to⟩ wat purpos we wote neuere.

A nother poynt ther is the same Thomas bad alle hys men þat non of þem schulde ben absent owt of his hows on þe morwyn whiche tyme þat þei seyn ony men comyn to þe ȝeldhalle but ⟨a⟩ non comyn hom and armyd hem and so dedyn and hym self Thomas Austyn was armyd at alle poyntys owttakyn his basenet and þat was rody stondynge be hym and also xv. or xvi. i armed with hym priuyly in his plase in trost þat ȝif Sire Nichol Brembir þat tyme meyr hadde y holdyn þe ȝeldhalle for to hau fallen up on hym with oþere diuerse companyes which he wende shulde hau ben there a ȝens the Kynge and þe pees and hollyche for to hau distroyyd hem þat weryn in the ryghte. And also his brother Roger Austyn cam to and fro be twenyn and warnyd Thomas Austyn alle here purpos þat þei weryn a bowtyn þe elexsion of Brembir and þer up on Thomas Austyn sente to Wigmours[a] where here fals comown counseil was holdyn þat nyghte þat is for to seigne þe meyntenours of Johan Norhamptone and warnyd hem for to ben ful redy of here purpos and what tyme on þe morwyn þat Brembir was chosyn meir he tok Chepe and þanne Thomas Austyn saw here strengthe and a non he keste offe his harneys and seide al is lost þat we hau ben a bowtyn and bad his meyne priuyly goeth to þe schoppe and settythe opyn as no þyng were don and so þei dedyn.

Also an oþer poynt þer was þat same day þat Hochoun of Lyuerpoll his seruaunt stod in his chambre in a wayte and þere cam Hewe Fastolfe and made water aȝens þe cherche wal of Seynt Laurenses and þanne seyde Hochoun of Lyuerpoll ȝonder is on of þe thefys and þanne he seide wit þou sen how I schal naylen hym with an arwe to þe wow and forthe þer withe

[a] Unidentified. Perhaps the house of Roger Wygemor, who was acquitted of involvement in disturbances following the election of Brembre; see Bird, 67, n. 1.

he teysed up his bowe for to hau keld hym *and* þanne seyde i Johan Hore
lad ben þou wilt on don us alle *and* so it was ileft.

An oþer poynt is this þat Thomas Austyn saw þat oþere false men weryn
ponsched for here on trowthe *and* was ferful þat his falshede schulde comyn owt *and* a noon he sente to his man be 3onde þe see þat he schulde
nat markyn his ware *with* his owne marke for a restynge whanne it came in

to Engelond *and* þere he lefte his trewe marke *and* tooke this marke
and þis was don in drede þat his falshed schulde hau comyn owt.

An oþer poynt is this þat þe same Thomas Austyn hathe seyd be diuerse
tymes be a wysement that it shulde neuere ben wel in Engelond whil this
kyng were kynge.

An oþer poynt is this in his presense be diuerse tymes his wiffe hath seyd
þat serteynly þat þe kynge was neuere þe prynses sone and also sche hathe
seyd þat his moder was neuere but a strong hore and þat same Thomas was
neuere þat man þat onys wolde beddyn here holdyn here wordys but cher-
schid here in here malyse.

And a noþer poynt is this þat what tyme þat þe same Thomas Austyn
saw þat þe Duk hadde nat his purpos a 3ens oure lige lord þane he seyde it
is non oþer helpe now but ho so mythe getyn ij. men and sodeynly stekyn
Brembir *and* gon her wey.

Also an oþer poynt þat whiche tyme þat þe Duk lay at Hertforde þat þe
bat was be twenyn oure lyge lord *and* hym he sente me Johan Banham to
Hertforde in al þe haste þat mythe ben don for to aspyen what tyme he
wolde comyn to Londone *and* wheþer he wolde comyn stronge or non *and*
þat man þat I Johan Banham schulde hau wist of he was nat there but he
was owte of Dukys message.

Also a nother poynt is þis þat þe same day of þe forseyde election was
Thomas Austyn bad me Johan Banham gon in to Chepe *and* aspyen 3if I
seghe eny compaignyes draughynge to þe Gildhalle þat is for to seyn Gold-
smythes Taillours Cordewaners *and* com hom *and* warne hym.

An oþer poynt is this þat diuerse tymes Thomas Austyn hath seyd þat
hit schulde neuere be wel til þe fals harlottes were honged which þat
gouerned oure lyge lord þe Kynge *and* seys Brembre be his name.

A nother poynt is this þat foure dayes byforne þat þe same election was
Thomas Austyn ⌈seyde⌉ to a man of Kydermynstre now þe mair wenethe
þat he shulde haue non mene a geynes hym at shuche a day he shal haue a
geynes hym mo þan a thousand let hym make hym as mery as he wel.

A nother poynt is þis þat he hathe stolne of oure lige lord þe Kyng a
thousand pounde.

A nother point is þis at diuerse tymes he seyde he roghte neuere who
were Kynge so he were in pees.

A nother poynt is this þat whiche tyme þat Norhamptones brother was in prisoun al þat euer he couthe aspyen he was þat man þat warned hym word for word als myche as he couthe by me Johan Banham and y Johan Banham wyl stonden herby þat withe outen eny fraude or male engyne þat þis is god and trewe.

Et quo ad tenorem alicuius indictamenti non habemus nec cepimus aliquod aliud indictamentum tangens personas in dicto breui domini regis nominatas nec aliquem illorum nisi super articulis et accusacionibus in ista cedula superius specificatis per quandam inquisicionem nuper coram nobis Nicholo Exton maiore ciuitatis London' Willelmo More et Willelmo Staundon' nuper vicecomitibus et Iohanne Charneye coronatore eiusdem ciuitatis captum cuius ⟨. . .⟩[b] indictamenti tenorem vobis mittimus in forma qua sequitur:

Inquisicio capta apud Gihaldam London' die lune proxima post festum Exaltacionis Sancte Crucis anno regni regis Ricardi secundi vndecimo coram Nicholo Exton' maiore ciuitatis London' Willelmo More et Willelmo Staundon' vicecomitibus et Iohanne Charneye coronatore eiusdem ciuitatis per sacramentum proborum et legalorum hominum ciuitatis predicte ad inquirendum super articulis et accusacionibus in predicta billa contentis et specificatis. Et iurati inquisicionum predicte super sacramentum suum presentant et dicunt quod omnia in dicta billa contenta sunt vera excepta illa articula continente þat he hathe stole of oure lige lord þe Kyng a thousand pounde. Et quod predictus Thomas Austyn culpabilis est de omnibus aliis articulis et accusacionibus in eadem billa contentis et specificatis set ubi in ⟨predicta⟩ billa supponitur quod predictus Thomas Austyn furatus fuit de domino Rege mille libras. Iidem iurati dicunt quod inde ignorant ⟨et⟩ dicunt quod idem Thomas Austyn diuersis temporibus concelauit et retinuit custumias domini Regis uidelicet de subsidis ⟨. . .⟩[c] pannis lineis velaminibus et aliis mercandisis suis ad dictam ciuitatem London' ex partibus externis adductis ad summam centum viginti et quinque librorum. Et dicunt dicti iurati quod omnia alia mala in predicta billa contenta facta fuerunt et preposita ante electionem Nicholo Brembre militis in maiorem ciuitiatis London' videlicet ante festum Translacionis Sancti Edwardi regis et confessoris anno regni domini regis nunc octauo et continuata usque circiter primum diem maii tunc proxima sequente et nichil postea in facte prout inter se inquirere possunt. Set dicunt iidem iurati quod predictus Thomas Austyn hucusque continuauit huiusmodi malum propositum suum in corde suo videlicet contra gubernacionem dicte ciuitatis ut intendunt.

Et nos Willelmus Venour et Hugo Fastolf vicecomites London' non habemus aliqua indictamenta appella siue accusaciones unde in dicto breui fit

[b] One word illegible.
[c] One word illegible.

mencio coram nobis aliqualiter residencia vel capta de tempore quo nos fuimus vicecomites ciuitatis predicte.

Et ulterius ego Nicholus Exton' maior vobis significo quod quedam horribilis accusacio facta fuit coram me et predictis Willelmo More et Willelmo Staundon' nuper vicecomitibus versus Rogerum Austyn tangens personam domini Regis de qua sine speciali mandato dicti domini Regis non audemus inquirere neque certificare tamen semper in secretis parati erimus ad eam dicendum et dominus Rex de materia inde plene est informatus.

Appendix 2

THE LITERATURE OF LIVERY

RICHARD II was wise to emphasize public order and the abuses of livery and maintenance during his 1388–1390 campaign for a return to sole rule. As demonstrated by the petitions in the Cambridge Parliament of 1388, these were already issues of the highest importance to the parliamentary commons. In fact, a highly developed legal and literary discourse on the abuse of liveries had been crystallizing for nearly a century and would endure for a century more. Articulating his own concerns within its bounds, Richard was able to display heightened responsiveness to a matter of importance to influential subjects with a minimal expenditure of energy and imagination. Yet a brief survey of the "literature of livery" demonstrates that such a discourse does not serve a single master.

The "botouns" of the "capel-claweres." Commentaries of the late thirteenth century begin to embrace a new explanation for local disorder (or at any rate an emphasis so new that it virtually constitutes a new explanation). Instead of treating disorder as a consequence of decline or dissolution of previously existing authority, they treat it as the result of a novel and disturbing proliferation of associative forms. Justices in York in 1294 reported, for example, that the administration of law was completely choked by "influential maintainers of false complaints and champertors and conspirators leagued together" (Harding, 148).

When Parliament acted against local felonies and transgressions in its 1305 ordinance against trailbaston, it acknowledged the potentially collusive nature of these acts by adding a separate definition of conspiracy. This definition begins with abuses of oath-taking, moves to judicial interference, and pauses over a perception about retinue-building:

> Conspiratours sount ceux qui s'entre alient par serment, covenaunt, ou par autre alliaunce, qe chescun eidra & sustendra autri emprise de fausement & maliciousment enditer . . . ou acquiter les gentz, ou faussement mover plees ou meintener. . . . Et ceux qui receivent gentz de pais a lour robes ou a lour feez pur meintenir lour mauveis enprises. (*RP*, 1:183)

> Conspirators ally themselves by oath, covenant, or other alliance, to aid and sustain each other in false indictments . . . and acquitals, or in maintaining false pleas, . . . and include those who enlist people from the countryside with liveries or fees to maintain their evil activities.

Each of the emphases of this ordinance would become enormously important in the course of the century, but it is particularly prescient in noting the new flexibility creeping into practices of oath-taking, and the new ease of retinue-building by liveries or fees.[1]

The perceptions of this ordinance are borne out in a nearly contemporaneous semialliterative poem, in which a jaundiced west-country poet blasts the behavior of lordly retinues and their vast proliferation to embrace a rout of ribalds, grooms, gadelings (or rascally companions), harlots, knaves, palfreyers, and pages, whose arrogance is fostered by association with the lord whom they serve (Robbins, 27–29). Seesawing between political satire and homiletically based castigation of worldly vanities, the poet launches a telling sarcasm, which may constitute the first poetic reference to the use of identifying clothing in retinue-formation:

> Nou beth capel-claweres with shome to-shrude [clothed];
> hue bosketh huem wyth botouns, ase hit were a brude,
> with lowe lacede shon of an hayfre hude [heifer's hide],
> hue pyketh [choose] of here prouendre al huere prude.
>
> (ll. 25–28)

These "capel-clawers" (literally, "horse-clawers" or "grooms") display pride, not only in stylishly cut leather shoes and fastidious eating habits, but in their attire, adorning themselves with *botouns* as if they were brides. These *botouns* may, of course, simply be buttons—adornments of a sort taken for granted today but regarded in the fourteenth century as fatuous and impractical, like leather shoes. But, within this poem's blistering condemnation of the lordly retinue, they probably possess an additional, nonstylistic implication, as *signa* or badges of liveried association, prideful not just in their quality of adornment but in their implication of seigneurial sponsorship.

The Yorkshire maintainers. Novel practices of association for mutual ad-

---

[1] Use of the term *recevoir*, or "receive," instead of the fourteenth-century *retenir* or "retain," may be understood in either of two ways. On the one hand, it may indicate a simple unawareness of the prevalent fourteenth-century usage. On the other, it may signal a desire to underscore an important difference, contrasting the easy availability of robes, short-term fees, and other epiphenomena of short-term attachment with the greater formality of retention. Seen in this respect, the recipient of livery acknowledges a tie, but a tie short of retention, and lesser in degree than that which would convey membership in the retinue, with others who have "been retained." This distinction is at least partially observed in the fourteenth century; the 1390 ordinance, for example, argues that the bestowal of livery should be reconnected to retention, that livery should be given only to those who have been retained. A virtue of J.M.W. Bean's *From Lord to Patron* is his insistence that retention, the granting of annuities, and the distribution of liveries are separate practices, though all interrelated as new forms of lordship originating in the requirements of the household (10–22).

vantage were not to remain the property of the lords.[2] A contemporaneous band, flourishing completely apart from aristocratic sponsorship and drawing its membership from tradesmen and laborers and other persons of unspecified vocation, is actually to be found in Yorkshire, in 1387–1393.[3] An indictment heard before the king's bench in 1393 alleges that some eighty malefactors organized a covin that endured for six years. Its members dressed themselves in the livery of a single company in a display of false allegiance and confederacy, each maintaining the other in all quarrels, true and false: various named persons

> cum aliis malefactoribus ad numerum quateruiginti malefactorum de eorum couina . . . per sex annos vltimo elapsos vestiti fuerunt in vna liberata de vnica secta per falsam alliganciam et confederacionem, quilibet eorum in omnibus querelis veris vel falsis alterum manutenendo." *KB*, 7:83–84.

The members of this covin showed up in their livery on numerous occasions during the seven years of their heyday, usually for purposes of coercion, and on several occasions recited a poem of their own composition.

John Berwald and his associates composed their poem within the understanding that practices of maintenance are prevalent and that neighbors must act reciprocally to defend one another. They suggest that "schrewes" have invaded their jurisdiction or *soke*, with schemes for self-advancement, and that precedents for such connivance exist among "frers . . . / And other ordres many mo." Their proposed solution is to embrace practices of maintenance on their own behalf, and they have plainly grasped its central prin-

[2] A proscribed 1306 alliance of merchants in the city of York was neither a traditional craft guild nor a religious fraternity, but a sworn association of tradesmen in a variety of occupations meant only to advance their prosperity by legal and economic collusion (Sayles, "Dissolution"). After mid-century, such associations began to appear among peasants and unorganized rural workers. A statute of 1377 complains, for example, of villeins and other tenants of lords who confederate themselves in great routs to aid each other to oppose their lords ("ils se coillent ensemble a grantz routes & sentrelient par tiel confederacie qe chescun aidra autre a contrester lours Seignours a fort mayn"), with the support of various "conseillours meyntenours & abettours" *Stat.* [335]. An accompanying statute of the same year, aimed at rural strata situated between the peasants and the great lords, complains that people of small revenue make retinues by easy means, gathering themselves in fraternities and distributing livery in order to maintain each other ("plusours gentz de petit garison . . . se coillent ensemble en fraternitez par . . . livere affaire meyntenaunce" *Stat.* [335]).

[3] The band included a farrier, two butchers, and numerous agricultural workers of unspecified occupation (*KB*, 7:83–85). They operated without apparent noble sponsorship, although Richard II's eventual pardon may suggest that, for all their comradely bluster, they were operating with the complicity of the lord of Cottingham, Thomas Holland, one of Richard's closest associates. After all, they apparently needed a good deal of pardoning; they stood accused of "divers trespasses . . . , contempts, maintenances, sworn conspiracies, assemblies, taking of fines and ransoms . . . , liveries of hoods of uniform suit contrary to the ordinance, confederacies, ambushes . . . , assaults . . . , false alliances by confederation that each would maintain the other," and so on (*CPR* [1391–1396], 249).

ciple, that one maintains a brother whether or not he happens to be in the right:

> And [y]et wil ilkan hel vp other
> And meynteyn him als his brother
>   bothe in wronge and righte.

Despite an appeal to neighborly sentiments ("also wil in stond and stoure / Meynteyn owre negheboure"), and an assurance that everyone is free to move "to and froo" among them, their primary allegiance is one to another and their mutual determination is to see that their members experience no "hethyng" or scorn. The nature of their tie is, they boast, such that an injury to one is an injury to all:

> And on that purpos yet we stand
> Who so dose vs any wrang
>   in what place it falle
> Yet he myght als wele
> As haue i hap and hele
>   do again vs alle.

The poem's central strategy is simply to embrace what everyone already knows about maintainers: that they stick up for each other, right or wrong. The poem is, in other words, produced within a matrix of mainly negative comment about maintenance, and its ingenuity is to stand these criticisms on their heads, to embrace them unapologetically.[4]

Richard II rides the discursive tiger. Richard's histrionic offer in the Cambridge Parliament of 1388 to set aside his own *signa* was an attempt to tap into his subjects' unease about the consequences of short-term affiliation. As signaled by the apparent approval of the Westminster chronicler, Richard was briefly successful in corralling an immense body of already articulated sentiment against the distribution of liveries and redirecting it for ends of his own. But, although so large, varied, and influential a body

---

[4] The Yorkshire maintainers seem to have realized that these appropriations and extensions of widely held sentiments about maintenance, stripped of apology and enlisted in an ideologically based offensive, could serve their cause well. The poem is written for accessibility, in a meter and rhyme scheme similar to those that Chaucer was concurrently parodying in *Sir Thopas*, and it was promulgated according to the ambitious schedule of public readings noted in the indictment. Along with their adoption of and frequent appearance in *una liberata*, and willingness to show the occasional strong hand, the poem seems to have been an element in a highly successful program of self-representation to the people of the countryside. This program may be seen as conceived and launched within the ideologically hostile terrain of the official discourse on livery and maintenance, and as—at least locally and temporarily—recasting and redirecting that discourse for purposes of their own. A sign of the Yorkshiremen's success, whether ideological or practical or both, is that they seem, however unaccountably, to have gained Richard's personal pardon, and the case against them seems to have been excused when they came before him on 21 May 1393 (*KB*, 7:85).

of discourse as that directed against liveries may be briefly turned to one account or another, it cannot be securely possessed—or not, at any rate, by anyone so deficient as Richard in the art of consistent self-portrayal. When Richard, having already set a standard for lavish distribution of *signa* in 1387, turned again to this practice with the new livery of the White Hart at Smithfield in 1390, he put himself at odds with the very discourse through which he had thought to gain advantage. And this discourse provided his detractors with the language and concepts of his rebuke.

As Richard languished in prison between August 1399 and February 1400, a west-country author began an alliterative poem of admonition that has come to be called *Richard the Redeles*. First contemplated as a poem of advice to Richard in his kingship (prologue, ll. 30–31), it is carried forward in that period of uncertainty between Henry's first successes (ll. 11–14) and some final determination of Richard's fate (ll. 25–29)—though prudently directed to a larger audience than the imprisoned king (ll. 53f.). It emphasizes Richard's failings as a guardian of good justice and local order, and, particularly, his abusive and puzzling overreliance on the livery of the White Hart:

> But moche now me merueilith / and well may I in sothe,
> Of youre large leuerey [livery] / to leodis aboute,
> That ye so goodliche gaf / but if gile letted,
> As hertis y-heedyd / and hornyd of kynde.

> (2.1–4)

An aspect of the genius of this poem is that it not only deplores Richard's use of signs but creates a phantasm in which "signes / that swarmed so thikke" (l. 21) overrun the country. In fact, as Nick Ronan has shrewdly pointed out (311–14), the *signes* themselves metonymically become the actors in this farce, swaggering about in every holt and town. The harts and hinds themselves "acombrede the contre" (l. 28), and the liveries poked into everyone's affairs: "Thus leueres ouere-loked / Youre liegis ichonne" (l. 35). Not only, finally, do they run riot through the realm, but they provide the poet with a tool of thought and elaboration: rather than imagining the behavior of harts to reflect that of the men who bear them, the poet finds the men to exhibit hartlike behavior. In fact, he wryly argues (in apparent allusion to Henry's landing in July, consolidation of his position in August, and triumph with Parliament in late September) that their failure might have been predicted, for the end of summer was near and molting-time was at hand:

> And also in sothe / the seson was paste
> For hertis yheedid [headed] / so hy and so noble
> To make ony myrthe / for mowtynge that nyghed.

> (ll. 10–12)

The herd that once held together, he observes, was to scatter into forests and fields. The actual effect of such signs is, the poet believes, to destroy allegiance, creating mistrust among subjects who all, initially, had every reason to love their king. For all their metonymic vitality, these signs are finally empty signifiers, which point to no established relationship, to nothing beyond themselves:

Thane was it foly / in feith, as me thynketh,
To sette siluer in signes / that of nought serued.

(ll. 44–45)

Speaking only of the period 1390–1399, when Richard devoted himself to the livery of the White Hart, the poet seems not to realize that Richard had a longer involvement with liveries—including his earlier (even less effectual) experiment with *signa* in 1387, and his emergence in 1388–1390 as a monarch so opposed to *signa* he was ready to forgo his own. So much the better, the poet would surely have concluded had he known the whole story, for Richard to have stuck with his own reformist program.

Fifteenth-century Yorkshire: "All is thrugh mantenance." In 1468, Parliament acted at the instance of Edward IV, noting that "dyvers Estatutes for punicion of such persones that gyven or resceyven Lyverees . . . have be made, and that yet dyvers persones in grete nombre . . . daily offenden ayenst the fourme of same," and seeking enforcement of all previous statutes.[5]

When the Wakefield *Second Shepherds' Pageant* was composed in the last third of the fifteenth century, maintenance was more a fact of life than it had ever been—and all the more eligible to serve in this play as one of several emblems of rural privation and subjection in a world unknowingly awaiting a new spiritual dispensation. Martin Stevens has observed that the Wakefield Cycle represents the transformation of the "city" plays of York into "manorial" drama in which contemporary society and its abuses are represented in terms of a county seat, run by landed gentry through the presiding agency of the manorial court (126). His perception is certainly borne out by the opening monologue of the first shepherd, whose troubled state involves not only physical discomfort, bewildering and unreadable signs, and images of sterility, but oppression as well. Oppression occurs at the hands of "gentlery-men":

---

[5] This statute may, as argued by J.M.W. Bean, represent an attempted extension of royal control (213–17). Even if so, the increased acceptance of practices of livery and maintenance is indicated by a lengthy list of appended exceptions, including liveries given by the king for the defense of the realm, or at the coronation, or the marriage of any lord, or the commencement of any clerk, or the making of sergeants of law, or given by any guild or fraternity or craft, or by any mayor or sheriff of any city . . . and so on.

We ar mayde handtamyd
With thise gentlery-men.
Thus thay refe us oure rest, Oure Lady theym wary!
These men that ar lord-fest, thay cause the ploghe tary.

(ll. 16–20)

The problem is not, in other words, the lord of the manor himself, but the gentlemen in his service, those who are "lord-fest" or bound in a form of service from which they derive their authority. This derivative authority, together with the form of its announcement, is then disclosed:

For, may he gett a paint slefe or a broche now-on-dayes,
Wo is him that him grefe or onys agane says!
Dar no man him reprefe, what mastry he mays.
And yit may no man lefe oone word that he says,
No letter.
He can make purveance
With boste and bragance;
And all is thrugh mantenance
Of men that ar gretter.

(ll. 28–36)

The retainer, bearing the livery of a painted sleeve or brooch, derives his authority through "mantenance" of a "gretter" man, his lord.

That signs of lordship might be as modest as a sleeve or brooch need not surprise us; we have already seen the early fourteenth-century use of *botouns* as well as the presumably simple *liberata* of the Yorkshire maintainers. Yet, as J.M.W. Bean points out, the 1468 statute is the most comprehensive thus far in its reference to signs other than suits or robes as evidence of retaining (178). That a liveried henchman on a fifteenth-century Yorkshire moor could serve the playwright as an emblem of worldly discomfort suggests both the continuation and the diversification of maintenance practices.[6]

---

[6] Emphasis on the derivative and attenuated status of symbolic lordship is then reinforced in an encounter with an irrefutably bogus authority: Mak the trickster, posing as a king's yeoman, deriving his claim to reverence on an imagined relation to an absent lord: "What! ich be a yoman, I tell you, of the king, / The self and the some, sond [messenger] from a greatt lording." Mak fools no one, but the point in this play is not success or failure but imposture itself—unwitting enactment, of both the false lordship that promotes continued oppression and disharmony and a portended birth that promotes liberation and harmony. More than just contemporary "satire," maintenance is converted to something else, an emblem of illegitimate authority and self-deception in a world that awaits revelation.

WORKS CITED

MANUSCRIPTS
Public Record Office:
  Close Rolls:
    C54/215, mem. 3d
    C54/226, mem. 26
    C54/229, mem. 32d
    C54/288, mem. 32d
  King's Bench:
    KB/27/507, mems. 40–41
    KB/27/508, mem. 4
  Miscellanea of the Exchequer:
    E163/5/28, nos. 9, 12
  Chancery Miscellanea:
    C258/24, no. 9
  Gaol Delivery:
    JUST 3/177, mem. 27a
    JUST 3/180, mem. 30a
Corporation of the City of London:
  Letter-Book G, fol. cccvii
  Letter-Book H, fols. ccxxiv, xxxxix
  Mayor's Court Roll 1, mem. 2
  Plea and Memoranda Rolls, A/25, mem. 3b, A/27, mem. 2

PRIMARY SOURCES

Adam of Usk. *Chronicon*. 2d. ed. Ed. Edward Maunde Thompson. London: Henry Frowde, 1904.

Annales Ricardi Secundi, Regis Angliae. Ed. H. T. Riley. Rolls Series, no. 28, pt. 3. London, 1866. [*Annales*]

Anonimalle Chronicle. Ed. V. H. Galbraith. Manchester: Manchester University Press, 1970.

Bracton, Henri de. *De Legibus et Consuetudinibus Angliae*. Vol. 2. Ed. Samuel E. Thorne. Cambridge, Mass.: Belknap Press, 1968.

Brut. Ed. F.W.D. Brie. EETS, o.s., vol. 131, pt. 2, 1908.

Calendar of Close Rolls, 1327–99 (numerous volumes, cited by year). London: Stationery Office, 1896–1927. [*CCR*]

Calendar of Early Mayor's Court Rolls, 1298–1307. Ed. A. H. Thomas. Cambridge: Cambridge University Press, 1924.

Calendar of Fine Rolls, 1307–99 (numerous volumes, cited by year). London: Stationery Office, 1912–29. [*CFR*]

Calendar of Inquisitions Post Mortem. Vol. 15. London: Stationery Office, 1970.

Calendar of Letter-Books of the City of London, Letter-Books G and H. Ed. Reginald R. Sharpe. London: Corporation of the City of London, 1907. [*CLBG, CLBH*]

Calendar of Patent Rolls, 1327–99 (numerous volumes, cited by year). London: Stationery Office, 1891–1916. [*CPR*]

Chaucer, Geoffrey. *Minor Poems*. Ed. George B. Pace and Alfred David. In *The Variorum Chaucer*, vol. 5, pt. 1. Norman, Okla.: University of Oklahoma Press, 1982.

———. *The Riverside Chaucer*. 3d. ed. Boston: Houghton Mifflin, 1987.

Chronicles of London. Ed. C. L. Kingsford. Oxford: Clarendon Press, 1905. [*Chronicles*]

Chronicque de la Traïson et Mort. Ed. Benjamin Williams. London: English Historical Society, 1846. [*Traïson*]

Creton, Jean. *Histoire du Roy d'Angleterre Richard*. Ed. and trans. J. Webb. *Archaeologia* 20 (1824), 1–402.

Dauzat, Albert. *Dictionnaire Etymologique des Noms de Famille et Prénoms de France*. Paris: Librairie Larousse, 1980.

Davis, Norman. *Paston Letters and Papers of the Fifteenth Century*. Vol. 1. Oxford: Oxford University Press, 1971.

Eulogium and *Continuatio Eulogii*. Ed. Frank Scott Hayden. Rolls Series, no. 9, pt. 3. London: Longmans, 1863.

Froissart, Jean. *Chroniques*. Ed. Siméon Luce. Société de l'histoire de France, no. 159, vol. 4. Paris: Renouard, 1873.

———. *Oeuvres*. Vols. 5, 9, 16. Ed. Kervyn de Lettenhove. Brussels: Devaux, 1868, 1869, 1872.

Gower, John. *Works*. Ed. G. C. Macaulay. 4 vols. Oxford: Clarendon Press, 1899–1902.

"Gregory's Chronicle." In *The Historical Collections of a Citizen of London*, ed. James Gairdner. Camden Publications, n.s., vol. 17. London: Camden Society, 1876.

Hardyng, John. *Chronicle*. Ed. Henry Ellis. 1812. Reprint. New York: AMS, 1974.

Historia Vitae et Regni Ricardi Secundi. Ed. George B. Stow, Jr. Philadelphia: University of Pennsylvania Press, 1977. [*Historia Ricardi*]

Index to Testamentary Records in the Commissary Court of London (London Division). Ed. M. Fitch. British Record Society, 1969.

Julius B II. *Chronicles of London*. Ed. C. L. Kingsford. Oxford: Clarendon Press, 1905.

Knighton, Henry. *Chronicon*. Vol. 2. Ed. Joseph W. Lumby. Roll Series, no. 92. London, 1895.

Lambarde, William. *Eirenarcha, or the Office of Justices of the Peace*. London: T. Wright and B. Norton, 1599.

Latham, R. *Dictionary of Medieval Latin from British Sources*. London: Oxford University Press, 1975.

Leadham, I. S. and J. F. Baldwin. *Select Cases before the King's Council, 1243–1482*. Selden Society, vol. 35. Cambridge: Harvard University Press, 1918. [*KC*]

le Bel, Jean. *Chronique*. Ed. Jules Viard and Eugène Déprez. SHF, no. 324. Paris: Renouard, 1905.

"Liber Regalis." In *English Coronation Records*, ed. L.G.W. Legg. Westminster: Constable, 1901.

Maidstone [Maydiston], Richard. *Concordia: Facta inter Regem Riccardum II et*

Civitatem Londonie. Ed. Charles Roger Smith. Ann Arbor: University Microfilms, 1972.

The Mirror of Justices. Vol. 7. Ed. W. Whittaker. London: Selden Society, vol. 7. London: Quaritch, 1893.

"Petition of the Folk of Mercerye." In *A Book of London English, 1384–1425*, ed. R. W. Chambers and Marjorie Daunt. Oxford: Clarendon Press, 1931. ["Petition"]

Pisan, Christine de. *Lavision-Christine.* Ed. Sr. Mary Louis Towner. Washington: Catholic University, 1932.

———. *Oeuvres Poétiques de Christine de Pisan.* Vol. 1. Ed. Maurice Loy. Paris: SATF, 1886.

Placita Corone. Ed. J. M. Kaye. Selden Society, supplementary Series, vol. 4. London, 1966.

Powell, Edgar. *The Rising in East Anglia in 1381.* Cambridge: Cambridge University Press, 1896.

Powell, Edgar, and G. M. Trevelyan, eds. *The Peasants' Rising and the Lollards.* London: Longmans, Green, 1899.

Rhetorica ad Herennium. Ed. Harry Caplan. Cambridge, Mass., and London: Loeb Classical Library, 1954.

Richard the Redeles. In *Mum and the Sothsegger*, ed. Mabel Day and Robert Steele. EETS, o.s. 199, 1936.

Robbins, Rossell Hope. *Historical Poems of the Fourteenth and Fifteenth Centuries.* New York: Columbia University Press, 1959.

Rolls of Parliament [Rotuli Parliamentorum]. Vol. 2 (1326–77), vol. 3 (1377–1411). London, 1783. [*RP*]

Royal Commission on Historical Monuments (England). *An Inventory of the Historical Monuments in London.* Vol. 1, *Westminster Abbey*. London: Stationery Office, 1924. [*Inventory*]

Rymer, Thomas, ed. *Foedera.* Vol. 3, pt. 4. The Hague: Joannen Neaulme, 1740.

Sayles, G. O. "The Deposition of Richard II: Three Lancastrian Narratives." *Bull. Inst. Hist. Res.* 54 (1981), 257–270.

———, ed. *Select Cases in the Court of King's Bench Under Richard II, Henry IV and Henry V.* Vols. 6–7. Selden Society, vols. 82, 88. London: Quaritch, 1965, 1971. [*KB*]

Second Shepherds' Play. In *Medieval Drama*, ed. David Bevington. Boston: Houghton Mifflin, 1975.

Select Cases from the Coroners' Rolls, 1265–1413. Ed. Charles Gross. Selden Society, vol. 9. London: Quaritch, 1896.

Select Pleas and Memoranda of the City of London, 1381–1412. Ed. A. H. Thomas. Cambridge: Cambridge University Press, 1932. [*Pleas*]

Statutes of the Realm. Vol. 1. London: Basket, 1763. Also: Vol. 1. London: Dawsons, 1810. [*Stat.*]

Steele, Robert. *Three Prose Versions of the* Secreta Secretorum. EETS, extra series, 74. London, 1898.

Stockton, Eric W., trans. *The Major Latin Works of John Gower.* Seattle: University of Washington Press, 1962.

Suggett, Helen. "A Letter Describing Richard II's Reconciliation with the City of London, 1392." *EHR* 62 (1947), 209–13.

Usk, Thomas. "Appeal of Thomas Usk against John Northampton." In *A Book of London English, 1384–1425*, ed. R. W. Chambers and Marjorie Daunt. Oxford: Clarendon Press, 1931. ["Appeal"]

———. *The Testament of Love.* In *The Complete Works of Geoffrey Chaucer.* vol. 7. Ed. W. W. Skeat. Oxford: Clarendon Press, 1897.

Virgoe, R. "Some Ancient Indictments in the King's Bench Referring to Kent, 1450–2." In *Documents Illustrative of Medieval Kentish Society*, ed. F.R.H. Du Boulay. Kent Archaeological Society, 1964.

Walsingham, Thomas. *Gesta Abbatum Monasterii Sancti Albani.* Vol. 3 (1349–1411). Ed. H. T. Riley. Rolls Series, no. 28, pt. 4. London: Longmans, 1869.

———. *Historia Anglicana.* 2 vols. Ed. H. T. Riley. 2 vols. Rolls Series, no. 28, pt. 1. London: Longmans, 1863, 1864.

The Westminster Chronicle, 1381–1394. Ed. L. C. Hector and Barbara Harvey. Oxford: Clarendon Press, 1966. [*West.*]

SECONDARY SOURCES

Alford, John A. *Piers Plowman: A Glossary of Legal Diction.* Cambridge: D. S. Brewer, 1988.

Althusser, Louis. *Essays on Ideology.* London: Verso Books, 1984.

———. *For Marx.* London: Penguin Press, 1969.

Amsler, Mark. "The Wife of Bath and Women's Power." *Assays* 4 (1987), 67–83.

Aston, M. "A Kent Approver of 1440," *Bull. Inst. Hist. Res.* 36 (1963), 83–90.

Baker, J. *Introduction to English Legal History.* 3d ed. London: Butterworths, 1990.

Bakhtin, M. M., *Rabelais and His World.* Bloomington, Ind.: Indiana University Press, 1984.

Bakhtin, M. M., and P. M. Medvedev. *The Formal Method in Literary Scholarship.* Cambridge: Harvard University Press, 1985.

Barnes, P. "The Chancery Corpus Cum Causa File, 10–11 Edward IV." In *Medieval Legal Records*, ed. R. F. Hunnisett and J. B. Post, pp. 430–76. London: Stationery Office, 1978.

Barron, Caroline M. "The Deposition of Richard II." In *Politics and Crisis in Fourteenth-Century England*, ed. John Taylor and Wendy Childs, pp. 132–49. Gloucester: Alan Sutton, 1990.

———. *The Medieval Guildhall of London.* Corporation of London, 1974.

———. "The Parish Fraternities of Medieval London." In *The Church in Pre-Reformation Society*, ed. Caroline M. Barron and C. Harper-Bill, pp. 13–37. Woodbridge, Suffolk: Boydell Press, 1985.

———. "The Quarrel of Richard II with London." In *The Reign of Richard II*, ed. F.R.H. DuBoulay and Caroline M. Barron, pp. 173–201. London: Athlone Press, 1971.

———. "Revolt in London: 11th to 15th June 1381." Museum of London, 1981.

Barron, W.R.J. "The Penalties for Treason in Medieval Life and Literature." *Journal of Medieval History* 7 (1981), 187–202.

Bean, J.M.W. *From Lord to Patron: Lordship in Late Medieval England*. Philadelphia: University of Pennsylvania Press, 1989.

Bell, Robert. *Poetical Works of Geoffrey Chaucer*. Vol. 8. London: Griffin, 1854.

Bellamy, J. G. *Crime and Public Order in England in the Later Middle Ages*. London: Routledge and Kegan Paul, 1973.

————. *The Law of Treason in England in the Middle Ages*. Cambridge: Cambridge University Press, 1970.

Bennett, Judith M. *Women in the Medieval English Countryside*. New York: Oxford Univerity Press, 1987.

Bercé, Yves-Marie. *Fête et Révolte. Des mentalités populaires du XVIe au XVIIIe siècle*. Paris: Hachette, 1976.

————. *Histoire des Croquants. Etudes des soulèvements populaires au XVIIe siècle dans le Sud-Quest de la France*. 2 vols. Paris: Droz, 1974.

Bird, Ruth. *The Turbulent London of Richard II*. London: Longmans, Green, 1949.

Bressie, Ramona. "A Study of Thomas Usk's *Testament of Love* as an Autobiography." *University of Chicago Abstracts of Theses*, humanistic series, vol. 7, pp. 517–22. Chicago: University of Chicago Press, 1928–29.

Brewer, D. S. *Chaucer*. 3d. ed. London: Longmans, 1973.

Bristol, Michael D. *Carnival and Theater*. London: Methuen, 1985.

Bronson, Bertrand H. *In Search of Chaucer*. Toronto: University of Toronto Press, 1960.

Brooks, Nicholas. "The Organization and Achievements of the Peasants of Kent and Essex in 1381." In *Studies in Medieval History Presented to R.H.C. Davis*, ed. Henry Mayr-Harting and R. I. Moore, pp. 247–70. London: Hambledon Press, 1985.

Brown, A. L. "Parliament, c. 1377–1422." In *The English Parliament in the Middle Ages*, ed. R. G. Davies and J. H. Denton. Philadelphia: University of Pennsylvania Press, 1981.

Brusendorff, Aage. *The Chaucer Tradition*. Oxford: Clarendon Press, 1925.

Bynum, Caroline Walker. *Holy Feast and Holy Fast*. Berkeley: University of California Press, 1987.

————. *Jesus as Mother*. Berkeley: University of California Press, 1982.

Carruthers, Mary. "The Wife of Bath and the Painting of Lions." *PMLA* 94 (1979), 209–22.

Chambers, R. W. and Marjorie Daunt. *A Book of London English, 1384–1425*. Oxford: Clarendon Press, 1931.

Clarke, M. V. and Galbraith, V. H. *The Deposition of Richard II*. Manchester: Manchester University Press, 1930.

Coakley, John. "Female Sanctity as a Male Concern among Thirteenth-Century Friars." Paper presented at conference "Gender and Society II." *Fordham University*, New York, New York, 1989.

Cohn, Norman. *The Pursuit of the Millennium*. London: Temple Smith, 1970.

Coontz, Stephanie. "History and Family Theory." *Rethinking Marxism* 2 (Winter 1989), 97–106.

Crane, Susan. "The Writing Lesson of 1381." In *Literature in Historical Context: Chaucer's England*, ed. Barbara Hanawalt. Minneapolis: University of Minnesota Press, 1992.

Cross, J. E. "The Old Swedish *Trohetsvisan* and Chaucer's *Lak of Stedfastnesse*—A Study in a Mediaeval Genre." *Saga-Book* 16 (1965), 283–314.

Crow, Martin M., and Clair C. Olson. *Chaucer Life-Records*. Oxford: Clarendon Press, 1966.

David, Alfred. *The Strumpet Muse*. Bloomington, Ind.: Indiana University Press, 1976.

Davis, Natalie Zemon. *Society and Culture in Early Modern France*. Stanford, Cal.: Stanford University Press, 1975.

de Certeau, Michel. *The Practice of Everyday Life*. Trans. Steven Rendall. Berkeley: University of California Press, 1984.

Delany, Sheila. "Sexual Economics, Chaucer's Wife of Bath, and *The Book of Margery Kempe*." *The Minnesota Review*, n.s. 5 (1975), 104–15.

De Smith, S. "The Prerogative Writs." *Cambridge Law Journal* 11 (1951), 45–48.

Dinshaw, Carolyn. *Chaucer's Sexual Poetics*. Madison: University of Wisconsin Press, 1989.

Dobson, R. B. *The Peasants' Revolt of 1381*. London: Macmillan, 1970.

Douglas, Mary. *Purity and Danger*. London: Routledge and Kegan Paul, 1978.

Dyer, Christopher. "The Social and Economic Background to the Rural Revolt of 1381." In *The English Rising of 1381*, ed. R. H. Hilton and T. H. Aston, pp. 9–42. Cambridge: Cambridge University Press, 1984.

Facinger, Marion F. "A Study of Medieval Queenship: Capetian France, 987–1237." *Studies in Medieval and Renaissance History* 5 (1968), 3–47.

Faith, Rosamond. "The 'Great Rumour' of 1377 and Peasant Ideology." In *The English Rising of 1381*, ed. R. H. Hilton and T. H. Aston, pp. 43–73. Cambridge: Cambridge University Press, 1984.

Farmer, Sharon. "Persuasive Voices: Clerical Images of Medieval Wives." *Speculum* 61 (1986), 517–43.

Ferris, Sumner J. "The Date of Chaucer's Final Annuity and of the 'Complaint to His Empty Purse.'" *Modern Philology* 65 (1967), 45–52.

Fisher, John H. *John Gower: Moral Philosopher and Friend of Chaucer*. New York: New York Univerity Press, 1964.

Flandrin, Jean-Louis. *Families in Former Times*. Trans. Richard Southern. Cambridge: Cambridge University Press, 1979.

Fraad, Harriet, Stephen Resnick, and Richard Wolff. " 'For Every Knight in Shining Armor, There's a Castle Waiting to Be Cleaned': A Marxist-Feminist Analysis of the Household." *Rethinking Marxism* 2 (Winter 1989), 9–69.

Fradenburg, Louise O. "The Wife of Bath's Passing Fancy." *Studies in the Age of Chaucer* 8 (1986), 31–58.

Frank, Robert Worth, Jr. *Chaucer and* The Legend of Good Women. Cambridge: Harvard University Press, 1972.

Gabel, Leona C. *Benefit of Clergy in England in the Later Middle Ages*. Smith College Studies in History, vol. 14. Northampton, Mass.: Smith College, 1929.

Galbraith, V. H. "A New Life of Richard II." *History* 26 (1942), 223–39.

Ganim, John M. *Chaucerian Theatricality*. Princeton: Princeton University Press, 1990.

Garay, Kathleen E. "Women and Crime in Later Medieval England: An Examination of the Evidence of the Courts of Gaol Delivery, 1388 to 1409." *Florilegium* 1 (1979), 87–109.

Geertz, Clifford. *The Interpretation of Culture*. New York: Basic Books, 1973.

Gibson, Gail McMurray. *The Theater of Devotion: East Anglian Drama and Society in the Late Middle Ages*. Chicago: University of Chicago Press, 1989.

Giddens, Anthony. *Central Problems in Social Theory*. Berkeley: University of California Press, 1979.

Gluckman, Max. "Gossip and Scandal." *Current Anthropology* 4 (1963), 307–16.

Goffman, Erving. *Relations in Public*. New York: Harper and Row, 1971.

Goldberg, P.J.P. "Female Labour, Service and Marriage in the Late Medieval Urban North." *Northern History* 22 (1986), 18–38.

Goodman, Anthony. *The Loyal Conspiracy: The Lords Appellant under Richard II*. London: Routledge and Kegan Paul, 1971.

Gray, Howard L. "Early Commons Bills." In *The Influence of the Commons on Early Legislation*, pp. 201–87. Cambridge: Harvard University Press, 1932.

Gurevich, Aron. *Medieval Popular Culture*. Trans. János M. Bak and Paul A. Hollingsworth. Cambridge: Cambridge University Press, 1988.

Hamel, Mary. "The Wife of Bath and a Contemporary Murder." *The Chaucer Review* 14 (1979–1980), 132–39.

Hamil, Frederick C. "The King's Approvers: A Chapter in the History of English Criminal Law." *Speculum* 11 (1936), 238–58.

Hammer, Carl I., Jr. "Patterns of Homicide in a Medieval Univerity Town: Fourteenth-Century Oxford." *Past and Present* 78 (1978), 3–23.

Hanawalt, Barbara A. *Crime and Conflict in English Communities, 1300–1348*. Cambridge: Harvard University Press, 1979.

———. "The Female Felon in Fourteenth-Century England." *Viator* 5 (1974), 253–68.

Harcourt, L. W. Vernon. "The Baga de Secretis." *EHR* 23 (1908), 508–29.

Harding, Alan. "Early Trailbaston Proceedings from the Lincon Roll of 1305." In *Medieval Legal Records*, ed. R. F. Hunnisett and J. B. Post. London: Stationery Office, 1978.

Harris, Olivia. "Households as Natural Units." *Of Marriage and the Market*. Ed. Kate Young et al, pp. 136–56. London: Routledge and Kegan Paul, 1984.

Henderson, E. *Foundations of English Administrative Law: Certiorari and Mandamus in the Seventeenth Century*. Cambridge: Harvard University Press, 1963.

Herlihy, David. *Medieval Households*. Cambridge: Harvard University Press, 1985.

Hilton, Rodney. *Bond Men Made Free*. New York: Viking Press, 1973.

History of Parliament, 1386–1422. Ed. Linda Clark and Carole Rawcliffe, London: History of Parliament Trust, forthcoming, 1992.

Howard, Donald K. *Chaucer: His Life, His Works, His World*. New York: E. P. Dutton, 1987.

Howell, Martha C. *Women, Production, and Patriarchy in Late Medieval Cities*. Chicago: University of Chicago Press, 1986.

Huneycutt, Lois L. "Intercession and the High-Medieval Queen: the *Esther* Topos." Paper presented at conference, "Medieval Women," University of Toronto, February 1990.

Hunnisett, R. F. "English Chancery Records: Rolls and Files," *Journal of the Society of Archivists* 5 (1974–77), 158–68.

———. *The Medieval Coroner*. Cambridge: Cambridge University Press, 1961.

———. "The Reliability of Inquisitions as Historical Evidence." In *The Study of Medieval Records*, ed. D. A. Bullough and R. L. Storey, pp. 206–35. Oxford: Clarendon Press, 1971.

———. "Treason by Words." *Sussex Notes and Queries* 14 (1954–57), 116–19.

Kellaway, William. "The Coroner in Medieval London." In *Studies in London History*, ed. A.E.J. Hollaender and W. Kellaway, pp. 75–91. London: Hodder and Stoughton, 1969.

Kenshur, Oscar. "Critique of Ideological Essentialism." In *Dilemmas of Enlightenment*. Berkeley: University of California Press, forthcoming.

Kingsford, C. L. *English Historical Literature in the Fifteenth Century*. Oxford: Clarendon Press, 1913.

———. "The First Version of Hardyng's Chronicle." *EHR* 27 (1912), 462–82.

Kiser, Lisa J. *Telling Classical Tales: Chaucer and the* Legend of Good Women. Ithaca: Cornell University Press, 1983.

Kristeva, Julia. "Stabat Mater." In *Tales of Love*, pp. 234–63. New York: Columbia University Press, 1987.

Lacey, Kay E. "Women and Work in Fourteenth and Fifteenth Century London." In *Women and Work in Pre-Industrial England*, ed. Lindsey Charles and Lorna Duffin, pp. 24–82. London: Croom Helm, 1985.

Lambrick, Gabrielle. "The Impeachment of the Abbot of Abingdon in 1368." *EHR* 82 (1967), 250–76.

Lapsley, Gaillard. "The Parliamentary Title of Henry IV." *EHR* 49 (1934), 423–49, 577–606.

Legge, M. Dominica. "The Gracious Conqueror." *Modern Language Notes* 68 (1953), 18–21.

Le Roy Ladurie, Emmanuel. *Carnival in Romans*. New York: George Braziller, 1979.

Lipson, Ephraim. *A History of the Western and Worsted Industries*. London: Black, 1921.

McFarlane, K. B. "Bastard Feudalism." *Bull. Inst. Hist. Res.* 20 (1943–45), 161–80.

McKisack, May. *The Parliamentary Representation of the English Boroughs during the Middle Ages*. London: Oxford University Press, 1932.

McNiven, Peter. *Heresy and Politics in the Reign of Henry IV*. Woodbridge, Suffolk: Boydell Press, 1987.

Mah, Harold. "Suppressing the Text: The Metaphysics of Ethnographic History in Darnton's Great Cat Massacre," *History Workshop* 31 (1991), 1–20.

Manly, John Matthews. *Some New Light on Chaucer*. New York: Holt, 1926.

Mann, Jill. *Chaucer and Medieval Estates Satire*. Cambridge: Cambridge University Press, 1973.

Marx, Karl. *A Contribution to the Critique of Political Economy*. New York: International Publishers, 1970.

Miller, J. Hillis. "The Triumph of Theory, the Resistance to Reading, and the Question of the Material Base." *PMLA* 102 (1987), 281–91.

Moore, R. I. *The Formation of a Persecuting Society*. New York: Blackwell, 1987.

Mullett, Michael. *Popular Culture and Popular Protest in Late Medieval and Early Modern Europe*. London: Croom Helm, 1987.

Myers, A. R. "Parliamentary Petitions in the Fifteenth Century." *EHR* 52 (1937), 385–404, 590–613.

Nightingale, Pamela. "Capitalists, Crafts and Constitutional Change in Late Fourteenth-Century London." *Past and Present* 124 (1989), 3–35.

Norton-Smith, John. *Geoffrey Chaucer*. London: Routledge and Kegan Paul, 1974.

Palmer, J.N.N. "The Authorship, Date and Historical Value of the French Chronicles on the Lancastrian Revolution." *Bulletin of the John Rylands Library* 61 (1978), 145–81, 398–421.

Parkes, M. B. "The Literacy of the Laity." In *The Mediaeval World*, ed. D. Daiches and A. Thorlby, 2:555–78. London: Aldus Books, 1973.

Parsons, John Carmi. "Esther's Eclipse? The Queen's Intercession in Thirteenth-Century England." Paper presented in an earlier version at conference "Medieval Women," University of Toronto, February 1990.

Patterson, Annabel. *Shakespeare and the Popular Voice*. Oxford and Cambridge: Blackwell, 1989.

Patterson, Lee. " 'No Man His Reson Herde': Peasant Consciousness, Chaucer's Miller, and the Structure of the *Canterbury Tales*." *South Atlantic Quarterly* 86 (1987), 457–95.

Pearsall, Derek. "Interpretative Models for the Peasants' Revolt." In *Hermeneutics and Medieval Culture*, ed. Patrick J. Gallacher and Helen Damico, pp. 63–70. Albany: State University of New York Press, 1989.

Pike, Luke Owen. *A History of Crime in England*. Vol. 1. London: Smith, Elder, 1873.

Pocock, J.G.A. "Texts as Events: Reflections on the History of Political Thought." In *Poetics of Discourse*, ed. Kevin Sharpe and Steven N. Zwicker, pp. 21–34. Berkeley: University of California Press, 1987.

Pollard, A. W. *Chaucer*. Rev. ed. London: Kegan Paul, Trench and Co., 1912.

Pollock, Frederick, and Frederic William Maitland. *The History of English Law*. 2d ed. Vol. 2. Cambridge: Cambridge University Press, 1968.

Post, J. B. "Jury Lists and Juries in the Late Fourteenth Century." In *Twelve Good Men and True: The Criminal Trial Jury in England, 1200–1800*, ed. J. S. Cockburn and Thomas A. Green, pp. 65–77. Princeton: Princeton University Press, 1988.

Prescott, Andrew. "London in the Peasants' Revolt: A Portrait Gallery." *London Journal* 7 (1981), 125–43.

———. "The Judicial Records of the Rising of 1381." Ph.D. thesis, University of London, 1984.

Reinhard, J. R. "Burning at the Stake in Medieval Law and Literature." *Speculum* 16 (1941), 186–209.

Réville, André. *Le Soulèvement des travailleurs d'Angleterre*. Paris: Picard et Fils, 1898.

Ronan, Nick. "1381: Writing in Revolt. Signs of Confederacy in the Chronicle Accounts of the English Rising." *Forum for Modern Language Studies* 25 (1989), 304–14.

Rörkasten, Jens. "Some Problems of the Evidence of Fourteenth Century Approvers." *Journal of Legal History* 5 (1984), 14–22.

Roskell, J. S. *Parliament and Politics in Late Medieval England*. Vol. 1. London: Hambledon Press, 1981.

Rowe, Donald W. *Through Nature to Eternity: Chaucer's* Legend of Good Women. Lincoln, Neb.: University of Nebraska Press, 1988.

Rowland, Beryl. "Chaucer's Working Wyf." In *Chaucer in the Eighties*, ed. Julian N. Wasserman and Robert J. Blanch, pp. 137–49. Syracuse: Syracuse University Press, 1986.

———. "On the Timely Death of the Wife of Bath's Fourth Husband." *Archiv* 209 (1973), 273–82.

Rubin, Miri. *Corpus Christi: The Eucharist in Late Medieval Culture*. Cambridge: Cambridge University Press, 1991.

Sabine, Ernest L. "Latrines and Cesspools of Medieval London." *Speculum* 9 (1934), 303–21.

Sanderlin, S. "Chaucer and Ricardian Politics." *Chaucer Review* 22 (1987–88), 171–84.

Saul, A. "Local Politics and the Good Parliament." In *Property and Politics: Essays in Later Medieval English History*, ed. Tony Pollard, pp. 156–71. New York: St. Martin's Press, 1984.

Sayles, G. "The Dissolution of a Gild at York in 1306." *EHR* 55 (1940), 83–98.

Scattergood, John. "Social and Political Issues in Chaucer: An Approach to *Lak of Stedfastnesse*." *Chaucer Review* 21 (1987), 469–75.

Scattergood, V. J. *Politics and Poetry in the Fifteenth Century*. London: Blandford Press, 1971.

Schlauch, Margaret. "Chaucer's Doctrine of Kings and Tyrants." *Speculum* 20 (1945), 133–56.

Schmitt, Jean-Claude. *The Holy Greyhound*. Trans. Martin Thom. Cambridge: Cambridge University Press, 1979.

Sherborne, J. W. "Charles VI and Richard II." In *Froissart: Historian*, ed. J.N.N. Palmer, pp. 50–63. Woodbridge, Suffolk: Boydell, 1981.

———. "Perjury and the Lancastrian Revolution of 1399." *Welsh History Review* 14 (1988), 217–41.

Simpson, A.W.B. *A History of the Land Law*. 2d ed. Oxford: Clarendon Press, 1986.

Skeat, Walter W., ed. "The Testament of Love." In *Chaucerian and Other Pieces, The Complete Works of Geoffrey Chaucer*, vol. 7. Oxford: Clarendon Press, 1897.

Spacks, Patricia Meyer. *Gossip*. New York: Knopf, 1985.

Spurgeon, Caroline. *Five Hundred Years of Chaucer Criticism and Allusion*. Vol. 1. Cambridge: Cambridge University Press, 1925.

Squibb, G. *The High Court of Chivalry*. Oxford: Oxford University Press, 1959.

Stafford, Pauline. *Queens, Concubines, and Dowagers: The King's Wife in the Early Middle Ages*. Athens, Ga.: University of Georgia Press, 1983.

Stallybrass, Peter, and Allon White. *The Politics and Poetics of Transgression*. Ithaca, N.Y.: Cornell University Press, 1986.

Steel, Anthony. *Richard II*. Cambridge: Cambridge University Press, 1941.

Stevens, Martin. *Four Middle English Mystery Cycles*. Princeton: Princeton University Press, 1987.

Storey, R. L. "Liveries and Commissions of the Peace, 1388–90." In *The Reign of Richard II*, pp. 131–52. ed. F.R.H. DuBoulay and Caroline M. Barron. London: Athlone Press, 1971.

Strohm, Paul. "Politics and Poetics: Usk and Chaucer in the 1380s." In *Literary Practice and Social Change in Britain, 1380–1530*, ed. Lee Patterson, pp. 83–112. Berkeley: University of California Press, 1990.

——. *Social Chaucer*. Cambridge: Harvard University Press, 1989.

Stubbs, William. *The Constitutional History of England*. Vol. 2. Oxford: Clarendon, 1880.

Swanson, Heather. "The Illusion of Economic Structure: Craft Guilds in Late Medieval English Towns." *Past and Present* 121 (1988), 29–48.

Taylor, John. *English Historical Literature in the Fourteenth Century*. Oxford: Clarendon Press, 1987.

Text collectif. " 'Young Mr. Lincoln' de John Ford." *Cahiers du cinema* 223 (1970), 29–47.

Thompson, E. P. "The Moral Economy of the English Crowd in the Eighteenth Century." *Past and Present* 50 (1971), 76–136.

Thrupp, Sylvia. "Medieval Gilds Reconsidered." *Society and History*. Ann Arbor: University of Michigan Press, 1977.

——. *The Merchant Class of Medieval London*. Ann Arbor: University of Michigan Press, 1948.

Tout, T. F. *Chapters in Mediaeval Administrative History*. 6 vols. Manchester: Manchester University Press, 1920–1933.

Trexler, Richard C. *Public Life in Renaissance Florence*. New York: Academic Press, 1980.

Tuck, Anthony. "The Cambridge Parliament, 1388." *EHR* 331 (1969), 225–43.

——. *Richard II and the English Nobility*. London: Edward Arnold, 1973.

Turner, Victor. *Dramas, Fields, and Metaphors*. Ithaca, N.Y.: Cornell University Press, 1974.

Ullmann, Walter. *Principles of Government and Politics in the Middle Ages*. New York: Barnes and Noble, 1961.

van Uytven, Raymond. "Cloth in Medieval Literature of Western Europe." In *Cloth and Clothing in Medieval Europe*, ed. N. B. Harte and K. G. Ponting, pp. 151–83. Pasold Studies in Textile History, 2. London: Heinemann, 1983.

Victoria History: Hampshire. London: Constable, 1912. [*VH*]

Walker, Simon. *The Lancastrian Affinity, 1361–1399*. Oxford: Clarendon, Press, 1990.

Wallace, David. " 'Whan She Translated Was': A Chaucerian Critique of the Petrarchan Academy." In *Literary Practice and Social Change in Britain, 1380–1530*, pp. 156–215. ed. Lee Patterson. Berkeley: University of California Press, 1990.

Warner, Marina. *Alone of All Her Sex: The Myth and Cult of the Virgin Mary*. London: Quartet Books, 1978.

Welch, Charles. *A History of the Cutlers' Company of London*. Vol. 1. London, 1916.

White, Hayden. "The Value of Narrativity in the Representation of Reality." *Critical Inquiry* 7 (1980), 5–27.

Wilkinson, B. "The Deposition of Richard II and the Accession of Henry IV." *EHR* 54 (1939), 215–39.

Williams, Gwyn A. *Medieval London: From Commune to Capital*. London: Athlone Press, 1963.

Williams, Raymond. *Keywords*. Rev. ed. Oxford: Oxford University Press, 1983.

Wright, H. G. "The Protestation of Richard II in the Tower in September, 1399." *Bull. John Rylands Library*, 23 (1939), 151–165.

INDEX

affinity. *See* retinue

Alceste. *See* Chaucer, *Legend of Good Women*

Althusser, Louis, 72, 74n.11, 125n.4

Amsler, Mark, 141n.20

Anne, of Bohemia, queen of Richard II, 6, 69n.9, 99, 105–19; and Alceste, 116–19; epitaph of, 106; intercedes for London, 107–11; welcome to London, 105–6

antifeminism, 136–37

Appellants, of 1387–88, 19, 21–22, 28, 29, 30, 63, 71, 155n.13, 159–60, 164

appropriation, 7, 45, 53, 71, 72–74

approvership, 148–50, 153, 165–67

Arundel, Thomas, Abp. of Canterbury, 85, 88, 90, 106

association, sworn, 39–40, 52, 57–63, 73, 179–82

audience, 3, 15, 16, 22, 134–35, 135n.12

Austin, Thomas, mercer: Alicia, wife of, 12n.3, 13, 28, 163, 171; appendix 1, *passim*; career of, 22–23; chapter 1, *passim*; Roger, brother of, 12, 13, 164, 171, 174, 175–77

authorship, 93–94, 166–67; and intent, 9

Babcock, Barbara, 38

Badby, John, 122n.1

baga de secretis, 164

Bakhtin, M. M., 45, 45n.9, 47–48, 71

Ball, John, servant of Andrew Wauton, 128–29

Banham, John, chapter 1, *passim*; 161–64, 166, 168–73; his "Accusation" against Thomas Austin, 173–77

Baret, William, alderman, 20n.9

Barron, Caroline, 23–24, 25, 26n.14, 61n.2, 75, 91n.14, 147n.3, 158n.14, 159n.16

Barron, W.R.J., 122n.1

Bealknap, Robert, justice, 128, 154

Bean, J.M.W., 180n.1, 184n.5, 185

Bell, Robert, 93

Bellamy, J. G., 8, 123–24, 124n.3, 139n.15

Bennett, Judith, 9, 126, 132, 132n.10

Bercé, Yves-Marie, 49n.10

Bere, John, citizen of London, 147, 147n.5

Berwald, John, Yorkshire maintainer and poet (?), 181–82

Bible, 98

Bird, Ruth, 28n.17, 29n.18

Blake, Robert, *capellanus*, 128–29, 129n.8

Boccaccio, Giovanni, 7

body: social, 48; and property, 138

Borges, Jorge Luis, 117

Bracton, Henri de, 148n.6, 149, 152

Brembre, Nicholas, mayor, 6, 172–75; chapter 2, *passim*; chapter 7, *passim*

Bristol, Michael D., 35n.1

Bronson, Bertrand, 116

Brooks, Nicholas, 43n.7

Burke, Kenneth, 72

Burley, Simon, 17, 106

Bynum, Caroline Walker, 101, 104

carnival. *See* revelry

Carruthers, Mary, 140, 142n.22

ceremonies, 3, 29, 47, 58, 107–11

Chambers, R. W. and Daunt, Marjorie, 161

champerty, 57, 179

Charlton, Robert, justice, 128

Charnes, Linda, 26, 138n.14

Charney, John, coroner, 15, 18, 145–46, 146n.2, 154, 158–59, 163, 176

Chaucer: as narrator, 16n.7; in 1388–90, 69–70; and Henry IV, 89, 92; and Richard II, 58, 69–74. Works: "ABC," 97; *Boece*, 111; *Canterbury Tales*, 143n.23; *Clerk's Tale*, 113; *General Prologue*, 139; *Knight's Tale*, 112; "Lak," 65–70, 72–74, 116n.18; *Legend of Good Women*, 98, 99, 112–19; *Melibee*, 98, 111, 113; *Merchant's Tale*, 98; *Miller's Tale*, 135; *Parson's Tale*, 143n.23; "Purse," 9, 75, 86, 88–89, 93; "Scogan," 22; *Sir Thopas*, 182n.4; *Wife of Bath's Tale*, 113, 136–37, 139–44

Cheyne, William, coroner, 15, 21

Christine, de Pisan. *See* Pisan, Christine de